THE TWENTYSOMETHING SOUL

THE TWENTYSOMETHING SOUL

Understanding the Religious and Secular Lives of American Young Adults

TIM CLYDESDALE

KATHLEEN GARCES-FOLEY

OXFORD
UNIVERSITY PRESS

OXFORD
UNIVERSITY PRESS

Oxford University Press is a department of the University of Oxford. It furthers the University's objective of excellence in research, scholarship, and education by publishing worldwide. Oxford is a registered trade mark of Oxford University Press in the UK and certain other countries.

Published in the United States of America by Oxford University Press
198 Madison Avenue, New York, NY 10016, United States of America.

CIP data is on file at the Library of Congress
ISBN 978-0-19-093135-3

1 3 5 7 9 8 6 4 2

Printed by Sheridan Books, Inc., United States of America

To the late
Dean R. Hoge
scholar, educator, friend

CONTENTS

ACKNOWLEDGMENTS

The Twentysomething Soul is dedicated to Dean Hoge, who helped envision and initiate the research on young adults that forms the basis of this book before his untimely death on September 13, 2008. Dean was a greatly respected sociologist who spent the last thirty-four years of his career at Catholic University of America where he taught classes on sociology and published dozens of books and over one hundred articles and book chapters. A lifelong Christian, Dean hoped his sociological research would be useful to church leaders as they sought to understand changing social structures affecting church life. We are deeply grateful to Dean for inviting us to join this study of young adults and to carry on this project in his absence. We hope that Dean would be pleased with the finished book.

We also wish to recognize the many contributions of Jim Youniss and Tony Pogerelc. Both have seen the project through from the beginning, offering thoughtful contributions and constant support at every stage. When Dean fell ill, Jim stepped in to oversee the (successful!) writing of the research grant proposal, and after Dean passed, he remained a senior advisor to the project even though transitioning to emeritus status. Tony took on the role of principal investigator of the project awarded by the Lilly Endowment. We greatly appreciate his gracious leadership, especially his deft handling of financial matters and keeping us on track.

Our gratitude goes also to the Lilly Endowment and Chris Coble for their early support of Dean's vision along with a four-year grant to gather the data presented in this book and to create a website through which to share expert information about twentysomethings with the public. Lilly's funding enabled us to commission essays by sociologists, psychologists, and media studies scholars summarizing current research on twentysomethings along with commentaries from church leaders on these essays. In addition, we shared descriptive case studies of the congregations with vibrant young adult communities that are further analyzed in this book. It was Lilly's and our hope that church leaders would find these freely available resources beneficial to their ministry. These resources are still available in the Catholic University of America's digital archives.

This project was housed at the Catholic University of America's Institute for Policy Research and Catholic Studies (formerly called the Life Cycle Institute), where Dean Hoge, along with colleagues Jim Youniss and Joseph Tamney, developed the initial plans for a national study of the religious lives of young adults. We are grateful to the Institute for supporting our work and especially wish to acknowledge the hospitality of director Stephen Schneck and administrative support of office manager Woinishet Negash.

A great number of people contributed to the research that forms the basis of this book. We wish to thank the project advisors Nancy Ammerman, Steve Warner, and Gerardo Marti, who shared their wealth of experience in congregational studies with us. Our gratitude also goes to the hard work of the research fellows who conducted the congregational studies and shared their insights with us: Walt Bower, Tricia C. Bruce, Richard Cimino, Justin Farrell, Ashley Palmer, Grace Yukich, and Hilary Kaell. We are also indebted to William D'Antonio for his thoughtful advice on our national survey of twentysomethings. We benefited greatly from the assistance of students who helped with interviews, observations, transcription, and coding of hundreds of interview recordings: especially Karen Nevin, Nana Marfo, Mollie Kennedy, Elizabeth Jahr, and April Westmark.

This book would not have been possible without the generosity of hundreds of people who allowed us into their lives to observe their congregations and interview them. We are especially appreciative of the pastors who warmly invited us in to their churches, gave us access to their staff and layleaders, and introduced us to their young adults. We also want to recognize the universities that allowed us to interview students who do not have a religious affiliation. To the hundreds of young adults and church leaders who gave us an hour (or two or three) of their time to be interviewed, we are immensely grateful, and we hope that you recognize your journeys in the pages that follow.

This book would also not exist without the many years of encouragement and advice from Oxford University Press editor Theo Calderara. We are also grateful to editorial assistant Aiesha Krause-Lee for ushering the manuscript through its final stages, and to Doreen McLaughlin for her careful indexing of this topically diverse volume.

Lastly, we wish to recognize the role our families have played in the completion of this work. Kathleen thanks her amazing husband, Anthony, for his unfailing support while managing to work full time, earn a PhD, and raise our beautiful children, Jonah, Eva Marie, and Elijah, who will be twentysomethings much too soon. Tim thanks his beloved wife, Dawn, for her infectious laugh and saintly forbearance that she generously shares with this less-than-cheery author, and the many teens and twentysomethings who pass through our home, courtesy of our passionate, soon-to-be twentysomething, Grace, and our talented and now legal twentysomething, Jonah; you all have taught me much.

THE TWENTYSOMETHING SOUL

CHAPTER 1

MEET THE TWENTYSOMETHINGS

Maria Martinez

Maria is a thoughtful 22-year-old graduate student studying speech pathology in Texas.* She hopes to contribute something to the treatment of autism. Her ultimate life goal, though, is to be a stay-at-home mom. We first met Maria at a parish focus group interview with seven other young adults at St. Ann's Catholic Parish in the diocese of Dallas. St. Ann's is a large parish, with 28,000 registered members and over a hundred different ministries. Because Maria did not get to say everything she wanted to say in the focus group, she asked to be interviewed individually. Maria is active in the parish's "Twenty-Something" ministry and attends Mass at St. Ann's about twice a month, but during the week she attends morning Mass at another parish near her job. This kind of commitment to religious practice is not common among American twentysomethings, but it is not exactly rare, either: about 1 out of 4 of today's twentysomethings makes it a priority to both worship regularly and grow spiritually. So Maria is not alone in her devotion to faith, even as her daily Mass attendance places her among the most devoted of American twentysomethings.

Maria was not always so devout. The youngest of five children in a Mexican American family, Maria had what she calls a "traditional Catholic upbringing." But Maria's family was far from traditional in that they had a *written* family mission statement, which "talked about upholding Catholic-Christian values in our everyday life and using that

* To protect Maria's privacy, her name, like all interviewee names in this book, is a pseudonym.

as the foundation for every decision that we made." Maria went along with her family's expectations, but she resented being forced to participate, especially during her adolescence. Maria sometimes joked with her parents that she would rather be a Unitarian Universalist, but she never looked into it seriously.

It was not until college that Maria came to embrace the Catholic faith. Maria chose a Catholic college in the Midwest: "I probably chose to go to Catholic school because I knew that I needed to learn more about it to see if that was something that I wanted to do for the rest of my life." In college, Maria says, she "came into her faith." She began attending daily Mass, performing Eucharistic Adoration, and praying the rosary. Nothing was more important to her than the small Sunday Masses held in the dorms. Students would gather around the altar for the consecration and hug each other at the sign of peace. We asked Maria what she loves most about being Catholic. She said:

> I think it's the opportunity to receive the Eucharist every day. I mean no other religion allows or believes in that [. . .] the wholeness of the Eucharist. So, I think the ability to receive those graces each and every day is a thing that is totally sacred and something that I won't let anyone ever take away from me. Because it's there for our taking it, and it's amazing and wonderful, and I don't know what exists beyond that. I mean I don't know how I could *exist* without that. It's gotten to the point where I need it every single day. If I don't go to Mass and I don't receive the Eucharist every day, then it's an off day because I know that I don't have the graces that come with it.

When Maria moved back to Texas after college, she began visiting different parishes. She heard that people at St. Ann's were excited about their faith—something that was not true, she said, at a lot of parishes. When Maria attended St. Ann's the first time what struck her was the way everyone was invited to gather around the altar for the consecration, just like Mass in her college dorm. She knew right then that this was the place for her. She joined St. Ann's Twenty-Something group shortly thereafter. Now a core member, Maria has come to love the camaraderie of doing things like Eucharistic Adoration together. For most devout twentysomethings, regular worship attendance and involvement in a young adult program would satiate their religious appetites. But Maria's extreme devotion pushed her still further. She sought out Opus Dei, a conservative Catholic organization that promotes holiness in everyday life. She visits an Opus Dei center nearby where she has a spiritual director and attends catechesis classes for women.

For Maria, the teachings of the Church are the universal truth, and at the heart of this truth is love. Catholic teachings, she explains, have been laid out concretely and consistently by the Church for 2,000 years. They are the foundation for everything she does. Some of those teachings used to be hard for Maria to accept, but that was because she "was ignorant." For example, when she was in high school she had a gay friend who decried the Catholic condemnation of homosexual activity. When he raised the subject with Maria, she agreed the Church's position sounded bigoted. But then she studied the teachings, talked to a priest, and came to accept the Church's view. The same thing happened on the subject of women priests. The ban on women priests was once difficult for her to accept, but now Maria understands the reasons and she fully accepts the Church's teaching. Even Catholic teachings on chastity, something many young adults struggle with, are not a problem for Maria since she studied Pope John Paul II's "theology of the body." According to Maria, you cannot argue with the truth of Catholicism, so there is nothing about the faith that unsettles her.

Being Catholic and rooting her life in the Eucharist brings Maria great joy. Indeed, Maria is optimistic that she will soon be able to start a family and share this joy with her children, even though she doesn't have a boyfriend. Maria's optimism flows, we believe, from her complete confidence in Catholic teaching. Many Catholic young adults we interviewed for this book do not share Maria's confidence, however. They express doubts about Catholic teachings, especially around sexuality, and they are not as deferential to the authority of the Church. Still, they describe themselves, like Maria, as committed Catholics who intend to pass on their Catholic way of life to their children. Such commitment, even with reservations, will likely produce future generations of Catholics, who will join an ever-more religiously diverse America.

Jeremy Harris

Jeremy grew up in New York City, where his African American-Hispanic family attended a large, prominent African Methodist Episcopal (AME) church. As a gay youth in a Black church, Jeremy had difficult moments, but he felt accepted and he never questioned his faith. He sang at his and other churches, and in the choirs being gay was unproblematic. "I always felt there are so many gay people in the church, it's really just part of church." He describes it as a "don't ask, don't tell" approach. What did bother Jeremy was his church's stress on John 3:16, because that meant his friends who do not believe in Christ were damned: "I never felt like I have to denounce all churches, but I also never had anyone in my face telling me, 'you're going to hell.' [. . .] What bothered me more was condemning people who were good people." For Jeremy, the core of Christianity is a variation of what "Jesus said [was] the best commandment: try to love yourself and try not to hurt people." When it was time for college, Jeremy enrolled in an elite university on the West Coast and attended church only on holidays. Unable to find a job after graduation, Jeremy moved back in with his parents in New York City—weeks before September 11, 2001.

In what he calls the "post-college, looking-for-work, and trying to save enough money to move out" period, church was not Jeremy's priority. He was busy with "a lot of temp work," and, when it seemed impossible to land a good job without an advanced degree, Jeremy went back to school. In graduate school, Jeremy become friends with an Orthodox Jewish woman named Sharon who shared his love of gospel music. They heard about a theologically liberal church with a great gospel choir: Middle Collegiate Church. Affiliated with the Reformed Church in America, Middle Collegiate is a Mainline Protestant church known for integrating the arts into worship. Sharon convinced Jeremy to check it out with her. Jeremy says he went to "Middle" for the choir, and the choir kept him there. But Jeremy was also drawn by the intellectual depth of the minister: "what I really like is [how she] teaches me something about the text. Because I really like to know how this text came about and what was going on which makes this text what it is. And I really get that from the church, the intellectual kind of ministry which really turns me on in a way and makes me want to come back and see, what are you going to preach about next?"

Jeremy was 28 when he first visited Middle. Currently he attends Sunday services three times a month and is involved in short-term mission projects. His partner, Eric, was appalled when Jeremy joined the gospel choir—at least initially. Jeremy knows lots of people who, like Eric, are skeptical of, if not downright hostile to, religion: "It's really hard to convince people and sometimes I forget, because I invite my friends to the gospel choir concert and my friends are like 'yeah, I'm busy.' And I forget you have this preconceived notion of what church is, and I have to remember that everyone doesn't necessarily see church the way I see church." Jeremy eventually convinced Eric to visit Middle: "So he came and, of course, he cried, and he kept crying every time he came. It's the same story everyone says." Jeremy is quick to point out that Middle is not a gay church; it is a "come as you are church" rooted in Christianity but open to people of every sort. It is exactly the kind of church he thinks young adults today would love.

Lee Chen

Lee grew up in an atheist family. His parents emigrated from China and continued a few Buddhist and Confucian practices in the United States, such as having Buddha statues around the home and burning incense at the cemetery. But Lee does not think they actually believe in anything. They never taught him about Buddhism, Confucianism, or anything else, so Lee grew up thinking "everything was random." His parents told him to rely on himself and focus on his schoolwork. Lee was a good student and was surprised at how difficult it was to find a good job after he graduated from college. His parents said he needed to work harder, but nothing he did helped him find employment in his field of graphic design. Then the 9/11 attack occurred. This was a wake-up call for Lee, who began thinking seriously about the meaning of life. He started paying more attention to his friends when they talked about God, and eventually he met with one of their pastors, who convinced him that God exists. "I accepted Christianity based on his arguments and basically when I first came to my first church, I started experiencing the acceptance and love that he was talking about." Lee was "born again" by the end of that conversation, joining 30% of American twentysomethings who call themselves Evangelical Protestants.

Lee had attended church before, at a Chinese church in Brooklyn. As a teenager, he used to go there "to play basketball and look at girls." But he returned to this church after his conversion looking for a relationship with God. Lee was happy at this church for many years, but his perspective changed after he read *The Emotionally Healthy Church*, by Peter Scazzero. Lee was convinced that there were unspoken dysfunctions within his congregation that could be fixed, but when he tried to start a conversation about this he met resistance. So, Lee decided to visit Scazzero's New Life Fellowship Church in Queens, to see if Scazzero's ideas could be put into practice.

Lee's first visit to New Life was eye-opening, "I was kind of shocked, because I usually only go to churches that were predominantly Chinese or Asian, but for me to come to a church where it was a very good mix of everybody . . . [it was like] a mosh pit of different people!" New Life is a large, multiethnic church, and through interactions with "Hispanics, Blacks, Puerto Ricans, Whites, Koreans, and everybody," Lee became a more open person with greater awareness of different cultural backgrounds. He joined a small group, and that ultimately convinced him to make New Life his home church. The group was studying Scazzero's second book, *Emotionally Healthy Spirituality*. Lee was astonished by the way group members let down their guard and shared their weaknesses. This group became for Lee "a small group *of truth* where we all weren't just pretending everything is fine in our lives, you know, which basically was the culture that I came from in my old church. Yes, it was *truth*."

We met Lee at New Life. He was an eager interviewee. Employed as a graphic designer, Lee was happy with his career but unhappy with being single—especially since he had passed his 30th birthday. Lee said he feels a lot of pressure, "being Asian," to get married and have kids—but he is trying to accept "whatever God's plan is" for him. At this point in his life, work takes up most of his time and he wishes he could be more involved in church. Unlike at his old church, Lee feels accepted at New Life. He explains, "back in the old church, right, there were some things that I wouldn't confess to anyone, any of those members because they might judge me or say, 'oh you know, he should pray harder or he should, you know, get your life back together and everything. You're not seeking Jesus enough.' " At New Life, Lee experiences empathy and acceptance, something he says young adults really need:

> I think especially for young adults who don't have . . . whose parents are not Christian . . . I guess they were never taught that kind of stuff. It could get kinda lonely growing up here, especially in New York City, where people are more or less disconnected and, as a result, they actually distrust others. So, it's what we need to hear and to eventually trust one another and to eventually have this community, where we let our guard down and everything. Because, we're young adults and it's tough, you know? We work a lot, many hours a week, and so we don't have social times and even the social times that we have, we sometimes do not know how to be closer and let our guard down.

Lee has been attending New Life for two years. He sings in the choir and helps organize events, but he is not yet an official member because he has been too busy to attend the required membership classes. Lee's experience of social disconnection is fueled in large part by his demanding work schedule. This is common among twentysomethings, as is the desire to be accepted by others without pretense. Like many young adults we met through churches, Lee is glad he has found a Christian community that accepts him as imperfect and helps him work through the challenges of adulthood. Not all twentysomethings find such acceptance and support in Evangelical churches, however, including some who grew up in them.

Abby Newton

We first met Abby when she was a sophomore at a small Catholic university in the mid-Atlantic region. A political science major, Abby is a White woman who describes herself as an introvert, but she talked openly with us about her religious journey and agreed to do a second interview when she was a senior. Raised by Evangelical parents, Abby attended mostly Baptist churches growing up. Her family spent its time, Abby reports, either outdoors or at church. Abby was not allowed to listen to mainstream music, watch movies that feature witchcraft, or read the Harry Potter books, but her parents did allow her to go trick-or-treating. Abby remembers her father became intensely engaged in his faith when she was around 6 years old. He was very interested in the Zionist movement, and as the year 2000 approached he saw signs of the Lord's imminent return. A few years later, her father quit his job and left his family—without saying goodbye—to preach the gospel to Jews in Israel. After three months, he returned home to financially support them, but the stress of his departure remained a source of tension in the family.

Abby was baptized at age 13 and was very active in church and on short-term mission trips. In her words, "I very much loved God and was really into God's creation." This started to change when she went to high school. Abby points to several reasons for her break with Christianity. In her early teen years she began questioning authority and wanting better answers about everything, including the Christian faith. Then her depression, which she struggled with for a long time, became worse. At 16, she was officially diagnosed and became suicidal. Her parents told her to pray for God's help. Abby did pray every night for years, but it did not help. She explained, "If I'm feeling suicidal, where's God in that? And suicide is a sin according to the Bible, and if I'm asking God for all this stuff, why isn't he helping me not want to kill myself, like not want to be in this situation? My mother kind of recognizes that it was a medical problem, but my father still does not believe it. He still thinks that I am being dramatic and that it was teenage angst and that I did not pray hard enough."

The last straw, according to Abby, came in her final years of high school. Some of Abby's friends started coming out as gay or bisexual. Her initial reaction was that homosexuality and gay marriage were wrong, but when they pushed back, she realized her reasons were weak. "I am not a person who enjoys hating other people for a baseless reason, and you know my philosophy is if it is not hurting you or anyone else, then I really do not care." Abby came to accept her friends' sexual orientation and participated in a day of silence to support lesbian, gay, bisexual, and transgender youth. Feeling good about her relationship with her friends, Abby found herself at odds with her church community.

> I went to youth group maybe a few days after, and they talked about the day of silence, and they were bashing on gays. They were like "gays wouldn't be bullied if they just didn't tell anyone they were gay." I got really upset . . . I started crying because, you know, those were my friends they were talking about, and I walked out of the church, and I never went back; I can't handle this religion any more. A lot of the Bible talks about being good to people and treating your neighbor as you want yourself to be treated, and the fact that people were just fervently bashing these people for a different lifestyle choice that they may not understand really got to me. So that's the background about why I stopped believing in the Christian religion.

Not only did Abby stop believing in the Christian religion, she also doubted God's existence since her daily prayers had not relieved her depression. By the time Abby started college, she was a firm, outspoken atheist, but when we reinterviewed Abby just before her college graduation, she no longer called herself an atheist. "I do not really fall in line with that because a lot of atheists are really condescending and pretentious towards people who are religious and think they know all and are better than everyone, and I cannot stand that, and so I do not really affiliate with them." When asked if she believes in any sort of transcendent being she offers a series of short thoughts with lots of pauses as she struggles to put them into words:

> I would say that I think . . . I have actually been reading up on this because I do like learning about religion. It's just that I have not found one that fits me. I do not think that there is a transcendent being or something, but I don't know. I mean there could be, but I have not seen any evidence for that. I definitely do not think it is the same as the Western conception. If there is any sort of divine energy, I think it is more of the kind that goes along the lines of indigenous religions, such as Native American with this whole spiritual divine reverence for Mother Nature, is kind of what I see. Because. I don't know. I feel the universe itself is an amazing kind of thing that has happened scientifically and spiritually. So, if there is anything, I do not think it is any sort of patriarchal Western conception that we have made over the last two thousand years. I think it is something that has always been and always will be. And it just kind of, it does not have any kind of interference [in] everyday life. It is like an energy, if you will.

Age 22 and about to graduate from college, Abby is "trying to find my own way to still be a spiritual person and connect with the world around me without religion." This is a largely solitary path, and community is one thing she misses about religion. She reads a lot about religion and loves to be in nature. She thinks the peace she feels in nature is a lot like what people get from religion. Abby wishes she had a community to share these experiences with but has no idea whether she will ever find one that fits her. She definitely believes in ghosts and demons, though her friends make fun of her, and she has done some experimenting in the realm of paranormal activity and says she has encountered evil forces. Though Abby believes in supernatural beings and forces, she doesn't think there is any given direction or purpose to life. She thinks life is what you make it and has decided her life will be about doing good in the world. She contrasts her philosophy with people, like her father, who are focused on the next world. "I am more concerned about what impact I am having on the world because I realize if I die there are still a whole bunch of generations behind me that have to live here and deal with my mess, so try to make as little mess as possible and maybe clean it up in the meantime."

Scholars of religion would have a hard time putting Abby into existing religious categories. She does not believe in God, so she is technically an atheist, but she rejects that label. Because the God question is not of concern to her, we could label her a "nontheist"—but that misses a key point, which is that Abby is a *spiritual* nontheist. She believes there is an energy connecting the natural world that is both scientifically proven and spiritually perceived. Abby experiences this energy most strongly when she is hiking or camping, as do many Americans today, but most interpret this experience within a theistic framework.[1] Abby has an eclectic spirituality, combining ideas about the paranormal and Native American religions with ecological and humanistic commitments. Abby is one of a growing population of religiously unaffiliated Americans.[2] In fact, when surveyed, 3 out of 10 twentysomethings today do not indicate any religious affiliation, choosing "None" instead. The worldviews of Nones, as they are called, vary widely, some being believers in a personal God, others proudly to indifferently secular, and still others, like Abby, spiritually eclectic. Many twentysomething Nones share Abby's desire to make a meaningful life by doing good, which is an important but often unrecognized common ground they share with twentysomething Christians like Maria, Jeremy, and Lee.

An Optimistic Story

Despite important research by psychologists, sociologists, and religious studies scholars, there is little popular understanding of how much Americans' journey through their 20s has changed during the past half-century or of how blatantly incorrect many assumptions are about young adults' religious, spiritual, and secular lives.[3] Today's twentysomethings have been labeled the "lost generation"—for their presumed inability to identify and lead fulfilling lives, "kidults"—for their alleged refusal to "grow up" and accept adult responsibilities—and the "least religious generation"—for their purported disinterest in religion and spirituality.[4] These characterizations are not only unflattering, they are also deeply flawed. Yet it seems everywhere we encounter parents, educators, and counselors who ask, like the *New York Times* did, "What is it about twentysomethings?"[5]

What is it, indeed? We have interviewed hundreds of twentysomethings and surveyed thousands across the nation. We met scores of young adults who, like, Maria, Jeremy, Lee, and Abby, have devoted years obtaining the training essential to our Information Age. We have spoken with lots of twentysomethings who, like Jeremy and Lee, have full-time careers, and plenty of young adults like Maria and Abby, who juggle part-time jobs on top of full-time course loads. The overwhelming majority of them were quite thoughtful about their lives. There are, to be sure, twentysomethings who seem lost, avoid responsibilities, or indicate no concern about the religious, spiritual, or even ethical dimensions of their lives. But there is no shortage of Americans over 30 who act likewise; wanderers, shirkers, and thoughtless jerks can be found in every age cohort. The truth, though, is stranger than the fictions so many repeat about young adults: Americans of every age have far more in common than you'd think, and understanding twentysomethings requires little more than an appreciation of the changed economic, cultural, and religious contexts that young adults navigate today.

We write, therefore, to tell a story that is more optimistic than most. We write to introduce readers to the full spectrum of American twentysomethings, many of whom—like Maria, Jeremy, Lee, and Abby—live purposefully, responsibly, and reflectively. Some twentysomethings, like Maria, Jeremy, and Lee, prioritize their commitment to Christian faith and spirituality. Other twentysomethings, like Abby, reject the religion in which they were raised but explore alternative worldviews to create their own personal spirituality. Still others sideline conventional religion and spirituality until they feel settled in the other parts of their lives. There is change occurring among young adults, but little of it is among the 1 in 4 American twentysomethings who have consistently prioritized religious commitment during the past half-century. The change is rather found among those whose affiliation with religion has been for the sake of familial tradition and the approval of fellow Americans, neither of which have remained strong during the last fifty years.

We observed and interviewed twentysomethings in universities, churches, coffee shops, ministry programs, and even bars (the latter two overlapped!). We particularly wanted to understand twentysomethings who prioritized their religious lives since so many headlines make it seem as though they are disappearing. For this, we recruited a team of ethnographers who studied eleven congregations and para-church ministries overflowing with twentysomethings, interviewing more than 200 young adult participants and church staff. We also interviewed forty-nine religiously unaffiliated young adults to hear how these twentysomethings described themselves and made sense of life outside a religious tradition. And we surveyed 1,880 young adults for the National Study of American Twentysomethings (NSAT). We therefore have a broad base of unique data, which we augment with existing survey data, to describe the 91% of American twentysomethings who are Catholic, Evangelical, Mainline Protestant, or religiously unaffiliated (i.e., Nones).

Unfortunately, this means that the diverse 9% of American twentysomethings who affiliate with other religions lie beyond the scope of this project. We lacked the time and resources to collect representative data from twentysomething Jews, Mormons, Muslims, Buddhists, Hindus, Orthodox Christians, or affiliates of other world religions.[6] This is surely disappointing to readers interested in young adults affiliated with these religions; we hope the voices and findings from the twentysomethings we were able to study will be of comparative value. We also encourage scholars to augment this book with studies of their own; this topic is important, and it is essential to hear from as many voices as possible.[7]

"Growing Up Is Harder to Do"

Americans are a pragmatic, self-reliant people—characteristics that observers since Tocqueville have documented.[8] We like to get things done, and we expect our fellow citizens to demonstrate initiative and persistence. These are not bad traits, on the whole. But they have a downside: we start from the assumption that troubles or difficulties in getting things done are a function of the doer, not the context. Take car troubles, for example. When hearing someone complain about their car's operation, we want to know if the driver changed the oil regularly, kept their engine tuned, paid attention to fluid levels, and checked for possible leaks. If the answer to any of these is "no," the driver will get little sympathy and possibly a lecture about car maintenance. Only after hearing confirmation that the car owner has acted responsibly will Americans ask about the type and age of the car. Why? Because only after ruling out individual choices and actions do we consider the relevance of larger factors.

Our point is this: today's twentysomethings must navigate paths to adulthood that have become as complex and at times as congested as the Los Angeles freeway system, which neither they nor members of social institutions that prepare youth for life's transitions—that is, families, schools, and congregations—fully recognize or understand. Consequently, today's twentysomethings are maligned, described as the "boomerang generation" for the 1 out of 3 who "return to the nest" after graduating from college, or patronized as "not quite" adults because they do not possess complete occupational, financial, and domestic stability.[9] To rightly understand twentysomethings requires seeing the world that twentysomethings have inherited: a place where global economic and macro-cultural changes have made secure careers elusive, where family life is often unstable, where marriage and parenthood have become lifestyle options, where the path to financial and personal independence is littered with a hundred obstructions, and where spiritual growth is promoted outside organized religions as well as inside.

We see evidence of this changed world in Maria, Jeremy, Lee, and Abby's stories.

- Maria is working on a graduate degree, which is virtually a requirement now for a secure, rewarding career in many fields. Having that credential will help her find employment after she has children, and even though she prefers not to be employed, she will likely regard good schools and a safe neighborhood for her children as essential and thus choose to work outside the home.
- Jeremy enjoys greater freedom than ever to live as an openly gay Black man, an indicator of America's macro-cultural change particularly apparent in places like New York City. But like many, Jeremy will need to move away from his beloved city if he wishes to climb an employer's career ladder.
- Lee found a good job in his primary field, but it demands many hours, and this has limited Lee's social life and left him frustrated about being single.
- Abby's college graduation is around the corner, and she does not want to move back to her Evangelical parents' home. But demanding senior year coursework left her no time to forge a different plan, making this scenario likely while she prepares applications and seeks interviews.

Abby, Maria, Jeremy, and Lee must navigate a world that is more diverse and more competitive than did those—like the authors—who came of age twenty-five years ago. While these four young adults enjoy more freedom than ever before, they have learned firsthand what cognitive psychologists have documented: more choices make decisions harder, not easier.[10] And while the world is at their fingertips, that means global competition and global dangers are that close too. We would not want to trade places with any of them: from establishing a career to finding a partner to paying for housing—growing up has become a lot "harder to do."[11]

The Journey Ahead

We wrote *The Twentysomething Soul* for those who want to understand how American twentysomethings find meaningful paths through the present cacophony of religious, spiritual, and secular options. There is no shortage of commentary about this. Perhaps you have read about the growing number of young adults who have no religious affiliation—the so-called Nones—and their desire to be spiritual but not religious. Perhaps you have heard religious leaders or parents opine about why young adults grow disinterested in their childhood religion and wonder whether they will come back. Or perhaps you know of young adults for whom religion has become the ordering principle for their entire lives. We think these are all important phenomena. Understanding the growth of Nones and discovering why some maintain theistic beliefs but are not interested in organized religion, others create an eclectic spirituality, while the rest reject or claim indifference to all things religious or spiritual is an important story to be told. But it is far from the whole story of twentysomething religiosity. Fully 71% of twentysomethings *do* affiliate with a religion, and 62% are Protestants or Catholics. One-third of twentysomethings go to church regularly and volunteer time and money to support their religion's activities—just as generations of American Christians have done before them. And the majority of twentysomethings value their religious *and* spiritual lives, seeing them as overlapping rather than exclusive dimensions. *The Twentysomething Soul* explores the range of ways young adults relate to religion and spirituality to better understand why some young adults steer away from and others steer toward religious institutions during "the long slog" to adulthood that begins at age 18 and may not end until the 30s.[12]

The Twentysomething Soul makes seven major claims about the religious, spiritual, and secular lives of American twentysomethings.

- First, the beliefs and practices of today's twentysomethings demonstrate continuity far more than decline. This is not an original claim, but few outside scholarly circles seem to know it. We hope to convey this reality more widely.

- Second, the 1 in 3 twentysomethings who attend worship regularly (i.e., a couple of times a month or more) do not distribute themselves evenly across religious institutions but cluster within young-adult-friendly congregations. Birds of a religious feather very much flock together.
- Third, the ranks of the religiously unaffiliated are permeable and include philosophical secularists, indifferent secularists, spiritual eclectics, and, yes, even those who believe in God. These ranks grow as twentysomethings age, but we found that philosophical secularism could be difficult for twentysomethings to maintain outside of higher education and cosmopolitan centers.
- Fourth, the 42.7 million Americans who fall between the ages of 20 and 29 settle into one of four strategies with respect to religious and spiritual life: (1) prioritizing religious and spiritual life, (2) rejecting organized religion and its traditional practices, (3) sidelining religious and spiritual life, or (4) practicing an eclectic spirituality. The latter is rarest, while the popular options are to sideline religion until feeling more "settled" or to demonstrate indifference to all things religious or spiritual.
- Fifth, twentysomethings organize spirituality into two broad types: traditional and nontraditional. The former includes practices and views conventionally encouraged in religion, such as prayer and spiritual growth, while the latter includes thinking of God "as a spiritual force" and regarding "any art or music as a way to communicate one's spirituality." *Both* forms of spirituality are most common among those who prioritize religious and spiritual life, undermining the common view that religion and spirituality are opposites among today's twentysomethings.
- Sixth, prioritizing religious and spiritual life correlates significantly with marriage, cohabitation, parenthood, college graduation, employment, voting, community engagement, and social engagement. And this holds true even when the effects of gender, income, race, ethnicity, and age are held constant.
- Seventh, today's twentysomethings experience the world less as sets of institutions prescribing standard life scripts and more as nodes

> on a network from which they can freely choose cultural symbols, strategies, and interpretations.[13] American twentysomethings, in other words, are practical and postmodern—and resolutely so.

In short, the pervasiveness of religion and spirituality in American culture is such that twentysomethings must make their peace with it: prioritizing, rejecting, sidelining, or innovating. These strategies, in turn, figure prominently into the statuses young adults attain during their 20s.

Both within the United States and across the Global North, the transition to adulthood has been profoundly altered.[14] Many young adults and observers intuit that a massive change has taken place—though they often mistake why. Just as the study of ecological life now requires a broad understanding of climate change, so too the study of young adults must be framed within an understanding of global economic and cultural change. We therefore begin Chapter 2 discussing young adulthood today in the context of the religious, spiritual, and secular lives of American twentysomethings during the past half-century.

We then focus our attention on twentysomethings who participate in American congregations. Regular worship attenders like Lee, Jeremy, and Maria do not need to be convinced about the importance of church involvement, but they do need to be convinced to join a specific congregation, and their church shopping provides invaluable insight into their priorities. In Chapters 3, 4, and 5, we explore the church selection process and what attracts young adults to Catholic, Mainline Protestant, and Evangelical churches. We show how religiously active twentysomethings, regardless of their specific affiliation, seek a community that includes a critical mass of young adults and promotes ideas they agree with. This is of paramount importance. But there are also other factors, involving issues of inclusivity, orthodoxy, passion, authenticity, intellectualism, outreach, preaching, music, and liturgy that make or break a young adult's choice of congregation. Rightly combined, these factors leave young adult visitors shedding tears of joy upon experiencing what they have "been looking for [their] whole life." If poorly combined, however, young adult visitors exit and never return.

Then, we report on twentysomethings who, like Abby, do not affiliate with religion. And one of the first myths we expose in Chapter 6 is that the unaffiliated have no experience with organized religion. Many have been involved in religious organizations as children, and others have observed religious people and settings closely. Their religious disaffiliation is intentional. Some who are unaffiliated, to be sure, have grown up non-religious and have no experience with religion, while others practice an eclectic spirituality that charts a novel path. Nones are a diverse and highly fluid aggregation. They are also a large population, second only to Protestants.

Finally, we explain how our results add to what is known about the religious, spiritual, and secular lives of American twentysomethings. We use Chapter 7 to compare the religious and spiritual lives of young adults with those of adolescents, and to examine the relative importance of spirituality and religion in the lives of twentysomethings. Religious affiliation plays a prominent role in the frequency of attendance and type of spirituality that American twentysomethings report, while attendance and spirituality in turn have robust associations with life statuses of lasting consequence. In short, religion and spirituality make a difference in the lives of young adults, and not just among those who prioritize these matters, but also among those who reject religion, postpone their decisions about it, or pursue a spiritual path of their own.

The stories of Maria, Jeremy, Lee, and Abby introduced us to important themes in the religious, spiritual, and secular lives of American twentysomethings. The full story, though, requires a more systematic overview, as well as comparisons of today's young adults with previous cohorts of twentysomethings and with older generations today. We tell this story in the next chapter, framing it within an understanding of what scholars call "emerging adulthood." Think of it as a helicopter tour of the twentysomething habitat.

CHAPTER 2

Young Adulthood and Religion

Dottie & Ted

Dottie was 19 when she married Ted, who was three years her senior. She first spotted Ted in his navy uniform, showing off some fancy footwork in the center of the roller skating rink. When the announcer called out "ladies choice" and the organist began a Nat King Cole tune, Dottie made a beeline to the rink's center. Ted was charmed, and he and Dottie skated and spun around the rink with surprising ease. It was spring of 1947. Dottie and Ted got engaged that next Valentine's Day, and in August they were married in Dottie's church by the same vicar who baptized her. For a couple of years, they lived with Ted's parents and worked for the city electric company—Ted as a lineman, Dottie as a payment cashier. Shortly before the first baby arrived in 1952, she and Ted bought a house, and Dottie left her job to rear that child and the next four. Ted worked thirty-eight years for the electric company, retired with a good pension, and both he and Dottie lived into their 80s, enjoying nine grandchildren, four great-grandchildren, and a life centered on church and family.

At the time, there was nothing remarkable about Dottie and Ted's story. Their lives were one more performance of an American cultural script that everyone knew and appeared to perform with ease. Seven decades later, however, this script not only shows its age, but few are able or willing to perform it anymore. If today a teenage Dottie came home exuberant about a sailor Ted, she would likely be advised to put her education and career first, be told to consider other romantic options, and if still resistant, she would likely lose the respect of friends, the support of family, or the blessing of her vicar. The same would happen to Ted, who would also discover that his service in the navy offered limited traction in the workforce, and his General Education Diploma (GED) provided no path to an income sufficient to afford a house, a stay-at-home wife, and five children. The script that guided Dottie and Ted's lives and millions of other Americans in the post–World War II era has been shredded by seven decades' worth of macroeconomic and cultural change. In its place is a crowd-sourced menu offering scores of potential life scripts—few of which promise the financial, familial, and religious stability that Dottie and Ted experienced. This is the reality of coming of age in America today. This is "emerging adulthood."[1]

In this chapter we describe the core economic and cultural factors that have combined to create emerging adulthood. We then focus on twentysomethings' religious, spiritual, and secular lives, and close with a comparison of successive cohorts of American twentysomethings. To do this we use our National Study of American Twentysomethings (NSAT) and supplement that with data from the National Opinion Research Center's General Social Surveys (GSS).[2] That means we cite a lot of statistics in this chapter, but we do so using a lot of figures to illustrate the most important patterns and work to keep the big picture foremost in the discussion.

Lengthening Transition to Adulthood

The names given to today's twentysomethings vary, from extended adolescents and emerging adults to the boomerang generation, but the basic causes of the lengthening transition to adulthood are widely agreed upon.[3] The secure jobs with living wages and good benefits provided by America's manufacturing dominance are gone; the global economy relocated manufacturing to developing nations where labor is cheap and regulations minimal. In its place is a service economy that largely offers two kinds of work: low-skill, low-wage jobs or high-skill, high-wage jobs.[4] The former offer limited possibility of financial independence, while the latter require college and graduate school training and considerable educational debt. Understanding the importance of a college degree, today's high school graduates overwhelmingly plan to get one.[5] But nearly half of those who begin college with the goal of a four-year degree never graduate, leaving millions of twentysomethings in the worst possible state: saddled with college debt and lacking a college credential.[6] Those that do graduate are better positioned in the workplace, but that does not mean they have moved to easy street. They face stagnant incomes despite possessing bachelor's degrees, housing rents that rise in good times *and bad*, and job competition from anyone, anywhere in the globe with an internet connection and English skills.[7]

Life is more than work, of course. And few appreciate this more than twentysomethings. To have a social life today, though, requires investing in and closely monitoring social media. That is because friendships require communication, and the chief means of contemporary communication is digital. Today's twentysomethings, like it or not, have to make their peace with the digital status quo. As for their love lives, there is little more frustrating to twentysomethings than the hazy complexities of meeting, mating, and romantic partnering. The sexual freedom afforded by changing mores and readily available birth control is widely taken, but when added to a wariness about marriage, given the 1 in 3 odds of divorce, means twentysomethings must navigate relational pathways that feel untrodden and spend much of their 20s unsettled domestically.[8]

The effect of these economic, social, and relational realities on young adults is palpable. Twentysomethings inhabit an uncertain status, seeing a world of possibilities and even exploring its options, yet often feeling indecisive and doubtful about what it is that they even want.[9] Nor is this unreasonable: the world is more accessible than ever, and personal freedoms virtually unparalleled, but threats of every sort and violence undermine any sense of security. Uncertainty, sociologically speaking, is religion's raison d'être; that is, religion's traditional function in society is to address uncertainties and help members live productive lives. Dottie and Ted, for all they knew of the disruption that World War II wrought, did not experience anything like the uncertainty that today's twentysomethings do. They depended upon the cultural script taught to them by their families, reinforced during their schooling, and sanctified in their churches, and—most importantly—*it worked*.

With the cultural script that guided Dottie and Ted now moribund, how do today's twentysomethings sort out life's uncertainties? How do they engage, adapt, or avoid religion—the institution traditionally responsible for resolving uncertainty—as they journey through their 20s and forge their adult lives? To answer this, we studied twentysomethings who affiliate with America's three-largest religious groups: Evangelical Protestants, Mainline Protestants, Roman Catholics; and the religiously unaffiliated (i.e., Nones).[10] Ninety-one percent of American twentysomethings, in fact, identify with one of these four groups (see Figure 2.1). In the first chapter, we introduced one young adult from each of these four groups. In this chapter, we examine twentysomethings for these four groups systematically, using data in the NSAT and cumulative GSS.

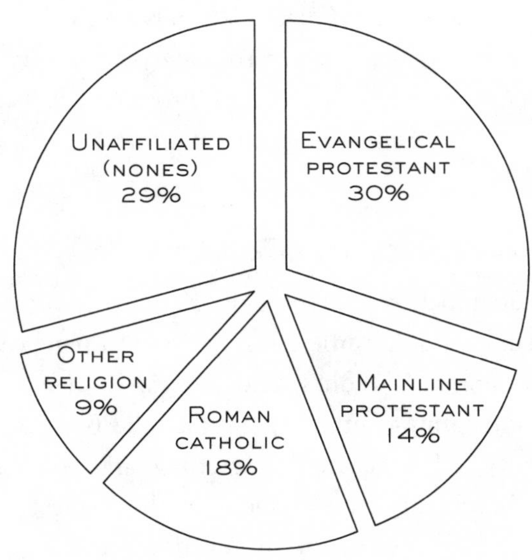

Figure 2.1

Religious Affiliations of American Twentysomethings

Source: NSAT 2013

Young Adults & Religious (Dis)Affiliation

Though the question is simple, "What is your religion?," the answers tell us much. Three out of 10 twentysomethings say they are Evangelical (i.e., Conservative) Protestants; for example, Baptists, Pentecostals, and nondenominational Christians.[11] Another 3 out of 10 answer "None"; that is, they indicate no affiliation with organized religion. Eighteen percent are Roman Catholic. Fourteen percent choose Mainline (i.e., Liberal) Protestant denominations; for example, Methodist, Lutheran, Presbyterian, or Episcopal churches. And 1 out of 11 indicate Mormon, Jewish, Muslim, Buddhist, Hindu, Eastern Orthodox, or "other non-Christian" religion (hereafter, "other" religion). Later in this chapter, and also in Chapter 7, we discuss findings from the NSAT about twentysomethings affiliated with other religions, but otherwise pass the investigation of this subpopulation of American young adults to future researchers. *The Twentysomething Soul* focuses on the lives of the 91% of American twentysomethings who affiliate with Christianity (Catholic or Protestant) or have no religious affiliation. In the next section, we discuss how the percentage of Protestants is declining and the percentage of religiously unaffiliated is climbing; the important points for now are the following: *7 out of 10 twentysomethings affiliate with a religion, 6 of these 7 affiliates choose Protestant or Catholic faiths, and 3 out of 10 twentysomethings do not affiliate with a religion.*

The Demography of (Dis)Affiliation

Young adults do not choose their religious affiliations at random. There are intriguing demographic differences between Evangelical Protestants, Mainline Protestants, Catholics, and Nones. Evangelicalism attracts many twentysomethings with its view that the Bible is God's Word, who then mostly self-segregate due to ethnic and political differences (see Chapter 5). Evangelicalism includes the highest percentage of Black young adults. Catholicism, by contrast, attracts the highest percentage of Hispanic and fewest Black young adults, while Mainline Protestantism draws a disproportionate share of White young adults.

It is the unaffiliated, however, that attracts the largest population of White young adults (see Figure 2.2). These race distributions fit with historic patterns; the oft-named "Black Church" refers to Protestant churches that are overwhelmingly Evangelical in theology, the dominance of Roman Catholicism among Spanish-speaking peoples is a worldwide phenomenon, and the declaration of no religious affiliation comes from those whose White privilege leaves them most confident in their rejection of a widespread social practice.

Male and female twentysomethings report Mainline Protestant, Catholic, and no religious affiliation equally. But there are notable gender differences in affiliation with Evangelicalism: more females than males affiliate with Evangelicalism (56% and 44%, respectively). This differential cannot, unfortunately, be interpreted with the data we possess. Perhaps certain young adult women find the traditional gender roles promoted by Evangelical churches to be particularly appealing, perhaps the sentimentalism of Evangelical

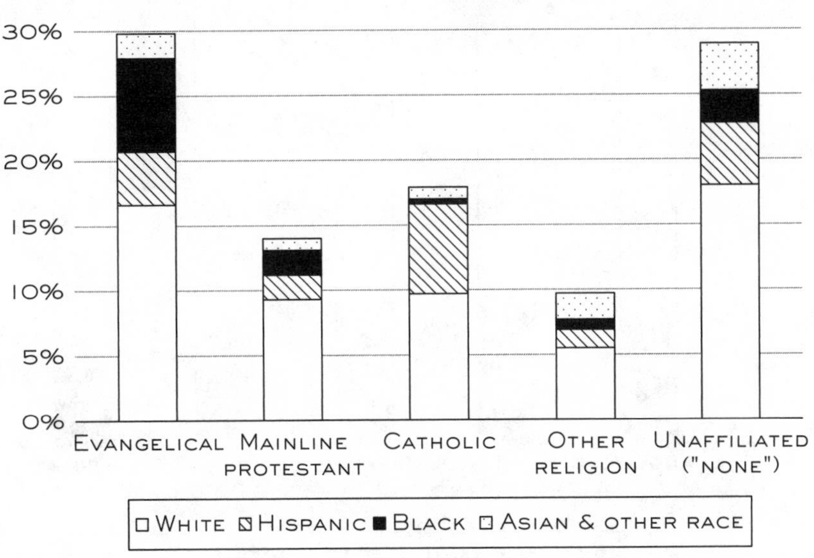

FIGURE 2.2

Race and Ethnicity of American Twentysomething Population by Religious Affiliation

Source: NSAT 2013

worship makes male twentysomethings uncomfortable, or perhaps the long-tilted gender ratios of Evangelical churches have become a self-fulfilling prophecy. We can confirm that the lower proportion of twentysomething Evangelical males supports anecdotal accounts from female twentysomethings at Evangelical churches, whose hopes of meeting marriageable males with similar religious commitments were not (yet) being fulfilled.

That marriage is important in Evangelical Protestant circles is more than anecdotal; however. More than 1 in 4 Evangelicals are married, while Mainline Protestant, Catholic, and unaffiliated twentysomethings have rates of 1 in 5 married or lower (see Figure 2.3). Cohabitation rates, by contrast, are lower among Protestant and Catholic twentysomethings, and highest among Nones. But cohabitation is not infrequent among Christian twentysomethings, despite its lack of religious approval: 1 out of 6 Catholic and 1 out of

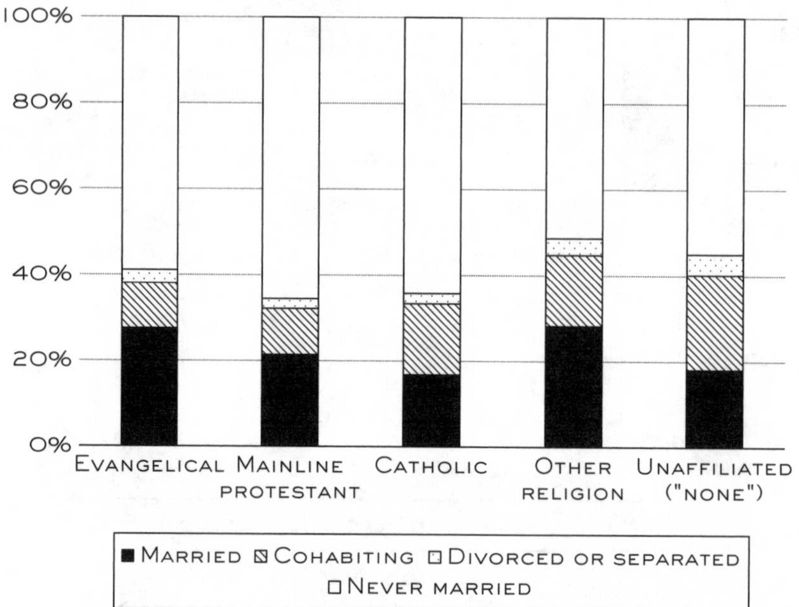

Figure 2.3

Marital Status of American Twentysomethings by Religious Affiliation

Source: NSAT 2013

9 Protestant twentysomethings currently cohabit. This is the first instance of cultural accommodation we have encountered, but there are more to come. It indicates that Christian twentysomethings take advantage of the personal freedom they enjoy as Americans and combine practices and beliefs according to their own consciences, not official church teaching.

Few statuses may be of greater social import than becoming a parent or graduating from college. And few may be more linked than having a child and completing one's education. Evangelical twentysomethings are a case in point: they are the most likely to be parents (28%) and least likely to graduate from college (29%; see Figure 2.4). So too are Mainline Protestant and unaffiliated twentysomethings: their lower rate of being parents (17%) pairs with their higher rate of graduation from college (36%). But odds are not always determinative, as

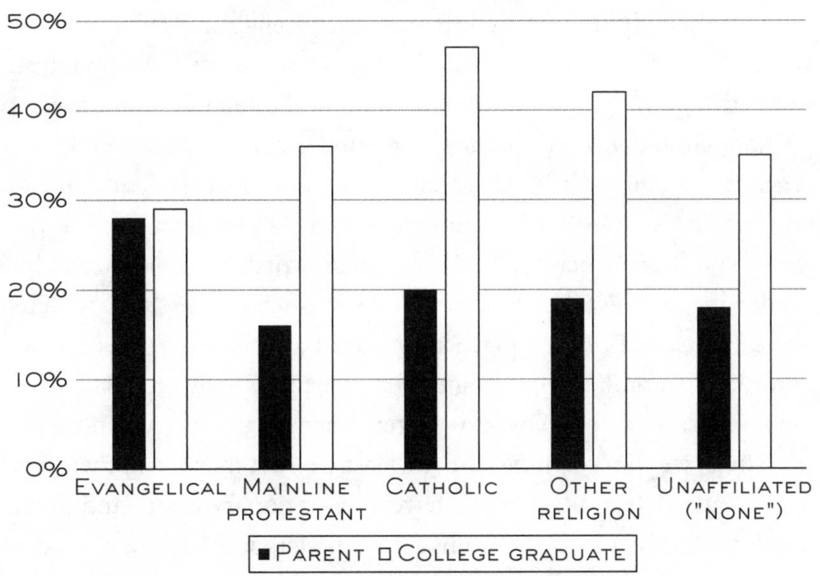

Figure 2.4

Parenthood and College Graduation Rates of American Twentysomethings by Religious Affiliations

Note: College graduation rates calculated for those 24–29 years of age only.

Source: NSAT 2013

Catholic twentysomethings are second-most likely to be parents (20%) but *most* likely to graduate from college (47%). These college graduation rates, in particular, are interesting because they demonstrate (1) the century-long social ascendancy of (White) American Catholics, (2) the parity of Mainline Protestant and unaffiliated twentysomethings with the national graduation average,[12] (3) the continued educational lag among Evangelicals, and (4) the changing relationship between higher education and religiosity. The last of these is most important: a half-century ago, there was a strong, negative relationship between higher education and religion; today, this relationship is neutral if not positive. In fact, college graduates are more likely to attend worship services regularly and volunteer with religious organizations than those who have not graduated college.[13]

Worship Attendance

There are, clearly, important differences between Protestants, Catholics, and Nones. Some of these are demographic, some are educational, and some involve religious practices as well as the relative importance of religion. Attendance at worship is a good place to begin our look at practices, as congregational worship requires time, travel, and interaction with a religious organization, its leaders, and its members. Several things stand out when we look at regular worship attendance, which we define as a few times monthly or more often (see Figure 2.5). First, we see that 2 out of 3 Evangelical, 1 out of 3 Mainline Protestant, and 2 out of 5 Catholic twentysomethings attend worship regularly. That is a remarkable rate of voluntary attendance—especially when we consider that twentysomethings are the least well-established in their work lives of all adults and have the fewest discretionary hours and dollars of all adults. Given all the grousing from clergy about the absence of twentysomethings in their congregations,[14] we expected far lower rates. It could be that twentysomethings are over-reporting their attendance, that clergy are undercounting young adults, or that twentysomethings are clustering with peers in a fraction of churches. There is extant support for the first and extensive research on misperception for the

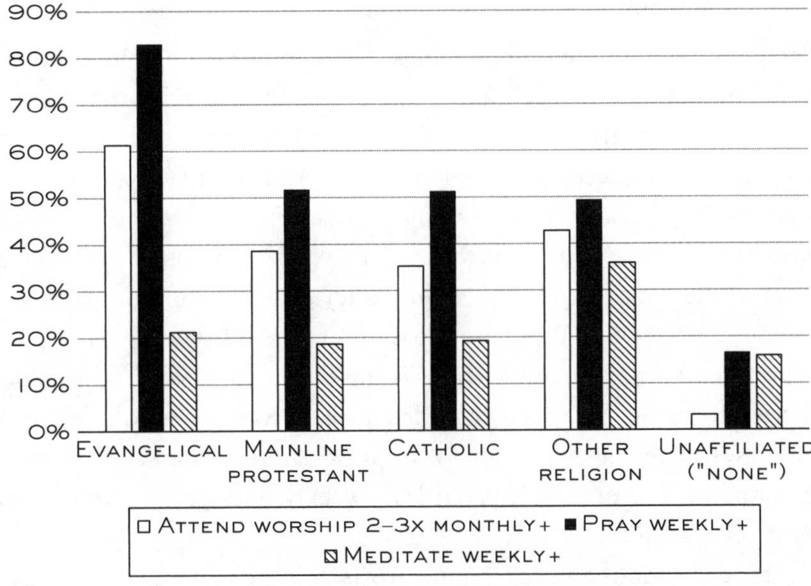

Figure 2.5

Worship Attendance, Prayer, and Meditation of American Twentysomethings by Religious Affiliations

Source: NSAT 2013

second,[15] but the latter is an original argument we extend based on our project's research.

Not all religiously affiliated twentysomethings attend worship. About 1 out of 11 Catholic and Evangelical, and 1 out of 6 Mainline Protestant twentysomethings in the NSAT indicate that they never attend worship services. That rate of nonattendance among Christians is dwarfed by the 3 out of 4 rate of nonattendance among unaffiliated twentysomethings. Yet, one might expect to find no attendance at worship among Nones, so hearing that 1 in 4 attend worship occasionally is intriguing (and especially the 1 in 25 Nones who reports attending regularly). Recent scholarship begins to explain this: a sizable proportion of Nones are "unaffiliated believers" or "culturally religious," and as such they attend worship occasionally or even regularly.[16] This finding is the first of several we relay about the considerable diversity among twentysomethings who are unaffiliated.

Prayer & Meditation

Prayer is, by far, twentysomethings' most frequent religious activity. Eight out of 10 Evangelical, 5 out of 10 Mainline Protestant and Catholic, and nearly 2 out of 10 unaffiliated twentysomethings report praying at least weekly (see Figure 2.5). And for twentysomethings who do pray, it is most often a daily activity. To be sure, there is wide variation in how twentysomethings define prayer; it could be anything from a "Help me, God" uttered during icy driving conditions to a recitation of the Lord's Prayer to a focused hour of private prayer. That prayer can occur in many settings is important to remember, as is the diverse forms it can take—from memorized recitations to anguished pleas. Whatever the setting or form, American twentysomethings do a lot of praying: 1 out of 2 pray at least weekly, and 7 out of 10 pray at least occasionally.

Less common than prayer, but surprisingly frequent given its lower emphasis in American Christianity, is meditation. About 1 out of 5 Christian twentysomethings indicate meditating at least weekly, with the highest rates reported by Evangelicals, while 1 out of 6 Nones report meditating at least weekly. The higher rate of meditation among religiously affiliated twentysomethings is important to note because meditation is often associated with the spiritual but not religious subgroup of the Nones, about which we will say more later (see Chapter 6). As with prayer, we did not define meditation but let respondents apply their own definitions as they answered the question. Some, perhaps most, may meditate for religious and spiritual reasons, but some may do so for its known physical and psychological benefits.[17] Whatever the reason, American twentysomethings meditate with impressive frequency—20% at least weekly and another 20% occasionally.

Importance of Religion

Another way to gauge the importance of religion among twentysomethings is to ask them directly. More than 6 out of 10 Evangelicals say their religious faith is "very" or "extremely important" in their everyday life. About 3 out of 10 Mainline Protestants, 4 out of 10 Catholics, and 1 out of 20 Nones say the same.[18] These proportions fit with worship attendance rates of religious twentysomethings and the nonattendance of unaffiliated twentysomethings, confirming the reliability of these NSAT measures. These measures also match results from other national surveys,[19] including the GSS results presented in the next section, demonstrating their validity.

Belief & Theology

So far, we have seen that American twentysomethings attend worship at a remarkably frequent rate, rank religion as very important in their lives, and pray frequently, with some even meditating regularly. We have also learned about unaffiliated twentysomethings, most of whom do not do these things, but some of whom do. In this section, we examine what twentysomethings believe about God, what doubts twentysomethings may have about their religious beliefs (or lack thereof), what they think of their religion's truth claims, and what importance they assigned to their religious faith as children. The former two convey the certainty of twentysomethings' beliefs, while the latter speaks to the continuity of twentysomethings' faith.

Christian twentysomethings believe, with certainty, in God—as the NSAT offered both "no" and "unsure" as additional options. Ninety-seven percent of Evangelical, 83% of Catholic *and* Mainline Protestant, and 26% of unaffiliated twentysomethings express belief in God (see Figure 2.6). When the question is narrowed to belief in God as "a personal being involved in the lives of people today," however, the percentages decline—and significantly so among Catholic, Mainline Protestant, and unaffiliated twentysomethings. What a sizable share of Catholic, Mainline Protestant, and unaffiliated twentysomethings opt for instead is a God that is not "personal" but rather "something like a cosmic life force." Disbelief in God, to be sure, represents the single largest category among the unaffiliated. This is not surprising. What may be surprising is that one in six Nones believe in a personal God who is active in people's lives, which indicates that these Nones

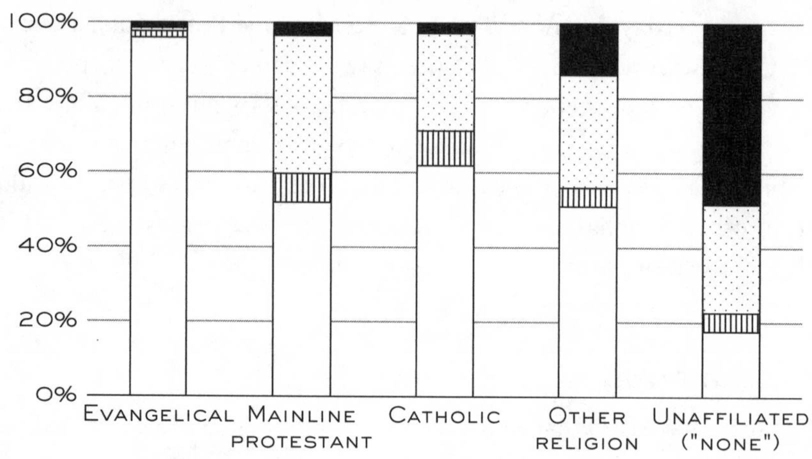

Figure 2.6

Beliefs about God Among American Twentysomethings by Religious Affiliations

Source: NSAT 2013

are traditional believers, and that their disaffiliation is with organized religion, not with belief in God.

Certainty about God's existence notwithstanding, Christian twentysomethings are less certain of religion's truth claims or their religious beliefs in general. Two out of 3 Catholic and 4 out of 5 Mainline Protestant twentysomethings believe "many religions may be true," rejecting the view that "only one religion is true." And half of Catholic and Mainline Protestant twentysomethings indicate having some doubts in the last year about their religious beliefs. Evangelical twentysomethings, however, indicate high levels of certainty: nearly 2 out of 3 affirm "only one religion is true," and the same proportion indicate "no doubts" about their religious beliefs.[20] But it is unaffiliated twentysomethings who express the highest certainty about their views: when asked if they had any doubts in the previous year "about being nonreligious," 3 out of 4 Nones said no. Moreover, 19 out of 20 unaffiliated twentysomethings reject the view that "only one religion is true," with 13 of the 19 indicating "there is very little truth in any religion." While many Nones do believe in God and pray on occasion, the terms "religion" and "religious" provoke strong and negative responses from the unaffiliated. They are, in short, quite certain about their nonreligiousness.

An important reason why belief in God may be so common among American twentysomethings is the importance of their faith as children. Seven out of 10 Protestants and 2 out of 3 Catholics agreed with the statement "as a child, my religious faith was very important to me."[21] Childhood religion was more important, in fact, than many twentysomethings said their religion was at present (see above). Yet a vital faith during childhood is no guarantee of vitality or even continued affiliation with religion in adulthood, as 1 out of 4 unaffiliated twentysomethings report their religion had been very important to them as children. The effects of childhood religion on twentysomethings are multifaceted, and we examine them further in the chapters that follow.

Religious People & Churches

One thing that all twentysomethings have in common is their *overwhelming* agreement that "too many religious people in this country" are "negative, angry, and judgmental" (see Figure 2.7). Three out of 5 Christian and 4 out of 5 unaffiliated twentysomethings endorse this statement, with Mainline Protestants being the most likely to agree of Christian twentysomethings. Given such broad disappointment with "religious people," we expected to find similar frustration with houses of worship. But there was little carryover. Three out of 4 Protestant, 3 out of 5 Catholic, and even 1 out of 3 unaffiliated twentysomethings agreed that most "churches and synagogues today" are "effective in helping people find meaning in life." Two out of 3 Christian and 2 out of 5 unaffiliated twentysomethings, moreover, *disagreed* that "mainstream religion" is "irrelevant" to "people my age," and slightly higher proportions of these respective twentysomethings *disagreed* that most

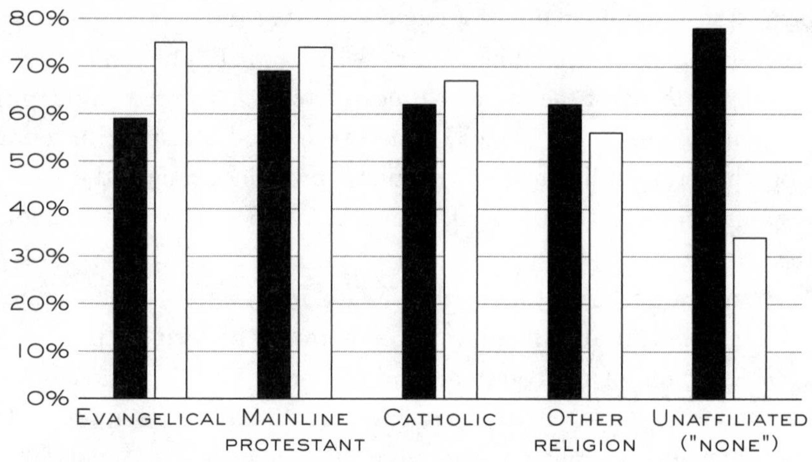

Figure 2.7

View of Religious People and Churches in America Across Religious Affiliations of American Twentysomethings

Source: NSAT 2013

"churches and synagogues today" are "not concerned enough with social justice."[22] This is fascinating, because it overturns a lot of claims that young adults are critical of churches.[23] They certainly object to angry and judgmental parishioners, but not to the parishes themselves. Today's twentysomethings are rather respectful of the role played by American houses of worship.

Spiritual Life

Spiritual life or spirituality means different things to different people; some consider it an integral part of living out a religious faith, while others regard it as independent and distinct from religion. We focus here on three survey items: the importance of spiritual growth as adults, personal experiences of spiritual and emotional connection, and view of God as a spiritual force.

First, we see that 6 out of 10 Evangelicals, 3 out of 10 Mainline Protestants, 3 out of 10 Catholics, and 1 out of 10 unaffiliated twentysomethings agree that spiritual growth is "very important to me" (see Figure 2.8). These are sizable differences in views of spiritual growth among religious affiliations, and they become quite important to our discussion of the comparative import of religious affiliation, attendance at religious services, and spirituality in Chapter 7. For now, the point to remember is that twentysomethings' religious affiliations and the importance that twentysomethings assign to spiritual life are not random, but distinctly patterned.

Second, 1 out of 2 Christian twentysomethings and 3 out of 10 unaffiliated twentysomethings agree that "I often feel a strong spiritual or emotional connection with all the people around me."[24] This is striking for two reasons: the high agreement among Christian twentysomethings that this feeling of connection happens "often," and that whether interpreted as spiritual or emotional, there is still a

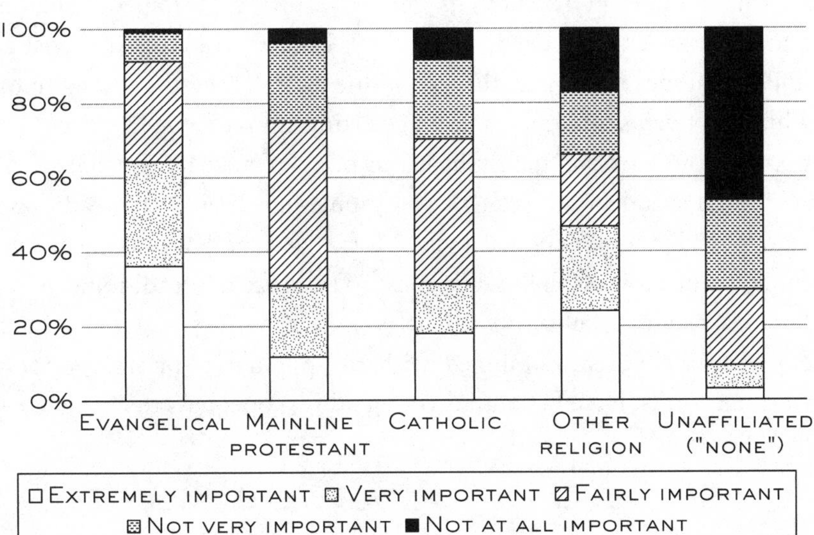

Figure 2.8

Importance of Spiritual Growth as an Adult Across Religious Affiliations of American Twentysomethings

Source: NSAT 2013

substantial gap in the experience of this between Christian and unaffiliated twentysomethings.

Third, we have already noted that a sizeable share of Catholic (26%), Mainline Protestant (40%), and unaffiliated twentysomethings (29%) indicate they believe God is "something like a cosmic life force." Moreover, 2 out of 5 Mainline and Catholic twentysomethings, 1 out of 3 unaffiliated twentysomethings, and 1 out of 4 Evangelical twentysomethings agree that "I used to believe in a personal God, but now I think of God as a spiritual force." This indicates the strong appeal of nontraditional views of God. So strong, in fact, that one-fifth of Evangelical twentysomethings affirm the following contradictory statements: "God is a personal being and involved in the lives of people today" *and* "I used to believe in a personal God, but now I think of God as a spiritual force."

So what does all of this tell us about the spiritual lives of twentysomethings? The high concern for spiritual growth along with experiences of spiritual or emotional connection with others reported by Christian twentysomethings demonstrate the overlap of religious and spiritual experiences in their lives. That is, traditional Christian understandings of spirituality continue to hold sway among most Christian twentysomethings, even as claims about being "spiritual but not religious" are frequently heard in popular media (see Chapter 6). At the same time, quite a few twentysomethings reject the traditional view of "God as a personal being" for a view of "God as a spiritual force," which reveals their willingness to embrace nontraditional views. Perhaps the toy light saber battles that today's twentysomethings enjoyed as children, combined with the popularity of stories about spiritual forces, have facilitated young adults' openness to cosmic spiritual forces.[25]

In a Nutshell

We have learned that 6 out of 10 American twentysomethings affiliate with Protestant or Catholic traditions, and 3 out of 10 do not affiliate with a religion. Many, but not most, Christian twentysomethings attend worship regularly, pray daily, and indicate their faith is important to their everyday lives, and some meditate regularly. A few unaffiliated twentysomethings do these things too. In addition, Christian twentysomethings overwhelmingly affirm that God is personal and involved in the world, and indicate their religious faith was very important to them as children. Sizable minorities of the unaffiliated also affirm these two statements. Yet American twentysomethings are pluralist when it comes to truth in religion: for example, most reject the view that "only one religion is true," and we saw earlier that solid majorities believe "too many religious people these days are negative, angry, and judgmental," and unaffiliated twentysomethings are especially disapproving of exclusivist and judgmental religious discourse.

Given twentysomethings' disapproval of judgmental religious people, it is surprising to see how positively they view "churches and synagogues today" and "mainstream religion." Most twentysomethings are not alienated from religion per se, and even among unaffiliated twentysomethings, there are many with benign views of churches and synagogues. Perhaps the high value that Christian twentysomethings assign to spiritual growth, or their experiences of spiritual connection to others, plays a role in twentysomethings' regard for houses of worship. At the same time, spirituality is no longer the exclusive province of organized religion, and Christian twentysomethings often disregard their religion's party line on views of God: about 1 out of 3 Christian *and* unaffiliated twentysomethings consider God to be a spiritual force rather than a personal being.

It strikes us that religion among twentysomethings is akin to the polar ice cap: there is plenty of ice now and likely will be for years to come, but the melt rate is rising and if sustained, the long-term impact will be staggering. Similarly, there is plenty of religious life among twentysomethings now and likely will be for years; but the disaffiliation rate from organized religion is significant and the long-term impact could be substantial. The analyses that follow examine religious change across successive cohorts of American twentysomethings, then contrast the religiosity of current twentysomethings with that of their older American counterparts. But first, some observations about American twentysomethings who affiliate with religions other than Protestant or Catholic Christianity are in order.

Other Religious Affiliations

Though our focus is on the 91% of twentysomethings who are Christians or Nones, we can report some basic findings regarding those who affiliate with other religions. They are a tremendously diverse group, and this presents a significant challenge for researchers. Within the other religious affiliations, the largest subcategory is Mormons (2.5% of American twentysomethings), then Jews (1.6%), Buddhists (0.7%), Hindus (0.5%), Muslims (0.4%), and Eastern Orthodox Christians (0.2%). That still leaves 2.5% of American twentysomethings who specify affiliations other than these. World religions are, moreover, as internally diverse as the American Christians we did study. American Judaism, for example, is understood by its practitioners as having four subdivisions: Reform, Conservative, Orthodox, and nondenominational[26]—and we would have needed at least fifty survey respondents and thirty in-depth interviewees from each to speak with confidence about any one of these groups. While we did not have the resources to tackle this challenge, we hope others will be able to shed more light on the lives of these twentysomethings.

That said, we can offer these observations about the 9% of American twentysomethings who affiliate with other religions. First, this category is demographically distinctive for having the highest proportion of twentysomethings indicating Asian and "other race," the highest proportion of married twentysomethings, and the second-highest proportion of college graduates (see Figures 2.2, 2.3, 2.4). Second, twentysomething affiliates of other religions report the highest rates of weekly meditation and second highest rates of worship attendance (see Figure 2.5). Third, while half of these twentysomethings affirm a view of God as personal and involved in people's lives, 3 out of 10 view God as a cosmic life force and 1 in 7 do not believe in God (see Figure 2.6). Fourth, these affiliates of other religions are comparable to Christian twentysomethings in their agreement that "too many religious people these days are negative, angry, and judgmental" and that "most churches today are effective in helping people find meaning in life" (see Figure 2.7). Fifth, this category divides rather interestingly over the importance of spiritual growth as an adult—ranking second highest in those answering "extremely" or "very" important *and* second highest in those answering "not very" or "not at all important" (see Figure 2.8).

Due to the wide differences among religions with which 9% of American twentysomethings affiliate, our interpretations must remain general. But we can say the following: there is significant devotion to religious life among young adults who are neither Protestant nor Catholic, and often in greater measure than found among their Christian counterparts. There is also evidence of greater interest in spiritual life—as seen in the importance assigned to spiritual growth, the frequency with which these twentysomethings meditate, and the sizable proportion who view God as an impersonal, cosmic life force. Exactly how this fits together, especially when combined with the high rates of marriage and college graduation of these twentysomethings, lies beyond the data we possess and underscores the need for continued research. For just as the 5% and 6% of yesterday's twentysomethings who affiliated with other religions became the 9% of today's twentysomethings so affiliated (see Figures 2.9, 2.12, and discussion in the next section), the 9% of today's twentysomethings will become 10%, 11%, or 12% of tomorrow's twentysomethings affiliated with other religions, and slowly, but oh so surely, the nature of Americans' religious and spiritual lives will shift as well.

When I Was Your Age

Memories are notoriously unreliable and generally grow worse with age. The purpose of this section is to compare the affiliations, rates of worship attendance, frequency of prayer, and some key religious beliefs of twentysomethings surveyed in the 1970s, 1980s, 1990s, and

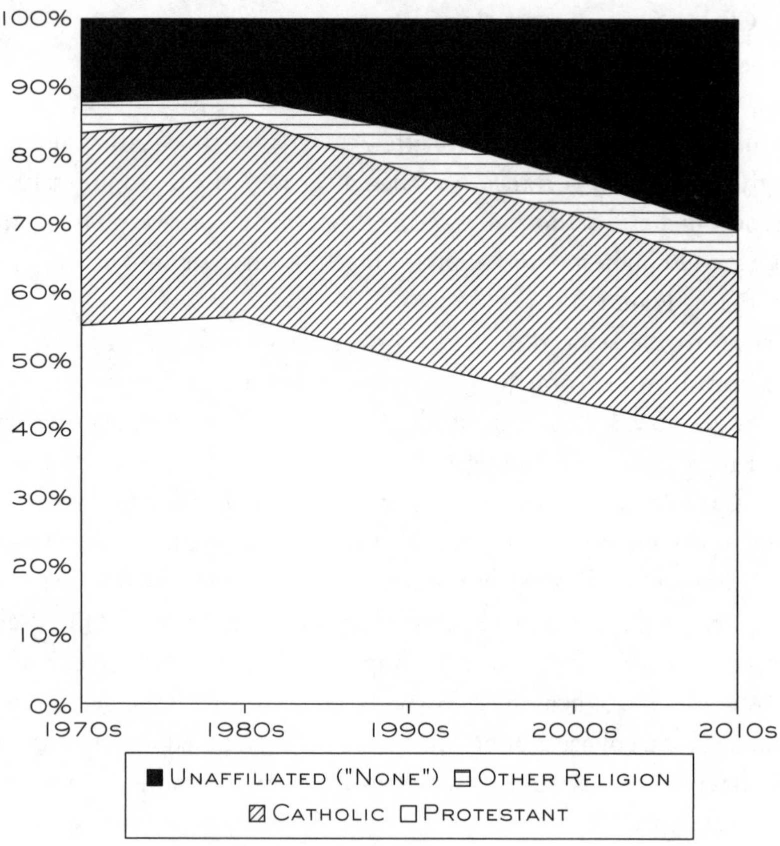

Figure 2.9

Religious Affiliations of American Twentysomethings Across Decades
Source: GSS 1972–2016

2000s with those surveyed in the 2010s. This way we can determine with precision how today's twentysomethings compare to their parents and grandparents *when they were in their 20s*. We can do this thanks to National Science Foundation's support of the GSS, a nationally representative survey of American adults conducted annually or biannually since 1972.[27] Limiting analyses to those age 20 to 29, grouping by decade, then presenting these results with the assistance of figures illustrates the persistence of religion as well as its changes across decades of young adults.

Young Adult Religion Across Decades

If you threw a stone into a randomly assembled crowd of twentysomethings in the 1970s, you would have had a better than 1 in 2 chance of hitting a Protestant; today your odds are 2 in 5 (see Figure 2.9). Protestantism is still, in aggregate, the largest affiliation of American young adults. But its popularity is slipping, and we know from other research that the decline among Mainline Protestants has been greater than the decline among Evangelicals.[28] A smaller proportion of twentysomethings affiliate with Roman Catholicism today than in the 1970s, but this decline would have been severe if not substantially offset by the infusion of Latino twentysomethings. White "cradle Catholics" have disaffiliated with the Church at a substantial rate during the past half-century, but their seats have been mostly filled by Latino immigrants.[29] Finally, twentysomethings indicating a religious affiliation other than Protestant or Catholic, though proportionately small, have increased, while twentysomethings choosing no religious affiliation have almost tripled between the 1970s and the 2010s.

Clearly, affiliation with religion is changing among Americans in their 20s. So, too, are rates of attendance at worship services (see Figure 2.10). These changes are smaller: where 2 out of 5 twentysomethings attended regularly in the 1970s, slightly more than 1 out of 3 do so in the 2010s. Where change is most evident is in the increasing proportion of twentysomethings who never attend worship and the decreasing proportion who do so occasionally. And yet, when viewed across five decades, we see these rates of regular worship attendance as being remarkably stable given the many other social and cultural changes that marked these years. Indeed, there is considerable stability in proportion of religiously active twentysomethings across decades, which becomes apparent when we examine prayer and beliefs.

Of all the images of American young adults that abound in popular media, few show twentysomethings praying. But that is a wholly appropriate image: in the 2010s, 2 out of 3 twentysomethings reported that they prayed weekly, and most prayed daily (see Figure

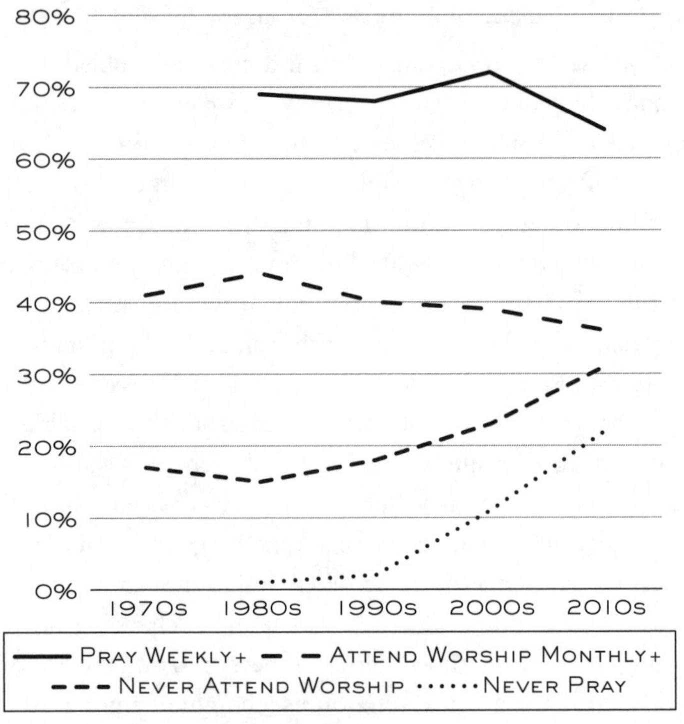

Figure 2.10

Frequency of Worship Attendance and Prayer Among American Twentysomethings Across Decades

Note: No data for prayer available before 1980.

Source: GSS 1972–2016

2.10). That rate of prayer has been relatively stable since the GSS first asked about prayer in the 1980s. What has changed is the proportion of twentysomethings who say they never prayed—from 1 in 100 in the 1980s to 1 in 5 in the 2010s. Not praying has gained a lot of ground among twentysomethings, but chiefly from territory vacated by twentysomethings who prayed less than weekly.

How are we to make sense of all this? This final set of comparisons is helpful. First, we see that 4 out of 5 twentysomethings affirm belief in life after death from the 1970s to the 2010s, with a slight increase in affirmation over the past half-century (see Figure 2.11). Second, we see the same proportion affirming belief in the Bible as God's Word

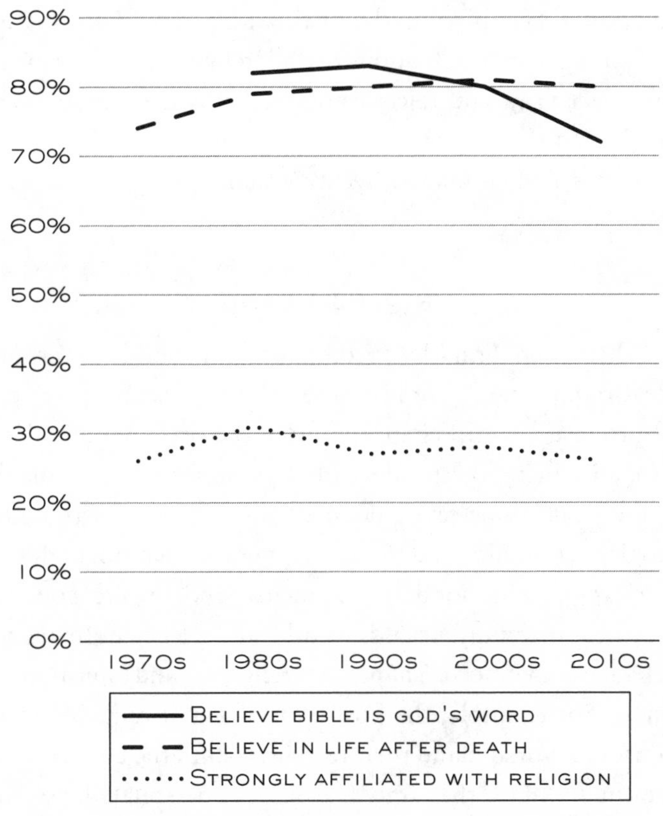

Figure 2.11

Beliefs and Strength of Religious Affiliation of American Twentysomethings Across Decades

Source: GSS 1972–2014

Note: "Believe Bible Is God's Word" combines "literal, word for word" and "inspired by God" answers; this item first asked in 1984.

during the 1980s through 2000s, with a decline in the 2010s. Third, we see a stable proportion of twentysomethings, more than 1 out of 4, who indicate their affiliation with religion is "strong." In other words, twentysomethings' belief in life after death and in the Bible as God's Word runs high and fairly stable, while strong religious affiliations are low but stable. American twentysomethings are overwhelmingly a believing and praying cohort, and have been across five decades, with a sizable minority (about 3 out of 10) strongly affiliating with religion and attending worship regularly. At the same time, there is a growing minority (about 1 in 4) who do not affiliate with religion, never attend worship, never pray, and reject traditional beliefs in the Bible and life after death, and this secular segment is gaining ground previously occupied by nominally affiliated twentysomethings.

Aging and Changing

In 1789, Benjamin Franklin wrote there are but two certainties in life: "death and taxes."[30] With more than two centuries elapsed, we humbly propose a third: change. During the first two decades of life, this change is chiefly the product of physical growth and maturation. During the next six or seven decades, this change is wrought by the technologic, economic, and social changes of nation and globe (of which emerging adulthood is testament), and by life course events involving health, family, friends, work, and place. Both macro- and micro-changes, therefore, shape the religious and spiritual lives of individuals. For example, the post–World War II religious resurgence filled houses of worship and their treasuries until the counter-culture of the 1960s undermined the same. The onset of personal illness, similarly, drives some to prayer and others forever out the door of any congregation. Beliefs and practices morph as individuals experience the life course, and past research indicates they shift toward increased spiritual and religious practice.[31] We certainly see changes in belief and practice when we compare today's twentysomethings with older age cohorts, but these changes are not always in the expected direction—which has important implications for understanding religion and spirituality across the life course (see Chapter 7).

Starting with the most basic indicator, affiliation with a religion, we notice several things when comparing today's twentysomethings with those aged 30–44, 45–59, or 60 plus (see Figure 2.12). First, we see that Protestants comprise the largest category across all age cohorts, and that the proportion of Protestant affiliates is greatest among those 60 plus and smallest among those under 30. This fits with the

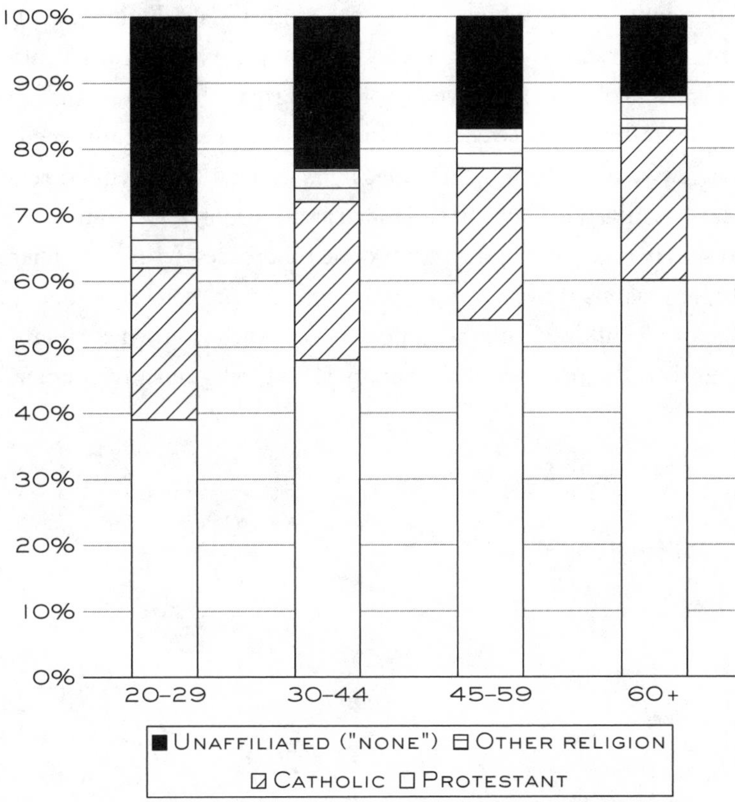

Figure 2.12

Religious Affiliation Across American Age Cohorts

Source: GSS 2014

shifting affiliations we observed earlier (see Figure 2.9). Second, we see *stable* proportions of Roman Catholics across age cohorts (23–24%), which actually indicates *dis*affiliation from Catholicism among older Americans (who as twentysomethings had 27–28% rates of affiliation with Catholicism). Third, we see religious disaffiliation concentrated among today's twentysomethings, and lower among America's older cohorts, but *not as low* as we would expect based on their cohorts' responses when they were twentysomethings: about 1% of the over 60 cohort, 6% of the 45–59 cohort, and 3% of the 30–44 cohort disaffiliated with religion *after* turning 30.

Attendance at worship rises across cohorts (see Figure 2.13). One out of 2 Americans over 60 attends worship services at least monthly, compared to 1 out of 3 twentysomethings, with 30–44- and 45–59-year-olds falling in-between. But look at Figure 2.10 again. See how 2 out of 5 twentysomethings in the 1970s and 1980s attended religious services regularly? Their attendance rate, presently, is 1 out of 2. This means that regular worship attendance increases with age. There are multiple reasons why: age correlates with being "settled"—being married, having children, owning a home—and these in turn correlate with civic and community involvement, including religious involvement (see

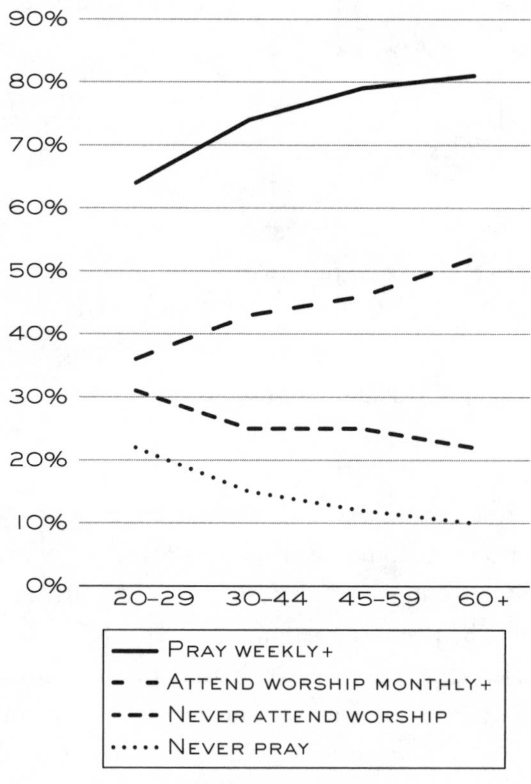

Figure 2.13

Frequency of Worship Attendance and Prayer Across American Age Cohorts

Source: GSS 2014

Chapter 7). At the same time, many Americans do not attend worship services. Three out of 10 twentysomethings, 2.5 out of 10 Americans aged 30–59, and 2 out of 10 Americans over 60 never attend religious worship. Older generations are least likely to never attend religious worship. Yet, consider this: 1 out of 6 Americans over 60 did not attend worship when they were in their 20s; today, 1 out of 5 of these Americans does not attend. This tells us that as Americans proceed through the life course, they mostly opt for regular attendance or consistent nonattendance. In other words, with respect to attending worship, Americans choose to "fish or cut bait."

Many things can affect worship attendance: work schedules, health, location, and more. Prayer is less affected by these things, however, making it a useful addition to our indicators of religiosity. Thus far, we have seen the popularity of prayer among American twentysomethings, and its popularity across decades. Here we begin to understand why twentysomethings pray a lot: they have learned it from older American cohorts (see Figure 2.13). Two out of 3 twentysomethings, 3 out of 4 Americans age 30–44 years, and 4 out of 5 Americans age 45 and over pray at least weekly. Had we seen these rates without the analyses above, we might conclude prayer is declining in America. But that would be wrong, because 2 out of 3 twentysomethings in the 1970s and 1980s prayed weekly (see Figure 2.10). In fact, Americans 45 and over who pray at least weekly have seen 10% more of their cohort peers join them in prayer. That is really interesting. But so is this: 10% of Americans 45 and over have joined the 1–2% of their peers who, when in their 20s, never prayed. The middle category of infrequent prayer, in other words, is vacated as adults age. They settle into regular prayer or none at all.

Other reasons why twentysomethings may pray as often as they do is their wide agreement with Americans over age 30 about the Bible as God's Word and about life after death (see Figure 2.14). Seven out of 10 twentysomethings believe the Bible is the inspired or even literal Word of God; 8 out of 10 Americans over 30 believe likewise. And wholly 4 out of 5 Americans age 20 and up believe in life after death. Few public issues find agreement this broad in the United States; President

Franklin D. Roosevelt's "landslide" election in 1936, for example, was built on winning 61% of the popular vote. Americans *overwhelmingly* believe there is more to life than meets the eye, whether we go up or down the age spectrum.

Finally, we must note that the strength of Americans' religious affiliation increases with age. Recall that a steady 1 out of 4 twentysomethings since the 1970s indicated that they were strongly affiliated (see Figure 2.11). Today, among Americans over 45, the rate jumps to 4 out of 10. We arrive then at an interesting conclusion: while religious affiliation is declining among Americans in general, among those who *do* affiliate, the proportion that does so strongly increases with age. We also arrive

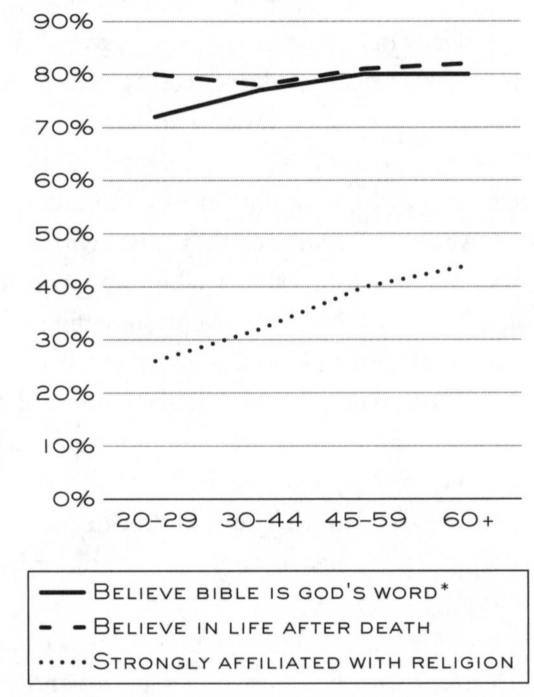

Figure 2.14

Beliefs and Strength of Religious Affiliation Across American Age Cohorts

Source: GSS 2014

Note: "Believe Bible is God's Word" combines "literal, word for word" and "inspired by God" answers; this item first asked in 1984.

at verse four of a now familiar song: the tepidly affiliated ranks thin out with age, while the confidently affiliated and unaffiliated ranks enlarge.

Why This Matters

The story we relay in this chapter is important because it contradicts popular complaints about young adults shirking their adult responsibilities, abandoning their religious roots, and reveling in their amoral lives. Today's twentysomethings, *like twentysomethings since the 1970s*, overwhelmingly uphold religious beliefs, attend worship, pray, and regard houses of worship with respect. Strongly committed twentysomethings are, moreover, as prevalent now as they were four decades ago. What has changed is the felt pressure to declare a religious affiliation and the disappearing stigma for those who choose "none," freeing many to disaffiliate and select their own life script.

Our goal in telling this story is to offer an accurate description of the religious, spiritual, and secular lives of American twentysomethings. We therefore commissioned the NSAT, whose results populate this chapter's pages and figure prominently into those that follow, to give us representative information about today's twentysomethings. But we did not begin this project with a survey. We began it with qualitative research because we knew there were millions of interesting and passionate twentysomethings who were charting meaningful paths through emerging adulthood, and we wanted to hear their stories told the way they tell them. Since our primary interest was in their religious and spiritual lives, and our resources were limited, we identified Christian churches and ministries that drew scores of young adults. We also recruited unaffiliated young adults for in-depth interviews, so we could hear and relay their stories as well. Our findings are thus generalizable to the 91% of American twentysomethings who affiliate with Protestant or Catholic churches, or who do not affiliate with religion at all.

The voices of twentysomethings that follow, then, represent the core of their respective religious and nonreligious groups rather than the periphery. They are, in other words, actively Catholic or Protestant and deliberately unaffiliated; the young adults from whom the future leaders of Christian, spiritual, and secular organizations will be drawn in America. There is much to learn from these twentysomethings, and we go deep into the worlds of Catholic, Protestant, and unaffiliated twentysomethings in the next four chapters. We then close by placing these findings into conversation with what is known of adolescent religiosity, with an examination of how twentysomethings make sense of their spiritual lives, and with a comparison of the relative importance of organized religion vis-à-vis spirituality. We think you will be surprised by these findings, as we certainly were.

CHAPTER 3

CATHOLICS

MICHAEL O'RILEY

Ever meet someone whose name suited them perfectly? We did, the day we traveled to Aquinas University to interview six students, Michael O'Riley among them. His father, an Aquinas alum, had newborn Michael wearing an Aquinas shirt and wrapped in an Aquinas blanket the day they brought him home from Mary Immaculata Hospital. And if that was not enough, later that evening Aquinas' basketball team upset Michigan in the Sweet 16, which Michael says "sealed" his fate. He would attend Aquinas, pledge Phi Kappa Theta, and study business, just as his father had done, then join his dad's equity management company after graduation. Michael's path in life was well defined, and he was content to walk it.

Perhaps a little too contented, Michael admitted. His grades had taken a slide, and his dad responded by cutting off Michael's spending money. Michael got a taste of what it meant to be "a broke college student," and it left him thirsty for cash, so he was quick to volunteer when he heard his professor announce our research project with its $20 interview incentive. "Frankly, I needed beer money," he explained. But a born extrovert, Michael also loved to meet people and talk, so the idea of getting paid to do what came naturally made an interview with us appealing.

During the interview, Michael made it clear that he loved his large and proudly Irish family and respected his family's deep Catholic faith. He told us how he grew up attending Mass each week, that he assisted the priest as an altar server for four years, and that he continued to attend Mass with his family whenever he went home. At Aquinas, Michael also attended Mass, "probably every other weekend" during his first two years, appreciating the music and the overall experience. "It's designed for college kids, so it's cool; they make it more enjoyable." But when he moved off campus, his attendance waned. "Now that I'm off campus, it's tough to drive over here on Sundays." The drive was not the only hurdle, however. Michael had begun to "question it more [. . .] thinking, analyzing a little bit more." He noticed, for example, how at his home parish, "it always seems like the priest is asking for money." He also decided that while his parents "believe it for real," Michael needed to "find out" what he believed: "I wanna do it for me, not because of what my parents do, or [because of] our tradition."

At 21 years of age and so near to graduating from college, however, Michael did not have time to sort out his religious views: "it's just not the time right now [. . .] I have to graduate college!" He would "figure out [religion] as soon as I get, like, settled down." Not that he intended to explore religions other than Catholicism: "I definitely don't have any desire to be a different religion." Rather, "it's just a matter of me getting more connected with the Catholic Church." Michael, like many college students, had settled into an ambivalent place with respect to religion.[1] Michael was furthermore ambivalent about his ambivalence—regarding his final year of college as neither the time nor place to undertake an examination of his religion. Engagement with religion belonged to his childhood family and his future family, but not his college years—at least, not any longer.

When we caught up with Michael three years later, it was apparent religion did not belong to his early twenties either. Living in an apartment with a friend from high school, and working in his dad's company, Michael continued to identify himself as Catholic but had attended Mass just four times in the past year—for Christmas, Easter, a wedding, and a funeral. He explained, "I'm still what I like to think is a good Catholic: my morals are the same, I still try to be a good person [. . .] it's just my attendance is lacking a little bit." For Michael, being a "good Catholic" equated to middle-class, traditional family life: "A wife and children, raising a family, being a good husband, being a good father, and being able to provide is one of the main staples of being a good Catholic." This equation is not unique to Michael. It is common among Catholic young adults, particularly among "cradle Catholics" (i.e., those born and reared Catholic) for whom family, ethnicity, and religion are tightly intertwined.[2]

We share Michael's story because it contains many of the elements we encountered in our observations of American young adults and in the research of others: religion viewed as marginal to young adulthood, relegated to the realm of family and ethnic tradition, and yet retained as a personal identifier.[3] Since many have documented this pattern, however, we focused our ethnographic research on less-studied phenomena: intentionally Catholic young adults and the Catholic congregations they prefer. We wanted to understand American twentysomethings who were deliberate about their involvement with Catholicism—that is, young adults who sought out Catholic churches on their own initiative and chose to participate in them regularly, and we wanted to explore the patterns and characteristics of the faith communities preferred by these committed young adults. We return to Catholic twentysomethings as a whole in the final section of this chapter, offering interpretations that include not only twentysomethings who prioritize religion, but also twentysomethings who sideline religion and those about to exit the religion entirely.

Active Catholics

Though cultural tides pull many Catholics toward religious ambivalence, fully 42% of Catholic participants in our National Study of American Twentysomethings (NSAT) choose to be active in a faith community. As we saw in Chapter 2, attaining financial independence requires young adults to be geographically mobile and prioritize work, which makes it all the more remarkable that more than one-third of American twentysomethings attend religious services often. Some attend Mass daily, as Chapter 1's Maria Martinez does, and many attend regularly: we estimate 3.2 million American Catholic twentysomethings attend Mass at least a couple of times each month.[4] Indeed, if all of these 3.2 million regularly attending Catholic twentysomethings resided in the same place, they would comprise America's third-largest city—coming in behind Los Angeles's 3.9 million and moving Chicago's 2.7 million into fourth position (see Chapter 7).

To understand why and how young adults participate in religious congregations as part of their journey to adulthood, we asked them. We recruited eight researchers to study Catholic, Evangelical, and Mainline Protestant congregations with vibrant young adult populations in different regions of the country. All together we studied eleven congregations along with two Catholic diocesan young adult ministries, observing 144 events and interviewing 234 members and paid staff over a twelve-month period. We found these young-adult-friendly churches the same way young adults do: internet searches, word of mouth, and physically "checking them out" to look for young adults. Once we selected the churches to study, we recruited young adult members willing to be interviewed using e-mail, Facebook, church websites, flyers, personal invitation, and word of mouth. In most cases, church staff helped with recruiting by sending e-mails or posting announcements online. In interviews lasting anywhere from forty-five minutes to two hours, we asked young adults about their religious upbringing, past church experiences, and what they looked for in a church. In short, they told us why they wanted to be part of a church, and why they chose to join and get involved in the church they did.[5]

Before we turn to their responses, we must clarify what we mean by "young adult members." Whereas our national survey, the NSAT, restricted itself to twentysomethings, our ethnographic researchers used each congregation's more fluid definition of young adult. Some churches define young adult with an age range (e.g., 21–35 years), others use a life phase (post-college), and still others leave it up to individuals to self-select as they see fit. There are also differences across Christian traditions: Evangelical Protestant churches, for example, usually cap the young adult group at 30, while Mainline Protestant churches and Catholic churches may extend the young adult category to 35 or even 39. We learned, too, that individuals generally opt out of the young adult group when they have children because they no longer share the priorities and concerns of their peers who do not have children.

Membership is another term that varies in meaning across Catholic, Evangelical, and Mainline Protestant churches. While some churches have a formal designation of membership, denoting a formal commitment, privileges, and responsibilities, others equate membership with regular financial contributions or regular attendance. For Catholics, the question of membership is complicated by the church polity. Parishes are churches and geographic territories; all those who live within the parish boundaries "belong to" the parish, though it is well-known that many American Catholics attend parish churches outside their locale. In the United States, Catholics are supposed to register with their local parish and make financial contributions, but they are not required to do so in order to participate in the life of the parish. Though many of the young adults we spoke with are not members in a formal sense, and many do not support their church financially, they think of themselves as active members by virtue of their participation and commitment. In this chapter on Catholics and the two that follow on Protestants, we use "members" in this same informal sense to denote those who are "highly engaged" and "very active" in the congregation. All those we refer to as members attend Sunday services several times a month and are involved in additional church activities.

Parsing out who exactly is a young adult and what it means to be a member in different congregations exemplifies a larger challenge that scholars face in cross-denominational research. While Christians share a common faith in Jesus Christ, they live out their faith in strikingly different ways. How do we ask young adults about their church experiences in language that will make sense to Christians as dissimilar as Pentecostals, Methodists, and Roman Catholics? In informal conversations and formal interviews, we used the vernacular of the Christian tradition to talk about issues relevant to Christian young adults in a variety of churches. This enabled us to be more efficient in the use of respondents' time, which was essential to our research and greatly appreciated (see Methodological Appendix).

With definitional and procedural issues clarified, we turn to describing the diverse places we encountered young-adult friendly ministries: a multigenerational mega-parish, a university student center, and urban parishes embedded in diocesan young adult ministry.

Multigenerational Mega-Parish

As she explained in Chapter 1, Maria Martinez attends different parishes throughout the week for daily Mass, but she identifies St. Ann's Catholic Parish as her church since this is where she finds camaraderie with other young adults who are similarly devout. St. Ann's, located in the diocese of Dallas, is a large, multigenerational, racially diverse church with a vibrant young adult community. This relatively new parish has grown quickly. St. Ann's became a parish in 1989; by 2011, when we conducted our research, this young church had 28,000 registered parishioners (8,500 families) thanks to the fast-growing Catholic population in greater Dallas.

St. Ann's is a proudly conservative parish that embraces "new dynamic orthodoxy," a phrase used by several parish leaders. The term was coined by New York's Cardinal John O'Connor in the 1970s and gained traction when Franciscan priest Michael Scanlan integrated the concept into the mission of the Franciscan University of Steubenville (Ohio) when he served as university president. According to the university's magazine, *Franciscan Way*, at the heart of "dynamic orthodoxy" is "fidelity to the Magisterium, Sacred Scripture, and Sacred Tradition" and "an energetic desire on the part of our students, faculty, and staff to apply Church teachings to contemporary culture and our own lives."[6] St. Ann's could be described as vibrantly traditionalist with an extraordinary number of ministry offerings (over 100). The Eucharist is central to parish life and celebrated in seven Masses on weekends, five in English and two in Spanish, and worshipped through perpetual Eucharistic Adoration.

Despite St. Ann's large size, there is a strong sense of community, high level of commitment and parish pride among parishioners, and consistency in messaging. In 2007, St. Ann's added a "Twenty-Something" group to serve recent college graduates who felt uncomfortable in the singles ministry, which rarely drew anyone under 35. Subsequently a "Young Marrieds" group for married twentysomethings split off. The "Twenty-Something" group advertises events through e-mail and social media, attracting several hundred young adults to weekly Bible studies, monthly "Holy Happy Hours," and seasonal retreats. It was this group that caught Maria Martinez's attention as she visited different parishes and decided that St. Ann's would be her faith community rather than just a place to attend Mass.[7]

University Student Center

It would be impossible to attend a Mass or any other event at St. Peter's Catholic Student Center without being overwhelmed by the youthful demographics. St. Peter's Catholic Student Center at Baylor University in Waco, Texas, is both a neighborhood church and a student center. It draws a diverse cross-section of Latinos, Anglos, and Asians from the local area, but most of its members are students, undergraduate and graduate students, along with staff and faculty from Baylor University. Uniquely connected to Baylor University—the largest Baptist university in the world—St. Peter's benefits from a campus culture where, in the words of one student, "it's cool to be Christian." At the same time, Catholics make up only 15% of the student population and are acutely aware of their minority status within its Evangelical milieu. For some students, St. Peter's serves as a Catholic refuge where they do not have to explain their devotion to Mary. On the Center's website, a student-made video features young adults talking about St. Peter's as their family. One student in the video explains, "these people here have become not my second family but a part of my family." As the video concludes, the word "home" flashes on the screen while two voices say in unison: "St. Peter's is *my* home."

At first pass, St. Peter's seems to attract young adults raised in traditional Catholic families, but several young adults told us there are two main "cliques" of students at the church. First, there are those who are very religiously conservative and typically from a traditional, often

Hispanic or African Catholic family. They want St. Peter's to be a sacred space and are concerned about the correctness of the teachings and liturgical practices. They promote the pro-life position that permeates St. Peter's and Baylor University and join with Baptist students in Baylor's Bears for Life student group to oppose abortion. The second clique consists of students raised in less-traditional Catholic homes, who, to put it in the language of one traditionalist, "did not receive a strong faith formation in the Church." This group of students wants St. Peter's to be a place of spiritual *and* social activities. They want the Center to be a place to relax and have fun with other Catholics. This "social" faction holds what one student called "Catholic parties," which are typical college parties with drinking but without the "hook-up culture."[8] We also observed a third clique of young adults who converted to Catholicism recently and align mostly with the traditionalist group.

During the academic year, St. Peter's is buzzing with activity. There are three Masses on Sundays, but the 9:00 p.m. Mass is the one dominated by students. The 9:00 p.m. Mass is considered a contemporary service with guitar music and casual dress. Every other Wednesday, dozens of students gather at St. Peter's for "The Rock"—a contemporary praise service with Catholic additions such as praying the rosary or candle-lit veneration of an icon of the Virgin Mary. In addition to worship services, students are at the Center at all hours, talking on the comfy couches and watching movies on the large screen. Mixed in with the socializing are intellectual discussions and debates that may involve fetching the Catechism from an adjoining room or seeking input from St. Peter's well-liked priest Father Anthony.

At the heart of the student experience at St. Peter's is the yearly retreat called Bear Awakening. Although the details are kept hidden from students, Awakening is a three-day retreat based on the Cursillo retreat model, which includes personal testimony from spiritually mature student-leaders and small group meetings and activities. The goal of Awakening is for retreaters to deepen their relationship with God or, for those just beginning a spiritual journey, to be awakened to that relationship and its possibilities. Once students have attended an Awakening, they are invited to serve as student-leaders and attend other retreats. Awakening and other retreats provide a mechanism for developing social bonds and deeper friendships that are rooted in St. Peter's and a shared Catholic identity. As we shall see, the desire to combine deep friendships and faith appears to lessen after college, but it remains important to many college graduates who seek out peers in parish-based young adult communities.[9]

Urban Parishes and Dioceses

At a typical Sunday evening Mass at St. Charles Borromeo Catholic Parish in Arlington, Virginia, five miles from Washington, DC, post-college-age young adults spill out of the sanctuary and into the narthex, standing six rows deep. While many parishes can scarcely find a young adult in their pews, St. Charles, with seating for over 400, is literally overflowing with them. Mass begins with singing led by a fifteen-person choir and small band. They set a festive tone that is carried further by the celebrant, Father Tony, who is welcoming and funny. Even more important to the young adults we spoke with is the large number of young adults in attendance. As one 26-year-old man explained, "I'd rather stand with people who look like me than sit with people who don't."

St. Charles has a reputation as a young-adult-friendly parish that allows it to draw young adults from far outside its parish boundaries. At the same time, many who attend St. Charles also attend and participate in other parishes, just as Maria Martinez does in the Dallas area. They may also attend events hosted by the diocesan young adult ministry office, the Catholic Information Center, and alumni groups from the Jesuit Volunteer Corp, FOCUS,[10] and Catholic colleges in the District of Columbia (DC). In other words, though some young adults are parish exclusive, others participate in multiple Catholic contexts drawn to events designed for young adults. The two local diocesan offices for young adult ministry play a critical role in providing a communication infrastructure (websites, Facebook pages, tweets) that in turn facilitate the interaction of a trans-parish, young adult Catholic network.[11]

The Washington, DC, region is home to the diocese of Arlington, Virginia, and the archdiocese of Washington, DC. Both dioceses have young adult ministry offices that provide spiritual, social, and service programming following the guidelines published by the U.S. Bishops in 1996. By far the most successful program, at least in terms of attendance, is "Theology on Tap." Held monthly in an Irish bar, 150–200 young adults gather on Monday evenings for beer and a lecture on a Catholic topic, such as relationships, vocations, and finding God in hard times. Parish young adult groups host tables with their parish name displayed so young adults can sit with their local group. One of the primary functions of diocesan-sponsored events like Theology on Tap is to help young adults connect with a "home parish," but there is little concern for official parish boundaries. When young adult Catholics move into the DC region, many will "check out" multiple parishes. In addition to St. Charles Borromeo, three other parishes have reputations as young-adult-friendly parishes: St. Thomas Apostle and Holy Trinity in Washington, DC, and St. Mary's in northern Virginia. We studied these four parishes over a twelve-month period, as well the programs offered by the Arlington and DC diocesan young adult ministry offices—observing events and interviewing young adult Catholics who identified themselves as active participants.[12]

Why Young Adult Catholics Go to Church

Having described the churches and diocesan context where we found young adult Catholics, what did we learn from the sixty-eight young adults we interviewed? Fifty-eight of our interviewees were cradle Catholics—meaning they were raised in a Catholic family—who had chosen a Catholic life for themselves. When they moved locations in their twenties, they would look for a new parish. But rather than join their local parish, almost all engaged in a period of "parish shopping," looking for a comfortable parish (or parishes) to attend Mass and get involved in a young adult group. The remaining ten young adults were converts to the Catholic faith with a similar commitment to finding a parish home. Both cradle Catholics and new Catholics responded in similar ways when we asked them how they selected a parish. The three most important factors were community, spiritual experiences, and church leadership.

Though canon law states that Catholics are obligated to attend Mass on Sundays and holy days, this was not a motivation for the young adults we spoke with. Since Vatican II, Catholic leaders have stressed love of God and neighbor over obligation and guilt. Given this shift, it was not surprising that out of the sixty-eight Catholic young adults interviewed, only one told us she looked for a church because it is "necessary." Baylor University undergrad Maribeth explained her decision to attend St. Peter's Catholic Student Center this way: "Because it was Catholic, and I didn't have a car so that was my only option. I have a car now, and I would not go anywhere else. But freshman year, in the beginning, I didn't like St. Peter's, so I just kind of went back because I knew it was necessary." Over time Maribeth's opinion of St. Peter's improved, and she no longer attends because it offers the most convenient location for fulfilling her Catholic duty. She is now involved in leading retreats and has formed close friendships with other young adults. Maribeth was unusual among the Catholic young adults we interviewed who typically engaged in some amount of parish shopping as they looked for a parish that offered more than a convenient way to fulfill their weekly Mass obligation.

The most frequent reason Catholic young adults give for selecting a particular church is "community." In future chapters we will hear a similar refrain from Mainline and Evangelical Protestants. What do young adult Catholics mean by community when looking for a church? From our interviews, we identified half-a-dozen distinct meanings. For example, community means friendly, welcoming, inviting, and nonjudgmental. It can also mean a critical mass of young adults who "look like me." A thirtysomething woman from St. Charles Borromeo explained that even though her peers did not actually talk to her when she first attended, she found the parish welcoming "because you see people like you, so it's a comfort zone." And the 26-year-old man from St. Charles who told us he would rather stand during a crowded 6:00 p.m. Mass than be seated at a service "with people who don't look like me" explained that he meant people his own age, not his own race or ethnicity (he was Korean). But given the similar demographic profile of the Catholics we interviewed, we would add educational attainment (at least a bachelor's degree) and socioeconomic status (aspiring middle class) to who qualified as "like me." When parish shopping, the importance of seeing a critical mass of young adult peers cannot be overstated. Beyond this, young adults told us that community means being able to "connect with" other young adults, which requires opportunities to socialize outside of religious services.

To help young adults establish relationships, parishes sponsor young-adult-only events. These events fall under the umbrella of Catholic Young Adult Ministry or YAM for short. Though the U.S. Conference of Catholic Bishops defines YAM as serving those 18–39 years of age, this range is way too large for the Catholic young adults we interviewed who want to interact with peers in a relatively close age range *and* similar life stage (post-college, unmarried, no kids). Several women in their 20s relayed stories of "creepy" older men (meaning those in their late 30s) at young adult events like Theology on Tap. The desire for peers to be in a similar life stage pushes young adults to drop out of YAM when they get married or get serious about starting a family. At St. Ann's in Dallas, this subset of young adults created their own "Young Marrieds" group, but few parishes have enough young adults to maintain two young adult groups.

Near Baylor University, St. Peter's Catholic Student Center was created to offer opportunities for Catholics students to form community. For the students we spoke with, community meant not only socializing but also forming strong friendships based on a shared Catholic faith. For 20-year-old Jasmina, faith and friendship blended perfectly at St. Peter's: "I guess it goes back to having God and your friends in the same place because you'll always have a place to go and worship, but it's great that you can have people to worship with and be with and it's the community of faith that I never had before and that's what I love about it." Jason, a 27-year-old graduate student, says the best thing about St. Peter's is "it's a social group that has faith interwoven into it." Though a few students told us there was too much socializing at the

Center—too much watching television, video games, and even parties with alcohol—the majority found the combination of socializing and spiritual development well balanced.

For some college students, the community of St. Peter's means more than socializing and friendships. Gabriela explained:

> We're all kind of going through the same phases in our life. We're trying to figure out what we want to do, what classes we want to take. It's kind of an ultimate support group, and that support group is also Catholic, so they're people who believe the same things that you do, who are experiencing the same things that you do, and kind of want the same things out of church.

These bonds are forged through intense religious experiences such as testimonials given on the Bear Awakening retreat. Gabriela is one of many young adults at St. Peter's who told us this community is her family, echoing the video on the Center's website. Since St. Peter's is largely composed of undergraduate students, many of whom are away from home for the first time, the appeal of a surrogate family is not surprising. We heard nothing like this from post-college young adults we met in parishes. They were not looking for this degree of closeness in a church community, but dating or the potential for dating came up as factor among the older twentysomethings and early thirtysomethings. Both men and women told us it would be nice to find a Catholic to go out with or possibly even marry. Indeed, many of their parishes host "Singles" groups to this end, but these groups are (perceived to be) dominated by those over 40 and desperate, and thus avoided by those in their 20s or early 30s.

As these examples illustrate, community signifies different things to different young adults. At one end of the spectrum, it means a critical mass of nearly anonymous, young adult peers, while on the other, it means a surrogate family. For most young adult Catholics, it means something in between that combines socializing and sharing faith experiences with people like them. Observers need to be alert to the complex layers of "community," which is clearly important to young adults and used in savvy church marketing to attract them. Still, community is not the only thing that young adult Catholics look for in churches.

Many young adult Catholics point to spiritual experiences as the primary reason for selecting their church. A 23-year-old student at Baylor, who spent two years visiting parishes before selecting St. Peter's, explained what draws her to church this way:

> I really kind of need that sense of time . . . that kind of pace just to keep the pace during the week. Sunday to go to church and stuff and then Friday I love going to church on Friday. It's just one of those things that I really like hearing like the scripture read and participating in that celebration really shape the way that I go through the week.

Daniel, a graduate student at St. Peter's, shared, "I wouldn't say I go for the music really or the people. That's not the important part. The Eucharist . . . receiving the Eucharist is the most important part for me." This view was also shared by Maria Martinez, whom we introduced in Chapter 1.

> I don't really consider myself as having a home parish because I go to all different kinds of churches—well not all different kinds, but I go to different parishes depending on the day and the time. Typically the Mass is the same everywhere [. . .] as long as the priest has the right intentions. I'm not there for an amazing homily and I'm there not to feel like I belong. The heart of it all is the Eucharist.

If receiving Eucharist is what matters most, then it should not matter which church one attends. Indeed, Maria told us she attends lots of different Catholic churches every week. But Maria also chose to visit St. Ann's because she heard it had a lot of people her age excited about their faith, and it reminded her of attending Mass in her college dorm. For Maria and Daniel, the spiritual experiences draw them to church—especially receiving the Eucharist at Mass, participating in Eucharistic Adoration and the Sacrament of Reconciliation, but they prefer to have these experiences with young adults like them. Seeing that there are other young adults who care deeply about their faith is important to them. Though Daniel said he does not go for the music, we heard from others that music is important to the quality of the spiritual experience. For example, we met Jesse, a 20-year-old male who had recently converted to Catholicism through the Rite of Christian Initiation for Adults (RCIA) program at St. Peter's. Jesse explained, "There was something in the Mass that just hooked me there, you know. I've been going ever since . . . and the songs sort of make you feel like you're in heaven or something."

The last set of responses to our question about selecting a church had to do with leadership. Specifically, we heard lots about the priests responsible for preaching on Sundays. The content of their message came up repeatedly, in two distinct ways: some young adults were looking for orthodoxy, while others were looking for openness. Twenty-three-year-old Alyssa checked out lots of parishes before deciding on St. Charles Borromeo near DC. She did not like hearing from priests who were too heavy on doctrine or preached fire and brimstone. Once, while she was sitting in the back of a church, the priest called all those in the back pews "lazy Catholics." Alyssa was incredulous and never returned to that church. Alternatively, Keith, a 21-year-old at St. Peter's, listened for orthodoxy: "I saw that Father Anthony was preaching the truth. I never heard anything that I could describe as not orthodox to the Catholic faith come out of his mouth. Other priests, though, I couldn't say that about." Another young woman said she did not want to hear anything political in a sermon, like helping illegal immigrants. Still other young adults in the DC parishes told us they would not attend a church in which the priest condemned homosexuals or cohabitation. For example, Teresa, a 33-year-old woman at St. Charles, put the matter plainly: "I don't come for the sermon, but a sermon could cause me to leave." Whether young adults align with the more traditional or progressive wings of the U.S. Catholic Church, they have strong opinions about what it means to be Catholic and are looking for a priest whose teachings align with their core convictions.

We also heard from some of our interviewees about the importance of finding a church with a priest whose homilies are interesting and challenging. Here are quotes about preaching from two men we spoke with at parishes in the DC region:

> Something unique, something that challenges me. Relate it to a story or make it relevant. I don't want to hear clichés; make it relevant or make it into a story. I understand that Jesus loves me, and you can say that in twenty different ways, but I want something that challenges me or makes me think about it with a completely new twist. I like it as almost academic in that sense. I want to be engaged mentally. I don't want to tune out. It is his ten-minute window to capture me.
>
> *30-year-old male, St. Charles Borromeo*

> One thing I like about Holy Trinity and a few of the priests [. . .] they are really smart men, and it's almost like going to a really good lecture. They talk about the message, they put it in a context of history, and they drop these connections between these messages you hear as a person from the church in general and they tie it in.
>
> *28-year-old male, Holy Trinity*

Young adults at St. Peter's Catholic Student Center similarly praised their pastor's preaching, but they also talked about his pastoral care skills. As the student chaplain, Father Anthony was often at the Center, available to talk with students for hours about the challenges they were facing. In contrast, post-college young adults in large, urban parishes did not expect to have substantial interaction with the parish priests, even though they would like to. One woman from St. Ann's put it this way: "I think just seeing the priest's face every once in a while, or having him stop by an event every once in a while, would be good. And I'm not in any way trying to downplay our priests here, they do wonderful things, [but] they're incredibly busy."

In the end, we found the three most important factors to young adult Catholics as they looked for a church: community, spiritual experiences, and the pastor, with the importance of each varying by age and life stage. The potential for forming close friendships is a major draw to church for college students. Post-college young adults, on the other hand, had made an intentional decision to be active Catholics and sought out a church where the liturgy and pastor inspired them. They often took time away—months or even years—from regular church involvement as their lives were in frequent transition. When they relocated for work, school, or relationships, they took their time choosing a church before settling in as a regular attender and becoming involved in parish life. Diocesan-wide young adult ministry events, like Theology on Tap, helped them meet other young adult Catholics and learn which parishes have vibrant young adult groups. While a critical mass of peers was a necessary staring point, the spiritual experiences offered at the parish and the priest's leadership, especially on controversial topics like gay marriage, were key factors in selecting a parish that aligns with, or at least does not offend, their core convictions.

Catholic Twentysomethings in America

In Chapter 2, we learned that Catholic twentysomethings had the highest rates of college graduation and second-highest rates of parenthood, matched the marriage rates of Mainline Protestant and unaffiliated twentysomethings, and included the highest proportion of Latinos. We also saw that 3 out of 5 Catholic twentysomethings viewed God as personal and involved in the world, that two-thirds reported their childhood faith was very important to them, that half prayed at least weekly, and that 3 out of 10 said spiritual growth as adults was very or extremely important to them. In this section, we compare different types of Catholic twentysomethings—from Active Catholics like those we encountered during our ethnographic research above, to Nominal Catholics like Michael O'Riley, who intend to re-engage religion when settled, to Estranged Catholics, who identify with the religion but virtually never attend church and indicate that their spiritual life is of little to no importance. And we will show that Active, Nominal, and Estranged Catholic twentysomethings self-segregate into different social worlds with religiously like-minded peers.

We deploy a typology of Catholics that is far from the first, nor the most advanced statistically.[13] But it is intuitive and easy to use, as it involves just two criteria: attendance at religious services, and the importance, "as an adult, to grow in your spiritual life."[14] We use it with the 333 Catholic twentysomethings in the NSAT, classifying them as Active, Nominal, or Estranged Catholics. Active Catholics attend religious services a couple of times monthly to more than weekly *and* indicate that growth in their spiritual life is "very" or "extremely important" to them as adults. Estranged Catholics, by contrast, indicate that spiritual life is "not very" or "not at all important" *and* their attendance at religious services is "once a year or less" or "never." Nominal Catholics include everyone else; that is, Catholic twentysomethings whose attendance at religious services or stated importance of spiritual life indicates that their practice of the Catholic faith is not a priority. Using the NSAT, we classified 22% of Catholic twentysomethings in America as Active, 20% as Estranged, and 58% as Nominal.

To understand what distinguishes these three types of Catholics from each other, we performed a statistical procedure called discriminant analysis. This identified two clusters of differentiating factors. The first cluster distinguished Estranged Catholics from their Nominal and Active Catholic peers: Estranged Catholic twentysomethings were more likely to be divorced or cohabiting, in their upper 20s, employed, from more affluent or White households, but not heads of households (see Figures 3.1, 3.2, and 3.3). This cluster is unsurprising, as even non-Catholics know the religion's rejection of divorce and cohabitation, which would leave divorced and cohabiting twentysomethings feeling unwelcome in church. It also fits with the pattern of declining participation among White cradle Catholics,[15] with the competing weekend options that affluent households enjoy, and with more years of life experience providing more reasons to withdraw from religious life (e.g., relocation, partner change).

The second cluster of factors identified by our analysis distinguished Active Catholics from Nominal, and to a lesser degree Nominal Catholics from Estranged: having children and being married, being Latino, not being Black or Asian, graduating from college, and not

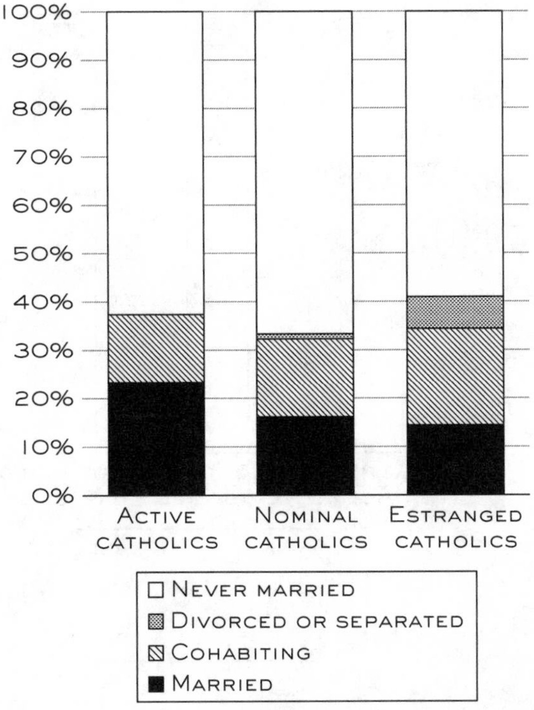

Figure 3.1

Marital Status of Active, Nominal, and Estranged Catholic Twentysomethings

Source: NSAT 2013

being employed (see Figures 3.1, 3.2, and 3.3). As above, this cluster fits with well-known patterns, like the Church's promotion of marriage and parenthood, Catholicism's dominance in Spanish-speaking nations, American college graduates' broader involvement in social institutions, the greater discretionary time afforded by not being in the labor force, and the reassurance unemployed twentysomethings might seek through religious participation.

Just as interesting to us, though, were the things that did *not* differentiate Active, Nominal, and Estranged Catholic twentysomethings. Neither loneliness or social media use varied across these three types, for example, nor did having a clear sense of purpose or meaning in their lives.[16] That is, no type is lonelier, more digitally immersed, or lacking in

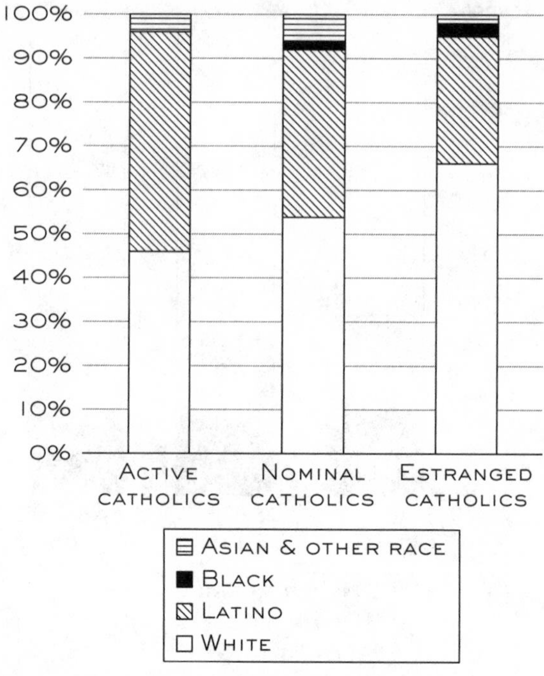

Figure 3.2

Race and Ethnicity of Active, Nominal, and Estranged Catholic Twentysomethings

Source: NSAT 2013

purpose than the other two types. All three types also indicated equivalent desires to marry, equally regarded gender identity as a private and inconsequential matter, reported comparable feelings of spiritual connectedness, saw art and music as similarly valid means of spiritual expression, and incorporated practices from other religious traditions at the same rate into their own spirituality. In other words, the desire to marry was the same across all types of Catholic twentysomethings as was viewing gender identity as socially inconsequential or being open to spirituality in settings beyond the Church's doors.

This is quite important, because it means that what sorts Catholic twentysomethings into Active, Nominal, or Estranged subtypes is different from what many assume: it is not Catholicism's provision of a sense of purpose, nor its sacrament of heterosexual marriage, provision

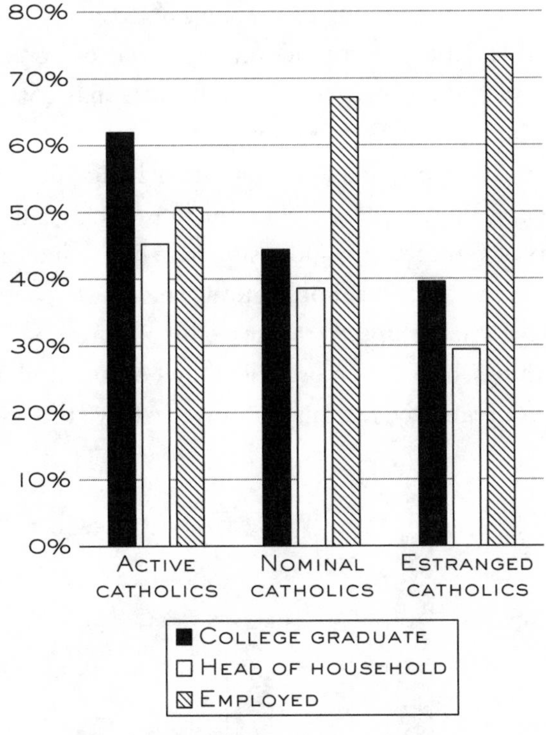

Figure 3.3

Education, Household Status, and Employment of Active, Nominal, and Estranged Catholic Twentysomethings

Source: NSAT 2013

of spiritual experiences, or community of the like-minded. Estranged and Nominal Catholic twentysomethings can find these things outside the Church as readily as Active Catholics find them within. Rather, what separates Catholic twentysomethings into Active, Nominal, or Estranged types are demographic factors like being divorced or graduating from college in conjunction with, as we demonstrate next, the depth of their identification with Catholicism and its core teachings, their view of helping others as an obligation, and their desire to give their own children the religious upbringing that was so meaningful to them.

The NSAT asked respondents about feeling part of a religion, regardless of current attendance, and about helping others. When we examine the answers Catholic twentysomethings gave, the results are striking (see Figure 3.4). Virtually every Active Catholic considers his- or herself as part of Catholicism, and 9 out of 10 affirm helping others as an obligation—regardless of its personal cost or demand. Among Nominal Catholics, these rates drop to 4 out of 5 feeling part of Catholicism and 3 out of 4 agreeing that helping others is an obligation. And among Estranged Catholics, the rates drop again—to 3 out of 5 feeling part of Catholicism, and a simple majority indicating helping others is a personal, sacrificial obligation. These differences are further reflected in the friendships twentysomethings form: Active Catholic twentysomethings have the most friends who attend church and do volunteer work regularly, Estranged Catholics have the fewest who do

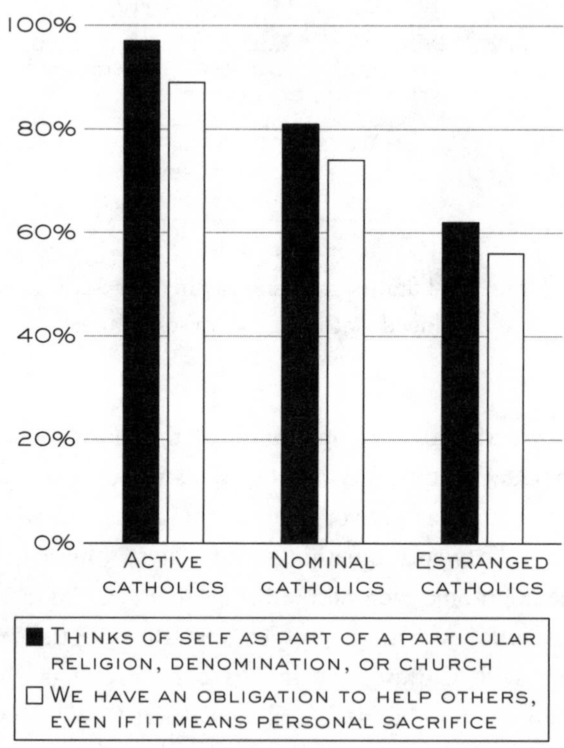

Figure 3.4

Religious Belonging, Helping Obligation by Active, Nominal, and Estranged Catholic Twentysomethings

Source: NSAT 2013

these things, and Nominal Catholics fall in the middle (see Figure 3.5). This shows us that Active, Nominal, and Estranged Catholics reside in fairly separate social worlds—they self-segregate into religiously committed, religiously marginal, or nonreligious subcultures that support their beliefs and facilitate connections to similarly minded persons.

Comparing Active, Nominal, and Estranged Catholics reveals distinct patterns of religious beliefs, practices, and importance of religion. Foundational is Catholic twentysomethings' belief that "God is a personal being involved in the lives of people today," which 97% of Active Catholic, 60% of Nominal Catholic, and 36% of Estranged Catholic twentysomethings affirm (see Figure 3.6). Gaps of this magnitude between groups are rare, and they underscore the centrality that viewing

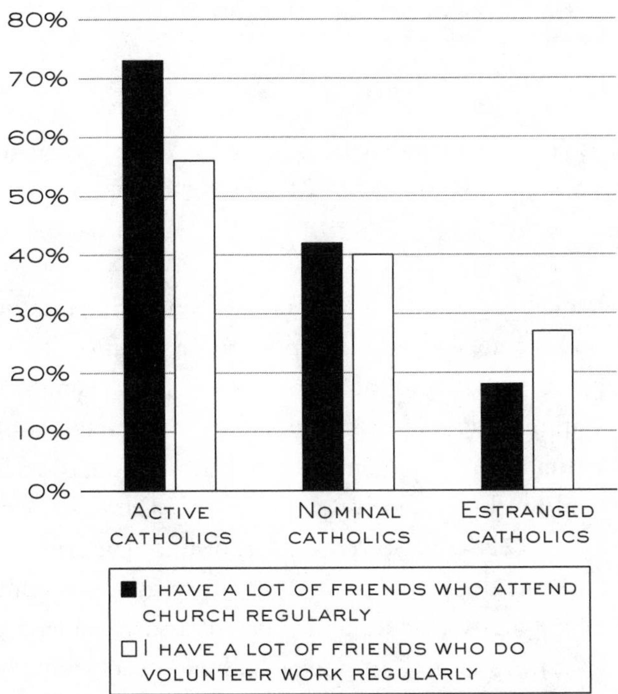

Figure 3.5

Church-Attending, Volunteering Friends of Active, Nominal, and Estranged Catholic Twentysomethings

Source: NSAT 2013

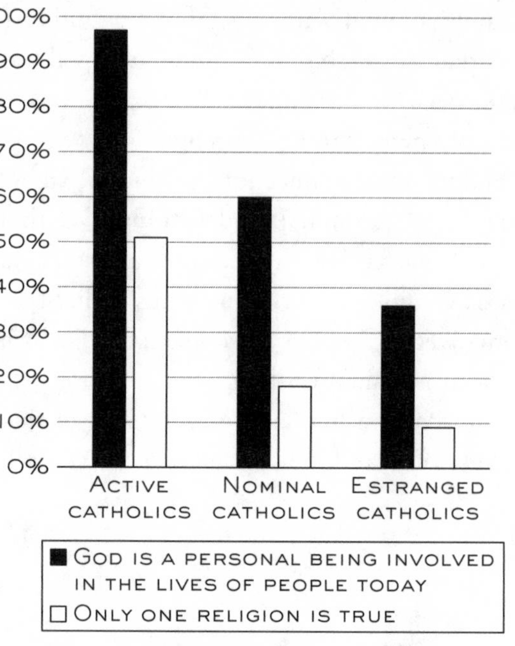

Figure 3.6

God as Personal, One Religion as True by Active, Nominal, and Estranged Catholic Twentysomethings

Source: NSAT 2013

God as personal and involved (or not) plays in differentiating Active, Nominal, and Estranged Catholic types. Such a traditional view of God in turn supports a high level of religious exclusivity, as more than half of Active Catholic twentysomethings affirm that "only one religion is true." Fewer than 1 out of 5 Nominal Catholics or 1 out of 10 Estranged Catholics affirm this exclusive view of the Catholic faith. These differences in beliefs are also reflected in distinct patterns of religious practice. Two out of three Active Catholics pray daily, compared to 1 out of 4 Nominal Catholics and 1 out of 100 Estranged Catholics (see Figure 3.7). About half of Active Catholic twentysomethings also meditate at least weekly, a practice shared by fewer than 1 out of 8 Nominal or Estranged Catholics. Not surprisingly, then, 3 out of 4 Active Catholics say their religion is "very" or "extremely important"

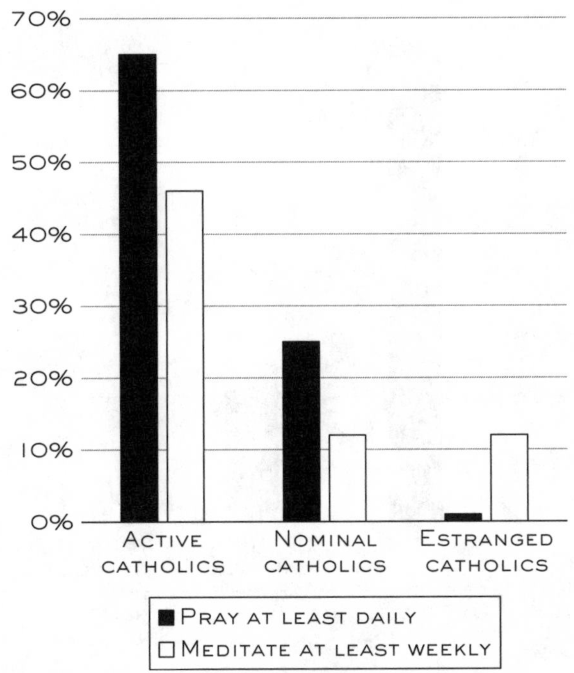

Figure 3.7

Prayer and Meditation of Active, Nominal, and Estranged Catholic Twentysomethings

Source: NSAT 2013

in their daily life, compared to 1 out of 4 Nominal Catholics and 1 out of 14 Estranged Catholics (see Figure 3.8).

Ethics likewise differentiate Active, Nominal, and Estranged Catholic twentysomethings. We saw earlier that Active Catholics overwhelmingly affirm helping others as a personal obligation; we see here that they are least likely to agree that "making a lot of money is very important to my happiness" or that "all I want out of life is a job that pays well and a partner I can trust" (see Figure 3.9). Estranged Catholics, by contrast, are the most likely to agree with these privatized, individualistic ethics.[17] And Nominal Catholics, once again, occupy the middle ground. This is also where Nominal Catholics settle on "my deep passion is greater social justice" (see Figure 3.10). Active Catholics are

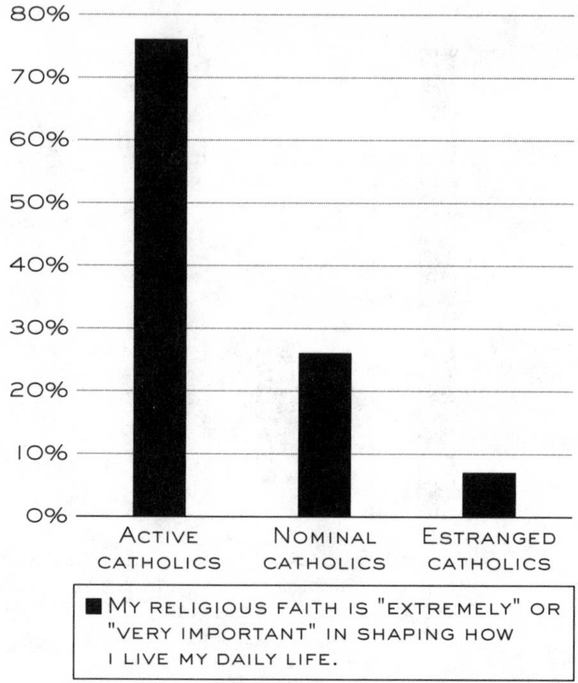

FIGURE 3.8

Importance of Religious Faith in Daily Life of Active, Nominal, and Estranged Catholic Twentysomethings

Source: NSAT 2013

the strongest supporters of this pro-social indicator, while Estranged Catholics are least likely to say their "deep passion" is "greater social justice."

The social worlds that divide Active, Nominal, and Estranged Catholic twentysomethings likely have their roots in childhood. Nine out of 10 Active Catholics report that "as a child, my religious faith was very important to me" (see Figure 3.11). Seven out of 10 Nominal Catholics report the same, as do 4 out of 10 Estranged Catholics. (And remember, these analyses are of American twentysomethings who still identify as Catholic. Twentysomethings who were raised as Catholic but have since left Catholicism are not included here.[18]) Differences born of childhood experiences clearly possess staying power, as nearly the same proportions of Active, Nominal, and Estranged Catholic

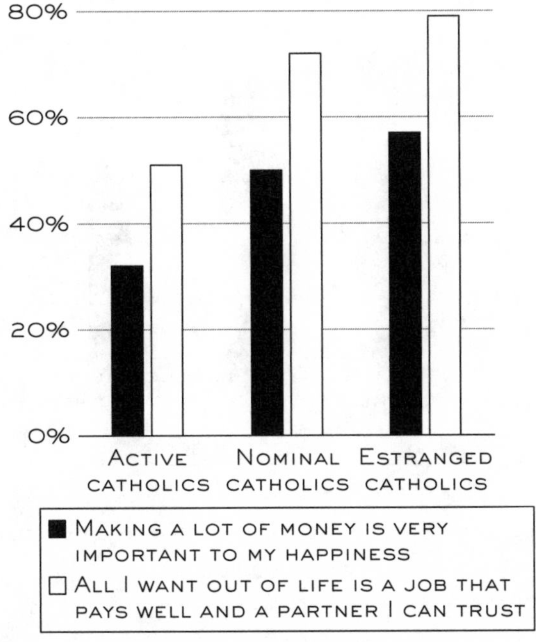

Figure 3.9

Individualistic Ethics of Active, Nominal, and Estranged Catholic Twentysomethings

Source: NSAT 2013

twentysomethings that report their childhood faith was very important also indicate that they "definitely plan to join a church" when they have children. To the extent that Catholic twentysomethings implement these plans, the distinct, socio-religious worlds of today's Active, Nominal, and Estranged Catholics will persist for another generation, and probably longer.

So what is the bottom line with respect to American twentysomethings and the Roman Catholic Church? In a word, durability. While individual twentysomethings' religious practice inevitably varies as they journey through their third decade, young adult Catholics *as a population* possess a remarkably stable proportion of actively committed adherents and a large contingent of nominally committed adherents who had important experiences in the faith as children that they wish to replicate for their children. Facilitating this durability is the

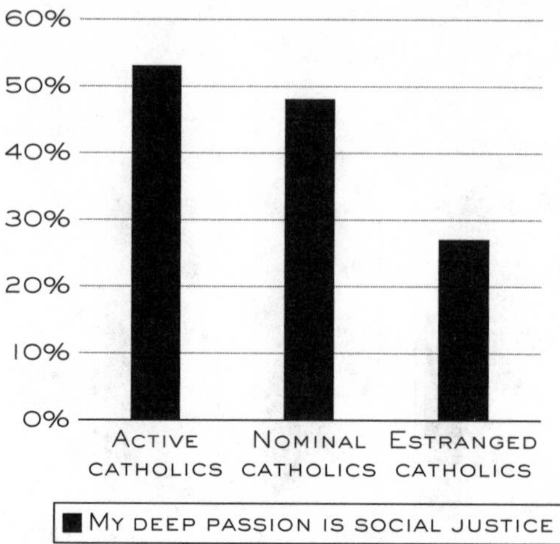

Figure 3.10

Passion for Social Justice of Active, Nominal, and Estranged Catholic Twentysomethings

Source: NSAT 2013

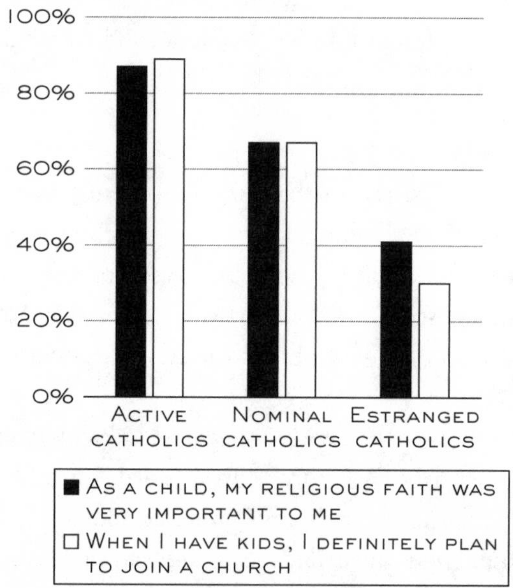

Figure 3.11

Faith Past and Future of Active, Nominal, and Estranged Catholic Twentysomethings

Source: NSAT 2013

willingness of Catholic parishes and diocesan ministries to adapt and serve interested Catholic twentysomethings. These factors, combined with immigration and fertility rates of Latino Catholics, should maintain the overall Catholic population for the next couple of decades.

CHAPTER 4

Mainline Protestants

Gillian Muller

Gillian's parents were not Christians. At 21 years old, Gillian had come to terms with this reality. For the first 18 years of Gillian's life, her mother and father attended Mainstreet United Church of Christ because they thought it would be good if their only child had a church upbringing. Gillian's dad even joined the church choir with her. Once Gillian left for college, however, her dad dropped out of the choir, and within a month her parents replaced weekly Sunday worship with a weekly Sunday brunch at one or another of Mainstreet's bustling cafes. But an interesting thing can happen when you raise a child in a church: their faith can become, as Gillian worded it, "real." Her years of attending church, singing in the choir, and attending children and youth programs left Gillian with a resolute identity as a Christian. Not a Bible-thumping identity, to be sure. "We didn't have to go *every* Sunday, and I'm not out proselytizing or anything like that." But a firm Christian identity, despite her mother and father's pretense: "I still consider myself a Christian . . . definitely."

We first interviewed Gillian when she was a senior science education major at Reformation Lutheran College, using a seminar room within its campus-dominating chapel. Gillian said that she liked the chapel's Sunday's service and attended "maybe once a month or so." She was particularly grateful that the service did not start until 1:00 p.m. on Sunday: "they understand that we need to sleep in on Sundays!" We asked Gillian her views on the Bible, as this is a key differentiating issue between Evangelical and Mainline Protestants.[1] Gillian's answer placed her squarely among the latter. "I don't think it should be taken literally. I think that's very dangerous and closed-minded. But I think it's good for a reference." We asked Gillian if she read the Bible. "I don't; I hear it in church, but I never read it on my own." And we asked Gillian if she prayed, and she answered "pretty much daily" because "I definitely find strength in it."

Gillian's four years of college, as with most college students,[2] did not alter her basic religious identity. "I'd say it's pretty much the same," though she acknowledged not attending church as frequently as she did before starting college. She described that infrequency as "bad," attributing it to being busy with her studies and liking "to sleep in," then declared, "but philosophically, I think I'm pretty much in the same place." Gillian's "faith," the term she preferred over "religion," answered "why we are here and what's the purpose [of life . . .] and I think that I kind of need that." The strength Gillian found in Christian faith was important enough that when we re-interviewed her two years after graduating from college, she had recently broken up with a boyfriend of four months. "He thought that raising children in the church would be brainwashing them, and I'm Christian and so that's an important thing to me." Though disappointed, Gillian appreciated that the breakup would lower her stress levels, as she was about to start graduate school to become a nurse midwife, and might give her time to start "church hunting [. . .] to find some place that I like."

We asked Gillian what she was looking for church-wise, and she answered something less "boring" than the United Church of Christ she grew up in. Churches with formal worship—with icons, candles, and somber music—did not appeal to her. For example, "Catholicism doesn't do a thing for me." Neither did the "Bible Baptist" church that she attended with a co-worker. "She kept asking why I stopped going after once, and I didn't really want to tell her that I thought they were all crazy." What Gillian hoped to find was "a basic, no-frills Protestant" church, that was "comparable to Methodist" churches. Yet the only place Gillian attended more than once since graduating from college was a Unitarian church that was up the street from her post-college summer internship. It was a fellow intern's idea to attend, but they both enjoyed themselves. "Everyone was so friendly," she explained, and the church provided "a chance to be spiritual and fill in the blanks as you wish." Since that internship lasted just ten weeks, Gillian was content to spend her final few Sunday mornings filling in the blanks with the friendly Unitarians. She had not, however, attended a Unitarian church since then.

Perhaps Gillian found a satisfactory, "no-frills Protestant" church after we re-interviewed her. If so, she might have sounded like the young adults we met at the three lively congregations described next. But it is more likely, given her relocation to a new city, enrollment in a demanding graduate program, and track record of not attending any Protestant church twice since graduating from college, that she did not. It is not Gillian's infrequent attendance at Mainline churches that we find most interesting about her, as she resembles most Mainline Protestant twentysomethings in that pattern. Rather, it is her resolute identification as a Protestant Christian *despite* her infrequent attendance at church. Gillian, in a manner akin to Chapter 3's Michael O'Riley, is content to reside somewhere between active involvement in a congregation and estrangement from church. We examine and contrast Mainline Protestant twentysomethings who are Active, Nominal, and Estranged in the latter part of this chapter, as the stories of all three types are essential to understanding young adults who identify with Mainline churches. But first, we examine those American young adults who despite relocations, career and graduate school demands, and extensive alternatives for their discretionary time, nevertheless choose to be active in Mainline churches. Who are these young adults who become active Mainline Protestants, and what congregations do they prefer? The answer involves far more diversity than one encounters among Catholic or Evangelical twentysomethings.

Active Mainliners

Everybody cries, Jeremy Harris told us in Chapter 1, the first time they come to New York City's Middle Collegiate Church. And while it may be hard to believe any church could have this strong an impact on young adults, we heard the same thing from others who attended Middle, including Melissa Pickett. Melissa, a 27-year-old graduate student and community organizer, grew up attending a Southern Baptist church and describes her family as a "very solid, Christian" family. She was part of a small core of kids who were involved in the church all the way through high school, doing everything from hand bells and plays to teaching vacation Bible school every summer. Though church life was woven into the fabric of her family, Melissa stopped attending church when she left home at 18 for college. Unlike Gillian and most college students, whose decline in church attendance is gradual and unplanned, this was a deliberate decision for Melissa. As a teenager, Melissa disagreed with her church's teachings on sexuality. In college, she gained an understanding of "systemic oppression" and came to embrace radical politics. Yet leaving church did not mean leaving her faith. Melissa explained, "I think that Christianity gives a, shall we say, mandate to look at the world differently, to look at the world radically, and to be transgressive." Even when she came out as queer, Melissa did not feel estranged from faith. Rather, she explains, "I left the church in the organized religion piece of it, really finding that it was no longer relevant to the things I believed in in the world, the person I was in the world, what I was doing in the world. If I have to make a succinct statement, really my politics and my life didn't jibe with the church anymore."

Melissa moved to New York City after college and for five years did not consider going to church because she could not imagine a church that would fit with her worldview. It was her partner Reagan's idea to find a church. Reagan had a similar church-immersed upbringing as Melissa. When she hit her "quarterlife crisis," Reagan began to search for a church community. She tweeted that she was looking for "a social justice, queer-friendly, critical thinking church that was not trying so hard to be youth-friendly," and someone told her about Middle Collegiate. At her first visit to Middle, Reagan saw a church handout with a child's drawing on it: "It was drawn by this little boy, and it was him in a dress, and said, 'Some girls wear dresses, but boys can wear dresses, too.' And I was, like, 'The church published that! That church put that in their bulletin!' " Melissa started attending to support Reagan, but she was also curious about what it would be like to attend church again. Here is how Melissa described her first visit to Middle when she was 26 years old.

> My first impression was actually sort of overwhelming to the point of perhaps crying; an overwhelming experience of . . . this is what I had hoped that church could be for me in the current place I'm situated in my life [. . .] Coming into that church and hearing within the first five or ten minutes, explicit dialogue about social justice movements [and] that the church was at the forefront of some of that work that was happening locally in New York was overwhelming to me. I definitely cried because I felt whole. I felt like I could be whole—that my faith that had sort of been on this shelf could now come out and be a part of my commitment to being a person who did radical, social justice work.

Melissa, like Reagan and Jeremy Harris, was surprised to find herself in church again. All three gave up on churches while in college and gave churches another try in their mid-20s. They were not expecting to find a church that would align with who they are, but they found just that in the progressive Middle Collegiate Church. Though far from a "typical" Mainline church, Middle is one of three Mainline Protestant churches we studied that are successfully attracting and engaging twentysomethings.

Mainline Protestant Churches and "Mainliners"

The term "Mainline Protestant" reflects the early twentieth-century divide between those Protestants who hold to traditional Christian teachings—namely Evangelicals, Fundamentalists, and Pentecostals, and those Protestants who, to varying degrees, accommodate their theology to cultural norms. Mainline Protestants regard the Bible highly but do not consider it free of error, for example, and they emphasize the "golden rule" of love over the historicity of a six-day creation or the miraculous feeding of 5,000 with five loaves and two fishes.[3] Once known as "mainstream" or "establishment" Protestants, this group has diminished in size relative to Evangelical Protestants during the past half-century and is now referred to as the "Oldline" by some scholars.[4]

Yet the story of Mainline Protestantism's decline can obscure the reality of its current size. There are 14% of American twentysomethings who affiliate with this branch of Protestantism, which equates to 6 million adherents between the ages of 20 and 29, of which 35% attend worship at least twice per month, or 2.1 million twentysomethings worshipping regularly in Mainline churches. If all of these regular worshippers were to occupy the same place at the same time, they would become America's fifth-largest city—coming in just behind Houston's 2.2 million and far ahead of Philadelphia's 1.6 million.[5] And the denominations that would dominate this Mainline Protestant "city" are the United Methodist Church, the Evangelical Lutheran Church in America, the Presbyterian Church (of the USA), the Episcopal Church, the American Baptist Churches, the United Church of Christ, the Disciples of Christ, Quakers, and the Reformed Church in America.

We selected three very different Mainline churches to study based on their local reputation: Middle Collegiate (New York City), The Crossing (Boston), and Clay Church (South Bend). In addition to observing forty-five events at these churches, we interviewed fifty-three young adults who were active in these congregations. Though our goal was to interview twentysomethings, we found that similarly to Catholic parishes, Mainline churches use a generous definition of "young adult" that includes the mid-30s. Thus, our interviews included participants between the ages of 18 and 35.

This chapter is about young adults who affiliate with Mainline churches and value its inclusive view of Christian faith. While it would be convenient to call these young adults Mainline Protestants, we did not meet a single participant who used this label. Some did identify with a specific denomination, such as Episcopalian and United Methodist, while others used more general labels: Christian, Protestant Christian, or "follower of Christ." Four interviewees, in fact, rejected the Christian label entirely—because they were either unsure about the centrality of Jesus in their beliefs or saw the Christian label as irreparably tainted by Evangelicals. We discussed how we should refer to this disparate group, deciding that what they had in common was a decision to become part of a Mainline Protestant church, so we call them "Mainliners." Before turning to these Mainliners, though, we profile each of our selected Mainline churches, to convey a bit of the range that exists within this branch of American Protestantism.

Arts-Focused Multiracial Church

Middle Collegiate Church is an old church—by its own account it is the oldest Protestant church in the United States. During its long history, the church experienced many periods of growth and decline and stayed afloat thanks to a large endowment. Today Middle feels like a young congregation. It is a progressive, innovative community that incorporates the arts and social justice into every aspect of church life. Sunday "worship celebrations" are a tour de force combining poetry, scripture, sermon, music, dance, and skits into an experience its members find emotionally moving, intellectually challenging, sometimes provocative, but always inspirational. Its website, bulletins, and other printed materials proclaim four words in vibrant hues of purple and gold: Bold, Inclusive, Artistic, Welcoming. Middle has attracted attention not only from twentysomethings like Jeremy, Melissa, and Reagan, but also from church leaders who want to emulate its success and researchers who want to understand it.

When we began studying Middle in 2010, it had a membership of almost 800 and a regular weekly attendance of approximately 250 people. Young adults comprise roughly 10% of those in attendance on a typical Sunday morning according to senior minister Reverend Jacqui Lewis. Middle is one of four Collegiate Churches in New York City affiliated with the Reformed Churches in America (RCA), which is one of the smallest Mainline denominations in the United States. Middle does not draw attention to its denominational affiliation, however. Of the twenty young adults we interviewed at Middle (median age of 27.5), only one had ever heard of the RCA prior to coming to Middle. Rather, the church emphasizes the diversity of its participants' backgrounds. It is proud of its substantial racial diversity and of its success in attracting young adults from religious and nonreligious backgrounds: Mainline, Evangelical, Catholic, Buddhist, and Jewish as well those raised without religion. Middle is inclusive of many religious traditions, but it is explicit about its identity as a Christian church. Middle is also inclusive of LGBTQ persons, as already noted, though it is not known as a gay church. Middle is a church for people who, as one interviewee put it, "get it" when Rev. Jacqui preaches about "intersectionality" and being called by God "to boldly do a new thing on earth."

Emerging Church with a Mission

Although the emerging church movement is largely associated with Evangelical Christianity, Episcopalians have long been part of the movement. The Crossing is a small emerging church sponsored by a large Episcopal parish in Boston, which provides the meeting space and a salary for the part-time minister. It began in 2005 when the Episcopal diocese hired Rev. Steph Spellers, a newly ordained priest in her early 30s, to lead the young adult ministry. Rev. Steph told us that a few years prior to this, she had had a vision in a New York gay bar that led her to feel called to create a radically welcoming ministry focused on celebrating God. With the diocese's financial support, she began gathering a handful of young adults for a process of discernment that entailed regular meetings in a pub to discuss what shape their Christian community might take. The result is a flexible, lay-led, liturgical community emphasizing "radical welcome." Weekly worship services began in 2006 with a few dozen attendees and a core of committed leaders. The Crossing was advertised by word of mouth and flyers left at spots with young adult appeal: yoga studios, gyms, thrift stores, coffeehouses, bookstores, co-op groceries, and university campuses.

When we studied The Crossing in 2010, it had roughly forty to fifty regular attendees, almost all of whom were in their 20s or 30s. One member described it as a young adult community rather than a community that attracts some young adults. A handful of local divinity students from Boston University and Harvard do field education hours at The Crossing, and the community includes recent college graduates interning through the Episcopal diocese of Massachusetts. The Crossing embraces a nonhierarchical, participatory model of church that combines traditional Christian liturgical forms with contemporary ritual practices such as meditation and fine arts. The participatory model requires a high level of commitment from members. From the beginning, The Crossing's mission has been to offer "radical welcome" to everyone, whether "churched, de-churched, or never churched." Most attendees come from Episcopal, Catholic, or Evangelical backgrounds and are highly educated. The majority are White, though Rev. Steph is Black. A large portion rejects the "cisgendered, heterosexual hegemony" of mainstream churches, however, and trans/queer justice issues are a major focus of the social action work of the community. We interviewed sixteen young adults involved in The Crossing between the ages of 22 and 31, with a median age of 27. The lay-led leadership structure and liturgical focus, combined with social justice work, are hallmarks of this young adult community.

Family-Oriented Church

Clay Church is worlds apart from The Crossing and Middle. Located in the Midwestern city of South Bend, Indiana, Clay is a family-focused United Methodist Church. Founded in 1966, Clay went through a period of decline and conflict in the 1990s until it hired Senior Pastor Herb Buwalda, who revitalized the church with new ideas—like appointing its first female pastor. Clay was well known for vibrant children and youth programming that attracted droves of families, but it had a hard time reaching young adults. A few years before our research, for example, it launched a "contemporary" worship service, but that drew "people who grew up listening to Neil Diamond," according to one staff member. So Pastor Herb commissioned a group of lay leaders and staff to study the issue and develop a strategy. They reported that young adults often perceive churches as being judgmental, legalistic, exclusive, and unkind. To counter that, Clay would need to emphasize the radically inclusive love of Jesus both internally through building relationships and externally through service opportunities.

Clay began to emphasize living out Christian faith through service, working with Habitat for Humanity, running an after-school tutoring program, and even building wells in Africa. In contrast to the large Evangelical churches nearby, Clay does not evangelize. Thus, its social ministry projects are open for everyone to participate in and intended to appeal to young adults who are more interested in "doing something positive in the world" than in "saving souls."

Clay's attendees are mostly White, and unlike Middle or The Crossing, its leaders avoid political issues that are potentially divisive. Instead they emphasize a traditional Methodist style of worship and organization, while embracing flexibility and innovation. The Clay staff, rather interestingly, describes their work with twentysomethings as "more like mission work" than a typical church ministry. They create informal opportunities for young adults to "just hangout" or get involved in a service project without feeling like it is an obligation. Clay expects little from young adults by way of participation, money, or commitment. The hope is that Clay's mission to young adults will yield results in the future. But it had already yielded results when we studied it in 2010—some 15% of its weekly attendance of 800 were young adults.

We interviewed seventeen Clay young adults between the ages of 21–33, with a median age of 26. Unlike the young adults at Middle and The Crossing, many Clay young adults are married and have young children. This reflects not only the family focus of this congregation but also the earlier age of marriage and childbearing among Midwestern young adults. Among the seventeen young adults we interviewed at Clay, twelve were married and five had children.

What Draws Young Adults to Mainline Churches?

Compared with the Catholics described in the last chapter, Mainliner young adults come from a wider variety of religious backgrounds, so it is not surprising that their reasons for choosing a congregation vary more than the reasons given by Catholic young adults. However, community is a primary reason cited by Mainliner young adults, just as it is for Catholic young adults. Mainliners want warm and friendly churches, but they do not want to be smothered with friendliness—something that none of the Catholic young adults mentioned. Mary Williamson, a married 26-year-old woman, was impressed by the welcome at Clay Church:

> Obviously, a lot of the churches around here are small, so you can just walk in and people will notice that you're new. As a couple, we kind of stick out, and we felt smothered. The nice thing about Clay is that after our first visit some people said hi to us, obviously people notice when you're new. [. . .] After the second time we visited, one day we came home and there was bread on our doorstep, which I think the bread thing is really cool. For me personally it's a nice touch without being too overwhelming.

Along the same lines, other Mainliners at Clay appreciate the "no pressure" approach of Pastor Herb, who sends out personal e-mails inviting young adults to social gatherings at his home, assuring them, "this is not a 'meeting,' not a 'committee!' "

For young adults at progressive Mainline churches—such as Middle, in New York City, and The Crossing, in Boston—community means much more than a warm and friendly congregation. Mainliners at Middle and The Crossing were emphatic that their church community is "radically inclusive." By this they meant, firstly, that their church is welcoming not only to gays and lesbians but also to bisexuals, transsexuals, and sexual-identity-questioning persons as well. Some of these young adults have been wounded by anti-gay churches in the past. For example, Andre, a 31-year-old man, came to The Crossing after attending Catholic and Pentecostal churches until his late-20s, says:

> I began to feel like, wow, this idea that homosexuality was wrong . . . wasn't really coming from God. It was coming from this organized church that has their great things but [also] this mandate that you have to fight these feelings [that] I felt was not really coming from God. It took me a long time to realize it came from this church

> community. And so that's how I came to The Crossing . . . because as I started feeling more comfortable [with my sexuality,] I didn't want to feel like I had to hide that part of my life.

Radically inclusive community also means that churches ought to include people of all ethnicities, nationalities, class backgrounds, and religious worldviews. It was the latter point that mattered most to Komika. Komika grew up in a culturally Buddhist family and attended Catholic schools from second grade through graduate school. She began looking for a church after finishing school and checked out Middle Collegiate at a friend's recommendation. Komika explains:

> So, the first thing I liked about it was, it was just eye-opening and a different type of church than compared to any of the churches I've been to. And then also I appreciated the fact that Jacqui [the pastor] and the whole church respects and shares and accepts, you know, other religions that believe in good. And then also the fact that it was open to diverse cultures, to different ethnic background and different sexualities, and I thought that was good.

Far beyond "accepting" diversity, Middle and The Crossing are strongly affirming, which explains why many young adults have an intense emotional experience when they first visit. For example, Andre grew up in a strict Catholic family but started going to what he describes as nondenominational, charismatic-type churches in his teens. He knew he was gay by age 14 and hid this from his church communities until his late 20s, when he attended a retreat for gay students offered by the university where he works and learned about The Crossing. Though the liturgical style is different from what he was used to, Andre felt at home from his first visit: "It's different, obviously, then you know an Evangelical service [is]. But I like it. I feel very accepted there. There's just, they are very intentional about being welcoming. And I feel like it's a great community where I don't have to hide any part of myself. I can bring my whole self to God in that community." Carla was in her mid-20s trying to become a professional actress in New York City when she stumbled upon Middle. She grew up in a strict Catholic family but left the church because it was "too judgmental." She described herself as a spiritual person who sees God in everything and everyone; she was not a fan of organized religion, but Carla began to long for a spiritual community. She was walking by Middle on a Sunday morning when she heard the church bells. She followed the sound to the steps of the church and read these words on a large banner: "Bold. Artistic. Inclusive." Struck especially by "artistic" and "inclusive," she walked into a Sunday morning "celebration service." She cried several times during the worship, describing it as a "safe space" for everyone: "I can love and be loved there . . . I am accepted, and everyone is accepted." Marianne, who is 30 years old, had a similar reaction to her first service at Middle: "I don't even know what made me go for the first time. Except that it was nearby. I'd been kind of thinking about it for a while, and then my mom came to visit, and we went together. And I was like, oh my God! This is the place I've been looking for my whole life!"

Mainliners also told us that the way the community worships together is important to them. Preaching was mentioned most often. Young adults at Clay Church described Pastor Herb's sermons as "real" and "genuine." Sam, 27 and married, shared: "I'd say that Pastor Herb has, gosh, just a real sensitivity for the pain that people experience in life, and I don't get that sense in other churches that I attend." Mainliners at Middle and The Crossing described the worship services as "transformational." For Middle, this results from worship experiences that thoughtfully integrate music, dance, and drama. Many young adults who attend Middle are themselves artists. Thirty-two-year-old Sarah commutes nearly an hour each way to attend services at Middle on Sundays. Though Sarah does other activities that feed her spiritually—yoga, meditation, and tai chi—only Middle offers a powerful experience of worship:

> There's a lot of arts in the worship [. . .] and the music is always very strong. I've gone to a lot of churches where, of course, the churches have music, but not like Middle's. Middle's music is "open up your heart" music [. . .]. The songs that are chosen and the way they are sung makes

> it different than other churches [. . .]. There's arts woven into it whenever it can be [. . .]. There may be modern dance, [and] four times a year there's some kind of puppet thing happening [. . .]. They celebrate people's creativity.

While Middle is known for its artistic worship, The Crossing is known for its experimental liturgies. Several young adults told us they found this emergent Episcopal church's worship style "weird" at first but came to love the juxtaposition of tradition and innovation. Most important to young adults at The Crossing was the centrality of the Eucharist in the worship service. Andre described it this way: "Everyone gets together in a circle and everyone serves one another. And then Reverend Steph, as she was tearing up the bread after praying, she was saying these words, 'Wherever you are on your journey, you are welcome. Wherever you find yourself, whatever questions you have, you can bring them to God. You can bring them to the table.' I was really moved by that, just by the words." Twenty-three-year-old Dave told us that The Crossing is a "Eucharistic community," by which he means it is "a community that gathers around Eucharist." For Dave, the way The Crossing does Eucharist expresses its theology of "radical welcome." He explained, "I think there's something about Jesus's gospel that is only transformative when it's accessible to everybody, especially the folks that are often on the margins and placed there by our society and structures, so if you took that away I don't know that I would need to be part of The Crossing. Actually, I know I wouldn't be."

Of all the reasons young adult Christians gave for choosing their church, one stood out as unique to Mainliners: the church's vision. Lots of churches have vision and mission statements featured prominently on the website homepage and bulletin, but Mainliners were impressed by churches that really try to live them. It was Clay Church's vision that caught the attention of Crystal when she first visited with her husband at age 23:

> When we were doing our church shopping, we said, "Well why don't we stop off there and see what's going on," and we stopped off, and it

> happened to be the weekend that Herb was talking about the vision that he thought God was putting in front of Clay, and we said, "That's what we want to be part of."

Crystal and her husband had recently stopped attending an Evangelical megachurch because of its theatrical production style and obsession with growth. They liked that Clay was intentionally moving from a "country club, inward focus" to an "external, community focus." For 26-year-old Sara, who also came from an Evangelical background, it was Clay's vision to be engaged with the local community without evangelizing that appealed: "I think the ministries outside of the church are most important. I'm not involved in the ministries that target strictly members, but I think the outreach without the evangelical twist is really, really important." While Clay's outward vision to serve the world inspires members to tutor underserved children and repair houses for impoverished families, Middle and The Crossing proclaim bold visions to transform the world. They connect the ministry of Jesus with building a society free of poverty, racism, and sexism. This boldness is attractive to young adult activists who previously thought of churches as part of the social problems they were trying to solve rather than as part of the solution.

Urban Progressives, Family-Oriented Midwesterners

Our study of three very different Mainline churches reveals a strong divide between urban progressive Mainliners and family-oriented Midwestern Mainliners. Protestantism's traditional assemblage of local congregation, declared membership, and family life is clearly continuing at Clay Church in Indiana, but not at all apparent at The Crossing in Boston or Middle Collegiate in New York City. Young adults at Middle and The Crossing were frankly surprised to find themselves in churches. While some grew up attending church, sometime in their late teens or early 20s, these young adults separated their "love of Jesus" from "organized religion" and acquired a wariness of churches, which they had come to associate with intolerance and oppression. Less than half of the young adults we met at Middle and The Crossing came from Mainline Protestant backgrounds. They came instead from Catholic, Evangelical, Pentecostal, Charismatic, Jewish, Buddhist, "spiritual but not religious," and even atheist backgrounds. They identify primarily as activists and liberals, but thanks to Middle and The Crossing, they are embracing a Christian identity too.

The church-going urban Mainliners we interviewed realize just how out of step they are with their peers. As Jeremy Harris told us in Chapter 1, his friends cannot imagine church in a positive light. Indeed, it took years for Jeremy's partner Eric to step inside Middle, and when he finally did, the experience of acceptance and love brought him to tears. Urban Mainliners also emphasize how busy they are, and they would never join a church unless it offered something too amazing to pass up: that is, a community with a visible cohort of young adults dedicated to transforming society, which celebrates life through radically inclusive, socially progressive, artistic and intellectual worship, demonstrates commitment to authentic truth-telling with love, and is tied together with great preaching delivered by funny and warm ministers. In other words, urban Mainliners have incredibly high expectations. And even when they find or stumble upon the whole package, they are slow to move beyond exuberance into a long-term commitment involving time and money.

The Midwestern young adults at Clay, by contrast, were raised in a Protestant church—either Evangelical or Mainline—or they married someone who was. They sought out a Protestant church to join because churchgoing and involvement in church life were normative for them and their peers. They "shopped" for a church using a few criteria: not-too-conservative theologically and socially, friendly but not smothering, some presence of young adults, a commitment to helping those in need, and good preaching. Using these criteria, they chose the best option from the available local choices. In their expectations of church life, these Mainliners share more in common with Evangelical young adults (see Chapter 5) than with Mainliners at Middle and The Crossing.

Mainline Protestant Twentysomethings in America

In Chapter 2, we learned that 1 out of 7 American twentysomethings affiliate with Mainline denominations—for example, Methodist, Lutheran, Presbyterian, and Episcopalian churches;[6] that 30% of these Mainliners consider religion to be very or extremely important in their daily lives; and that a majority of Mainliners pray weekly or more often. We also learned that Mainliner twentysomethings had the lowest rates of attendance at religious services of all Christian twentysomethings (35% attend weekly, 16% never attend) and were the most likely of religiously affiliated twentysomethings to agree (69%) that "too many religious people" are "negative, angry, and judgmental." These results, when joined with our ethnographic findings, confirm two things. First, the wariness about religion encountered among our interviewees is a nationwide phenomenon, and Mainline churches that draw twentysomethings anticipate and preemptively address this wariness. Second, Mainliner twentysomethings spread out along a continuum—from active types like Melissa Pickett or Jeremy Harris (from Chapter 1), to nominal types like Gillian Muller, whose priority on career and graduate school squeezes out time for regular participation in church, to estranged types, who say their religious affiliation is with Mainline Protestantism but indicate that their spiritual life possesses little to no importance presently and virtually never attend worship services. To examine this diversity, we applied the same Active, Nominal, and Estranged typology among Mainliner twentysomethings as we did among Catholic twentysomethings (see Chapter 3).

Of the 262 Mainliner twentysomethings in the NSAT, one-fifth (19%) met the criteria for being Active—that is, they attended church regularly and indicated growth in their spiritual life as adults was very important to them. One-sixth (17%) met the criteria for Estranged—that is, they attended church never to at most once per year and indicated their spiritual life was of little to no importance to them. And two-thirds (64%) met the criteria for Nominal—that is, their church attendance and importance of spiritual life fell in-between their Active and Estranged Mainliner peers.

Like we did in Chapter 3, we used a statistical procedure called discriminant analysis to see what demographic factors differentiated these three types. This identified a cluster of statistically significant demographic factors, with several important patterns. First, White twentysomethings exclusively comprise the Estranged Mainliner category, while Black, Latino, Asian, and twentysomethings identifying as some "other" race cluster in the Active and Nominal categories. Second, married and younger twentysomethings had higher rates of involvement than single, divorced, and older twentysomethings. And third, college graduates, single heads of households, and members of more affluent households had lower rates of involvement than their respective counterparts (see Figures 4.1, 4.2, and 4.3). Each of these is worth a closer look.

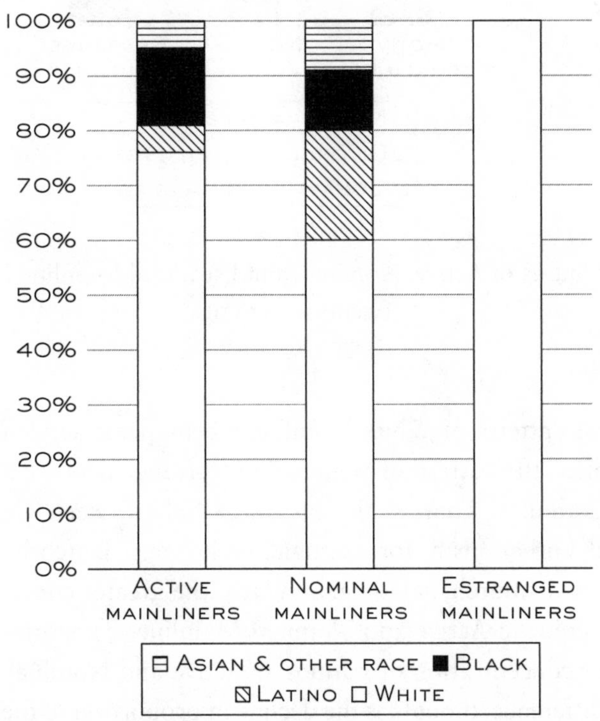

FIGURE 4.1

Race and Ethnicity of Active, Nominal, and Estranged Mainline Protestant Twentysomethings

Source: NSAT 2013

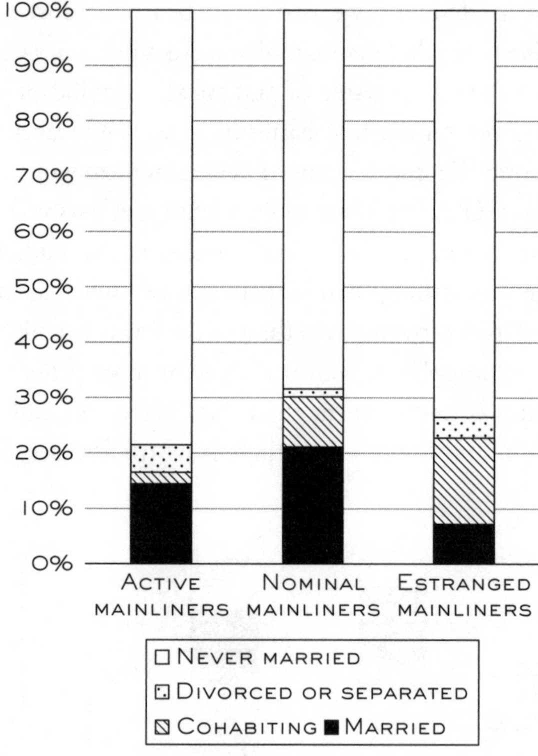

Figure 4.2

Marital Status of Active, Nominal, and Estranged Mainline Protestant Twentysomethings

Source: NSAT 2013

The first pattern, of White Mainliners being least active (see Figure 4.1), parallels the pattern of White ethnic estrangement we saw among Roman Catholics. That is, the historical link between German ethnicity and Lutheranism, for example, or between Dutch heritage and the Reformed Church, is fading. Similarly, the greater concentration of people of color in Active and Nominal Mainliner categories is akin to the greater concentration of Latinos as Active and Nominal Catholics. A major difference, though, is the decline in proportion of the American population affiliated with Mainline Protestantism, which is not occurring with Roman Catholicism. Mainline Protestantism *is* increasing in its racial and ethnic diversity, and that racial diversification is adding Active

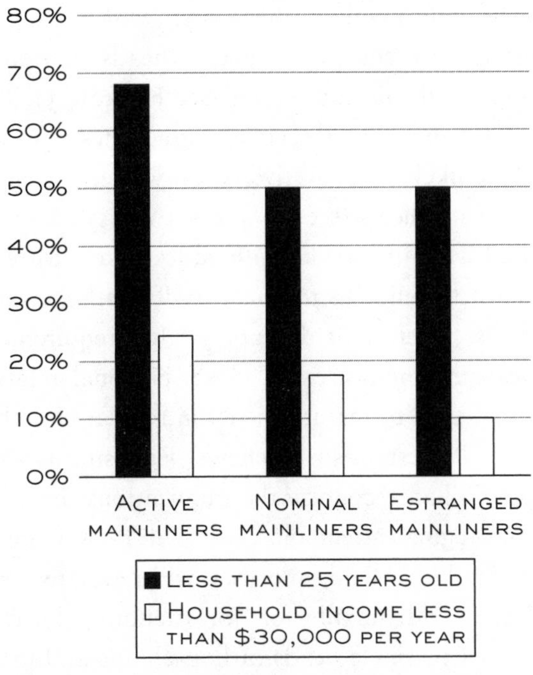

Figure 4.3
Age and Household Income of Active, Nominal, and Estranged Mainline Protestant Twentysomethings
Source: NSAT 2013

and Nominal twentysomethings. But it is not doing so at a rate sufficient to offset the declining involvement of White Mainliners.

The second pattern involves greater involvement by Mainliners under the age of 25 compared with those 25 and over, and by married twentysomethings compared to single (i.e., never married) or divorced twentysomethings (see Figures 4.2, 4.3). The former fits with the relatively less encumbered lives of those under 25, especially since our discriminant analysis held constant marital status, employment status, parental status, and head of household status. The latter fits with the more settled lives of married twentysomethings, especially compared with the less settled lives of their never married counterparts, and with the real or anticipated stigmatization of divorced twentysomethings in congregations.

The third pattern involves the lower rates of involvement in Mainline churches by college graduates, heads of households, and members of more affluent households (see Figure 4.3). This is important because, as a general rule, college graduates who affiliate with religion are *more* likely to be Active types; we see this among Roman Catholics and Evangelicals (see Chapters 3 and 5). So why, then, are college-educated Mainliners, like Gillian, less likely to be Active? The answer may lie with religious teaching itself: Catholicism requires attendance at Mass (even as it downplays that requirement publicly), and Evangelicalism emphasizes a "close, personal relationship with Jesus" that is expected to manifest itself in regular church attendance, while Mainline Protestantism eschews legalism. College-educated Mainliners like Gillian recognize the implications: being a Mainliner does not require regular attendance, they will be welcomed no matter how infrequently they attend, and they will never receive a scolding from the pulpit or individually for not attending church. As for the lower involvement of single heads of households and members of affluent households, we argue it is a function of discretionary hours and opportunities: the former have few, while the latter have many. When either is the case, involvement in Mainline congregations is one of the first things eliminated.

We were also intrigued by factors that did not differentiate Active, Nominal, and Estranged Mainliners. For example, Active, Nominal, and Estranged Mainliners equally and overwhelmingly agree "that it is OK to pick and choose [one's] religious beliefs without having to accept the teachings of their religion faith as a whole."[7] Similarly, 2 out of 5 Mainliners, regardless of type, indicate that they view God as a spiritual force and not personal; this demonstrates Mainliners comfort with holding beliefs outside the orthodox box. This openness to nonorthodox positions sets Active Mainliner twentysomethings apart from their Active Catholic and Active Evangelical counterparts, both of which are less likely to support "cafeteria" theologies or views of God as an impersonal, spiritual force (see Chapters 3 and 5).

Mainliners of Active, Nominal, or Estranged types also agree on the importance of marriage, with a majority (55%) saying they "would be very unhappy" if they never married, and on the desire to have children, with 3 out of 4 saying this was "very important" to them. It is a telling indicator of emerging adulthood (see Chapter 2) that marriage's importance falls below that of parenthood. It is also a poignant indicator of (the once) Mainline Protestantism's shift from the center of the American "establishment," that a majority of its twentysomethings are untroubled by the thought that they might never marry. Children are another story; they remain quite important to Active, Nominal, and Estranged Mainliners.

There are still other items that Mainliners agree on. Their use of social media, for example, occurs at comparable rates among Active, Nominal, or Estranged Mainliners.[8] Reports of having no close friends, or of feeling lonely, also occur at equal rates across these types.[9] Viewing gender identity as a private and inconsequential matter is widely and equally agreed upon by Mainliners.[10] Any work of art or music, moreover, can be a valid expression of spirituality; Mainliners do not restrict creative expression to traditional religious subjects or dissemination within religious venues only.[11] Finally, Active, Nominal, and Estranged Mainliners express similar levels of satisfaction with concern for social justice in "most churches and synagogues" today.[12] Taken together, these commonalities tell us that Mainliners have equivalent rates of social engagement and friendships, wide agreement about the inconsequence of individuals' gender identity, nearly complete openness to encountering spiritual expression in any setting, and similar levels of satisfaction with congregations' efforts to promote social justice.

These commonalities also tell us that what distinguishes Active, Nominal, and Estranged Mainliners is not what many presume. For example, it is not the case that Active Mainliners are more oriented to traditional American family life than Nominal or Estranged Mainliners. Nor are Estranged Mainliners loners who prefer social media, while Nominal and Active Mainliners prefer face to face engagement. Rather, what distinguishes Mainliner types are demographic factors like ethnicity and household income in conjunction with, as we describe next, the depth of their identification with Mainline churches, the daily relevance of Mainline teachings to them, the extent to which their friends attend church, and the desire to give their children a church experience as meaningful as the one they had as children.

Though all Mainliner twentysomethings indicate their religion as Protestant or Christian, only half of Estranged Mainliners think of themselves "as a part of a particular religion, denomination, or church" (see Figure 4.4). Among Active Mainliners, by contrast, virtually all think of themselves "as part of" a Protestant church or denomination, and 3 out of 4 Nominal Mainliners do so as well. A sense of belonging is the proverbial canary in the coal mine; research shows that new college students who do not feel like they belong are quick to leave, leading universities to invest millions into fostering connections among

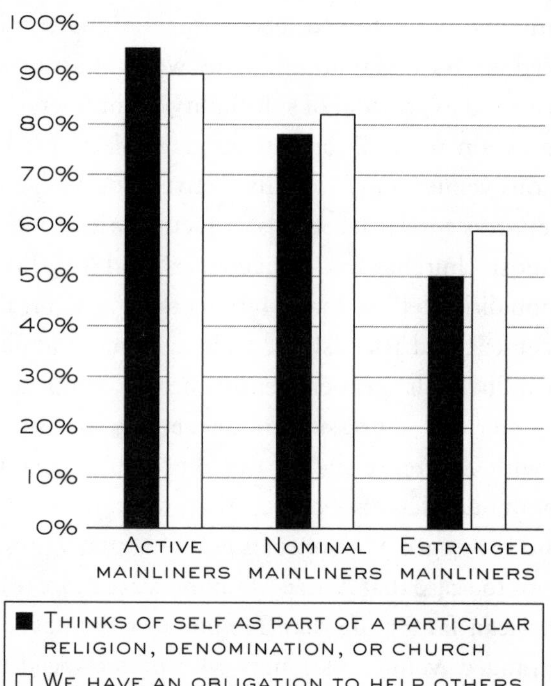

Figure 4.4

Religious Belonging, Helping Obligation by Active, Nominal, and Estranged Mainline Protestant Twentysomethings
Source: NSAT 2013

new students.[13] That more than 1 out of 5 Mainliners do not think of themselves as part of a Mainline denomination or church indicates the decline in adherents to Mainline churches is not over.

Because Mainline churches emphasize doing good in the world over believing in a particular creed, their adherents have been labeled "Golden Rule Christians."[14] That gospel rule says "in everything do to others as you would have them do to you; for this is the law and the prophets" (Matthew 7:12 NRSV). We therefore polled Mainliners about having an obligation to help others. They overwhelmingly agree with this obligation, even if it requires personal sacrifice, with Active Mainliners indicating highest agreement, followed by Nominal and then Estranged Mainliners (see Figure 4.4).

Not surprisingly, Active Mainliner twentysomethings report the highest proportion of friends who attend church and who volunteer regularly, followed by Nominal Mainliners, and trailed by Estranged Mainliners (see Figure 4.5). Active Mainliner twentysomethings, moreover, frequently report feeling "extremely," "very," or "somewhat" close to God "most of the time" (see Figure 4.6). These feelings are uncommon among Nominal Mainliners and rare among Estranged Mainliners. Feelings of closeness to God, and the religiousness of one's social network, are not coincidental. Since Emile Durkheim's classic study of religion, we know shared religious feelings are products of religious rituals.[15] Having many church-attending friends and feeling close to God, Durkheim would argue, are flipsides of the same coin.

Prayer is perhaps the most common religious activity in America. In Chapter 2, we learned that 1 out of 2 Mainliners pray at least weekly, with most praying daily. Here, we examine daily prayer, and learn two things more. First, Active Mainliner twentysomethings are substantially more likely to pray daily than Nominal Mainliners, and Nominals substantially more than Estranged Mainliners (see Figure 4.7). Second, only a minority of Active Mainliners report praying daily. This is in striking contrast to Active Catholics and Active Evangelicals, where we encounter an overwhelming majority praying daily (see Chapters 3 and 5). We have seen above that Mainline churches emphasize doing good works over theological orthodoxy. What we see here requires us

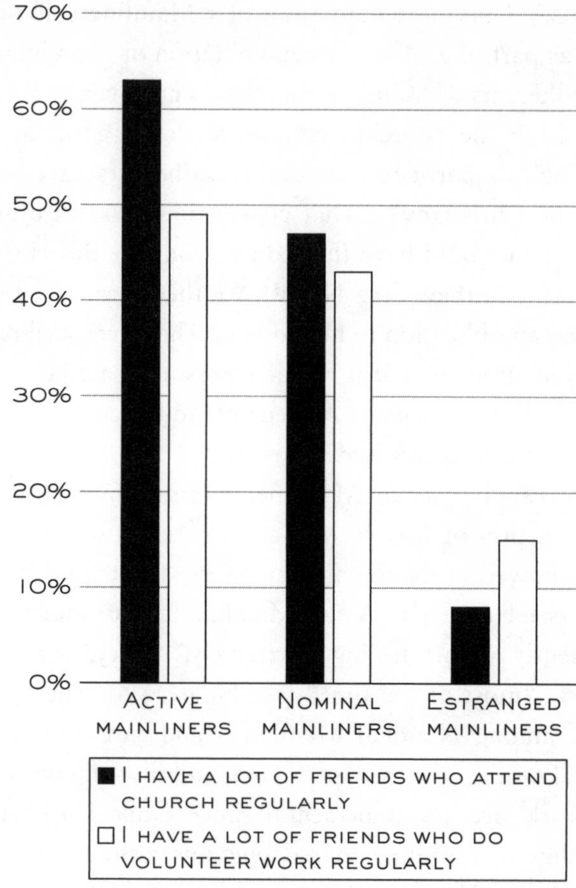

Figure 4.5

Church-Attending, Volunteering Friends of Active, Nominal, and Estranged Mainline Protestant Twentysomethings

Source: NSAT 2013

to augment that statement: Mainline churches emphasize good works over theological orthodoxy *and personal piety*. Daily prayer is less important to Mainliners than it is to other Christians, and similarly, regular meditation is less important to Mainliners than other Christians. Which is not to say these things are unimportant to Mainliners who practice them—this is only an observation about the proportion of Mainliners to whom these things are important. As we will see next, faith is very important to many Mainliners.

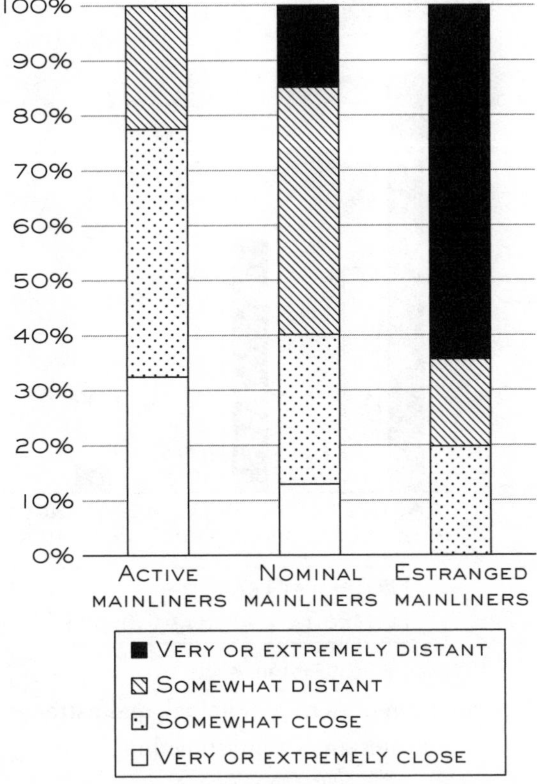

FIGURE 4.6

Feelings of Closeness to God Most of the Time Among Active, Nominal, and Estranged Mainline Protestant Twentysomethings
Source: NSAT 2013

Scholars are increasingly, and rightly, paying attention to the role of religion in everyday life. That is, does religion make a difference in how people live their daily lives? We asked American twentysomethings about this, and the answers by Active, Nominal, and Estranged Mainliners could not have been more different (see Figure 4.8). More than 4 out of 5 Active Mainliners said their religious life was "extremely" or "very important" in "shaping how I live my daily life." Only 1 out of 4 Nominal Mainliners said likewise. And from Estranged Mainliners, we got a big zero. This result conveys the powerful, everyday influence that religious faith has among Active Mainliners, and the total absence

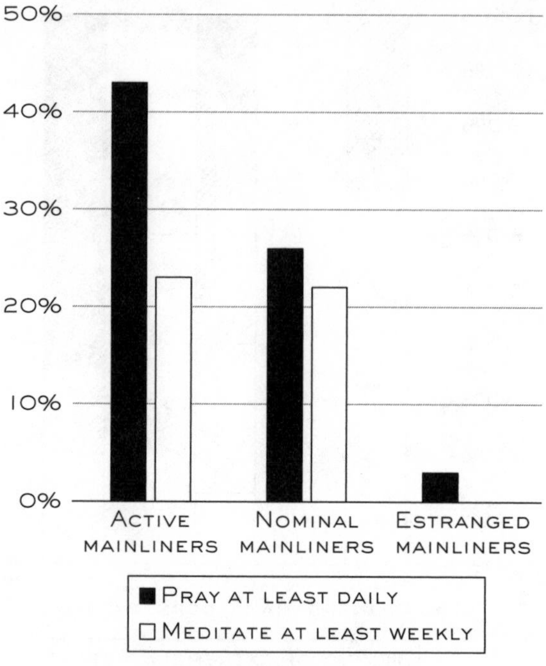

FIGURE 4.7

Prayer and Meditation of Active, Nominal, and Estranged Mainline Protestant Twentysomethings

Source: NSAT 2013

of the same among Estranged Mainliners; it also validates our Active, Nominal, and Estranged typology. When religious faith is relevant to everyday life, it is valued by twentysomethings. When it is not relevant, it is not valued.

This raises the issue of what makes faith relevant to Mainliner twentysomethings, and in what ways. Gillian told us she found strength in her faith, because it answered questions about life's meaning and her purpose. Her Mainliner peers seem to concur, as 7 out of 10 Estranged Mainliners, 9 out of 10 Nominal Mainliners, and 10 out of 10 Active Mainliners agree that their life "has purpose and meaning" (see Figure 4.9). Active Mainliners, moreover, are most likely to say they often ponder "the meaning of life," followed by Nominal Mainliners and trailed by Estranged Mainliners. A consequence of that increased

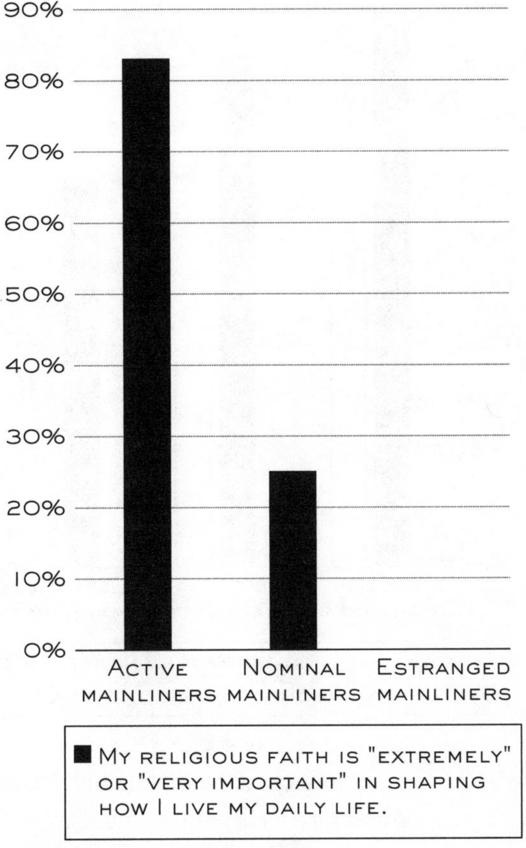

Figure 4.8

Importance of Religious Faith in Daily Life of Active, Nominal, and Estranged Mainline Protestant Twentysomethings

Source: NSAT 2013

pondering may be twentysomething ethics, with Active Mainliners' understanding ethical living to involve more than their private lives. Fewer than 40% of Active Mainliners agree that "making a lot of money is very important to my happiness" or "all I want out of life is a job that pays well and a partner I can trust" (see Figure 4.10). About 60% of Nominal Mainliners agree with both items, and over 70% of Estranged Mainliners do as well. As we saw earlier, Active Mainliners view helping others, even at the cost of personal sacrifice,

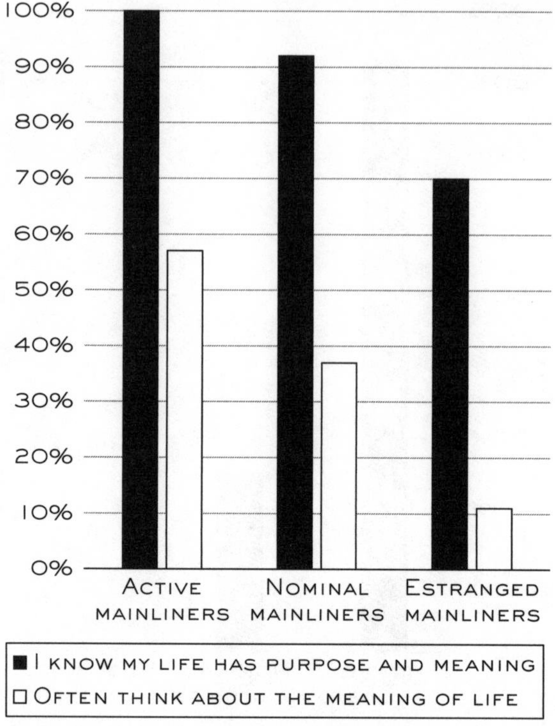

Figure 4.9

Life's Purpose and Meaning by Active, Nominal, and Estranged Mainline Protestant Twentysomethings

Source: NSAT 2013

as an obligation (Figure 4.4); they rank this helping ethic far higher than their income or even finding a life partner. Nominal Mainliners also rank helping others higher than income or partnership. Estranged Mainliners, however, do not: they place private satisfaction ahead of the obligation to help others. Reported values and actual behavior can, of course, vary widely. At the same time, values and behaviors are not uncorrelated, so these patterns merit reflection. We relay our reflections in Chapter 7.

Predicting the future may be social scientists' least favorite activity, as unforeseen factors powerfully alter social conditions. We will attempt it, nonetheless, with the proviso that our prediction presumes

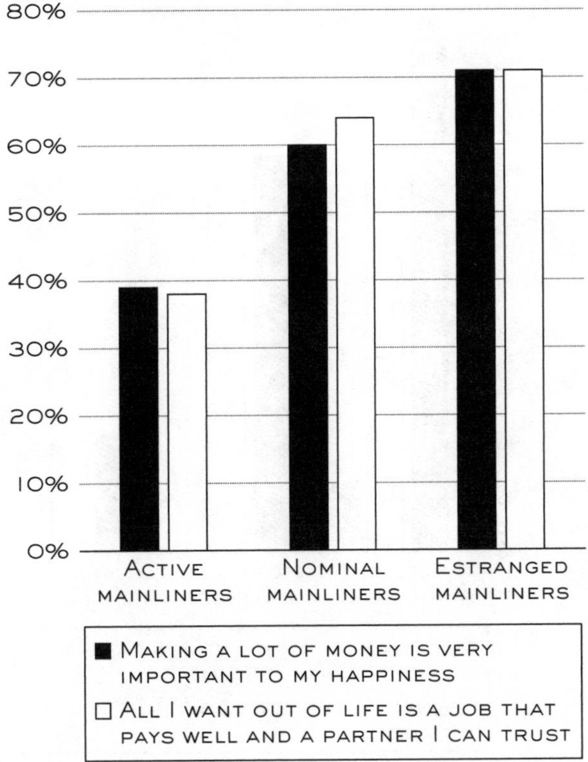

Figure 4.10

Individualistic Ethics of Active, Nominal, and Estranged Mainline Protestant Twentysomethings

Source: NSAT 2013

steady, gradual social change and generally settled lives for ordinary Americans. We predict that there will be a future generation of Mainline Protestants, because so many current Mainliners value their own childhood religious experience, and so many intend to join churches when they become parents (see Figure 4.11). Amazingly, 30% of Estranged Mainliners intend to join churches with their kids, which is more than the proportion whose own childhood faith was important. Still, this future generation is unlikely to match the 14% of American twentysomethings who are currently Mainliners, since only 71% of all Mainliner twentysomethings plan to join churches, and since Mainline

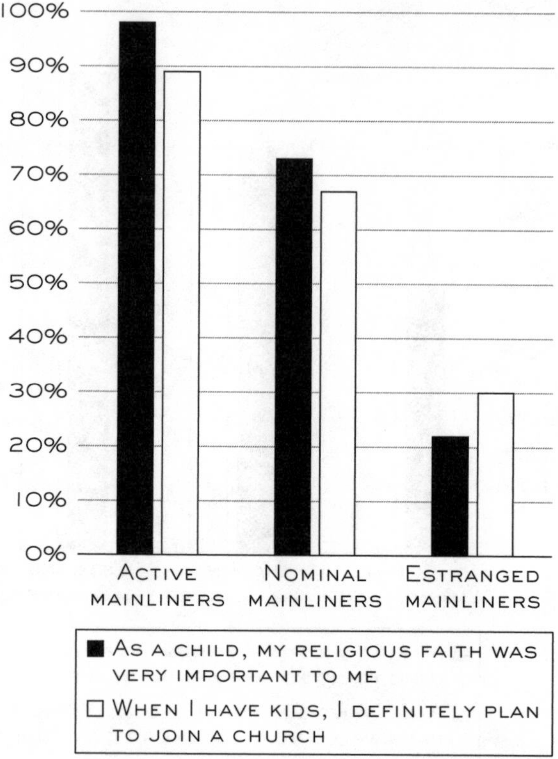

Figure 4.11

Faith Past and Future of Active, Nominal, and Estranged Mainline Protestant Twentysomethings

Source: NSAT 2013

churches place proselytizing on a continuum between uncomfortable and odious. Unless some larger social disruption prompts hordes of conversions to Mainline churches in specific, or something triggers a distinctively Mainliner spike in fertility rates, we expect a 40% decline in twentysomethings affiliated with Mainline churches by the latter part of the 2040s.[16] This will keep progressive Protestantism alive, but it will also result in shuttering a lot of Mainline church doors.

CHAPTER 5

EVANGELICALS

DIAMOND LEWIS AND ROBERT RINALDI

Throughout her childhood, Diamond was "very, very involved in church." And not just any church, either. She attended Seventh Baptist Church, founded by her Great-Grandpa Lewis, a powerful preacher whose legacy is revered at this historic Black church. Today, many of Diamond's family members still attend Seventh Baptist Church, as did Diamond and her mother, until Diamond was in eighth grade. At that point, Diamond's mother and father divorced, and when several deaconesses criticized her mother for doing so, she announced, "We're getting out!" Diamond, her siblings, and her mother moved 100 miles and one state away, and found a new church with more compassionate leadership. Diamond was thrilled with her new church. She explained how Seventh Baptist "was a very boring church," and its "older congregation" resisted doing anything differently. But her new church "is the best church in the world," and Diamond loves "my pastor, because he's so real [. . .] he will put it to you plain and simple." For example, "he talked about 'fleeing fornication,' [and] he was like, 'How can you *not* understand those two words? Do you understand the word *flee*?' He is just so funny." Now 21 and a senior at a public college in her state, Diamond prefers the church's third service on Sundays, which does not start until 11:30 a.m. Her pastor refers to the audience at this later service as "the 'after club crowd,'" because it is packed with "the early twenties, early thirties crowd." Diamond loves "the people" at this service and loves how well her pastor communicates with young adults—"he's funny and comical and biblical at the same time."

Robert Rinaldi also grew up "very involved" in church, despite his White, middle-class family's decision to switch churches four times during his childhood. When he was born, the family attended a Pentecostal church. Then they switched to an Evangelical Free church. Then to a nondenominational church. Then back to the Evangelical Free church. Part of the reason behind the "church hopping" was his parents' intense level of involvement, which set them up to know things about the congregation that few others did, and when "something wrong happened within the church, my parents got kind of ostracized for it—undeservedly." That did not poison Robert's or his parent's faith; it only lowered their opinion of that congregation, and they moved their involvement to the next church. Robert, in fact, attended a college affiliated with the Evangelical Free church, which is where we interviewed him at age 22, just weeks before his graduation.

Both Diamond and Robert made clear that they believe traditional Evangelical doctrines about the divinity of Christ, his death on the Cross as atonement for sin, and the absolute trustworthiness of the Bible. But Diamond admits she has not attended church as often since starting college. Some of this is due to Diamond's work schedule, which can include weekends. But even when Diamond is not working weekends, the 90-minute drive to her church leaves her hitting the snooze button rather than her car's ignition. When we caught up with Diamond for her second interview, she was a 24-year-old graduate student living in a small university town in the Midwest. She found a church in town that she occasionally attends, but "it's definitely not the same" as her home church. She's "trying to not constantly compare" this church with her home church, but it is clear Diamond is struggling with disappointment. Two years after our first interview with her, neither Diamond's beliefs nor her attendance had palpably changed. Diamond was still Evangelical in her theology and still attending church at the same rate—a few times a semester.

Robert, by contrast, attended church every week during college, up to and including his senior year. But after graduating from college, he moved to a new city, started a new job, and bought a house; and he began to struggle with his faith. He said he became "stagnant" in his spiritual life and met with a couple of pastors to "rethink my views on Christianity and how I handle the church." Robert explained that he was experiencing a delayed reaction to the critical approach to the Bible and Christianity taught at his Evangelical college. He was sure that he would come out on the other side of his "questioning" with a stronger faith, and he did identify a church that he attended occasionally. Still, realizing that "the world isn't so black and white, it's mainly gray" has been "the toughest thing" he has had to work through since his undergraduate years ended.

Robert's and Diamond's stories are unique, just as they are, but the place they find themselves with respect to Evangelical faith is crowded with other twentysomethings. Neither estranged from their faith nor "all in," they occupy a middle place while they wait for something—like graduate school or a time of questioning—to finish. The stories of Nominal Evangelicals like Robert and Diamond are important, and we return to Evangelicals like them in the latter part of this chapter.

Our focus is not Evangelical twentysomethings who stay on the periphery of congregations, however. We sought to understand those twentysomethings who are "all in" as Bible-believing Protestants and the congregations that draw them in across cities and even counties. We estimate there are 6 million Active Evangelical twentysomethings in America,[1] and if these devout young adults all gathered in the same place at the same time, they would bump Los Angeles' population of 4 million residents down to third place and become the nation's second-largest city—surpassed only by New York City's 8.5 million. A "city" of this size has much to explore and learn from, and much, too, that is interesting about the churches preferred by these 6 million American twentysomethings who identify with Evangelical denominations and congregations.

Active Evangelicals

We met 26-year-old Sarah Kim at New Life Fellowship Church in New York City. This is the same church where we met Lee Chen, whose story we relayed in Chapter 1. Sarah and Lee are fellow church members now, but they traveled different religious paths to reach the same congregation. Lee converted to Christianity in his early 20s, while Sarah's family has a Presbyterian heritage that goes back generations. Involvement in churches, then, has been a constant in Sarah's life; she's neither a convert nor a revert (i.e., a returnee to religion). Where Sarah's and Lee's stories overlap is growing up in strict Asian-immigrant families, with deep roots in New York City, and transferring to multiracial New Life Fellowship from ethnic-specific churches, which both found too restrictive. New Life Fellowship attracts immigrants and children of immigrants who seek an Evangelical congregation that permits them to be *American* twentysomethings instead of requiring them to retain the ethnic traditions of their parents.

In Kentucky, we met African American twentysomethings who wanted to retain their parents' traditions by joining historically Black churches, but they also wanted to update these traditions. We met 25-year-old Quenesha Smith at Consolidated Baptist Church in Lexington, Kentucky. Quenesha had moved to Lexington from Memphis for graduate school. She had attended a Baptist church in Memphis since she was "in the womb." But most of the kids she grew up with dropped out when they turned 18 because there were no activities or mentorships for them. Quenesha never thought about dropping out of church completely because churchgoing was ingrained in her by her parents. When she moved to Lexington, she looked for a Black church with great, scripture-based preaching and people her age. Thanks to a friend's invitation, she found both at Consolidated Baptist.

In this section, we hear from Active Evangelical twentysomethings—that is, church-committed, theologically conservative, young adult Protestants. Under this category we group together those who affiliate with Fundamentalist, Pentecostal, neo-Evangelical, and most historically Black churches.[2] Though different in many ways, Evangelicals share an unwavering commitment to Jesus Christ as Savior and to the Bible as God's revelation. Since several ethnographic studies of Evangelical churches that successfully reach young adults have already been published,[3] we sought to complement this research by choosing to study twentysomethings in a historically Black church and a multiracial Evangelical church. We begin by describing these church sites and then turn to our interviews with young adults who claim these churches as their own.

Multigenerational Black Church

Consolidated Baptist Church in Lexington, Kentucky, is a large, Black congregation born through the merger of two Baptist churches in 1895. This "Bible-believing church" is affiliated with the Southern Baptist Convention and emphasizes evangelism through preaching God's truth of salvation. In keeping with its conservative theology, Consolidated does not allow women to serve as ministers and is actively opposed to same-sex relationships. It holds three worship services every Sunday morning and a prayer service on Wednesday nights. One staff person described the services this way: "We have a good time. If you want to come and just hang out and just listen, you can do that. But if you want to come and exalt God and lift up your hands and shout and praise, you can do that too. We are really accepting of both of these pieces. We are lovers and huggers and smilers and kissers. If you want to be loved on, then this is the place to be." The mood changes at the end of the services on the first Sunday of each month, when "the ordinance of Holy Communion" is observed. With the dimming of lights, everyone becomes silent and reverent as deacons serve wafers and grape juice consumed in unison by the congregation. The other ordinance observed regularly at Consolidated is full-immersion baptism. Evangelism is central to Consolidated's mission, and members are frequently urged to share Christ with nonbelievers. As a large and growing church, Consolidated offers lots of ministries, such as a men's ministry, Bible studies, and even fitness programs. It also helps those in the wider community through a financial assistance program and a Feeding Ministry to persons who are homeless.

In 2003, Consolidated moved to a state-of-the art campus to accommodate the 1,500 individuals who attend its Sunday services. The new campus includes a worship space, administrative offices, a full-size gymnasium, and a café. Prior to moving into this new space in 2003, Consolidated was located two blocks from the University of Kentucky campus, where it had established a strong relationship with students. Pastor Richard Gaines, who was hired in 1996, would frequently walk around the campus encouraging students to visit Consolidated. When the church relocated too far for students to walk, the bonds between the church and the University nevertheless remained strong, with students and parishioners organizing dozens of carpools.

University students and alums thus comprise the core of young adults at Consolidated (which again, like other congregations described in this book, includes ages 18–35 as young adults). The largest contingent of young adults attends the 11:30 a.m. service, where the current college students sit together in one section. The 11:30 a.m. service is unofficially the contemporary service with many twentysomethings singing (and dancing) in the choir. Consolidated has a full-time young adult minister who is 24. He leads the popular Monday night Bible study called Real Talk, which focuses on issues of interest to young adults and draws about forty attendees weekly. When we studied Consolidated in 2009 and 2010, we interviewed twenty-three people between the ages of 20–33, with a median age of 26.

Multiracial Evangelical Church

New Life Fellowship, in Queens, New York, began as a house church in 1987. Today, it resides in an imposing former Elks lodge in one of the most ethnically diverse neighborhoods in the United States. Yet on Sunday mornings, the congregation appears even more diverse than the surrounding neighborhood, a feat it accomplishes with seemingly little effort. Perhaps the diverse membership results from New Life's long focus on care for the poor and the community development corporation, founded in 1994, through which many members volunteer. What this non-denominational church is most known for, though, is its focus on what founding Pastor Peter Scazzero calls "emotionally healthy spirituality." After experiencing a period of "spiritual burnout" and marital conflict in the 1990s, Pastor Pete took a sabbatical from New Life, which led to major changes in his ministry. He realized that spiritual maturity is impossible without emotional health. This led him to focus on family and marriage ministry and integrating sexuality, spiritual formation, and marriage.

Since his return from sabbatical, Pastor Pete began to introduce to New Life spiritual practices from the Christian tradition such as *Lectio Divina*, Daily Office, Ignatius Loyola's Daily Examen, and Sabbath observance. He adapted these for contemporary Christians and published guides to help members develop them. These spiritual practices are meant to help New Life congregants slow down and seek God in silence during their busy daily schedules in a frenetic city. In 2008, Pastor Pete introduced a "Rule of Life," adapted from the Benedictine model to fit New Life congregants' needs. According to the introduction, New Life's Rule of Life "is meant to be a framework for freedom, providing healthy boundaries while leaving plenty of room for flexibility and individuality." New Life's adapted monastic practices, emotionally healthy spirituality, and multicultural mission were integrated into the Rule of Life.

New Life has grown rapidly, reaching a Sunday worship attendance of about 1,200 during the period of our study. It feels like a welcoming, casual place. People dress informally, and the pastors have a down-to-earth way of speaking that sets the tone for the rest of the community. At the same time, there is an enthusiasm and expressiveness in worship that is hard to miss. The people sing and sometimes dance fervently during worship, pray expressively, and listen to the sermons intently. New Life draws people of Asian, Black, Latino, and White ethnicities in almost equal proportions, and roughly 25% of the congregation consists of young adults. Young adults have been active in the church from the beginning, especially young families and married couples.

In the mid-2000s, the growing number of twentysomethings led the church to form a distinct young adult ministry. Rich Villodas, a young adult himself, was hired to lead this ministry full time until 2013 when he succeeded Pete Scazzero as New Life's lead pastor. At the time of our study, there was also a college group called "Crossroads" with a part-time staff person. New Life young adult ministry offers events, gatherings, and groups where young adults can connect and build social ties. They range from parties to Bible studies. The church also started a coffee house ministry, where musicians and artists showcase their talents and attendees hear about social justice issues in the neighborhood and city. Young adult retreats have been held for the last five to seven years. But the main way that young adults become active in New Life is through involvement in small groups. Since it began in 1987, New Life has stressed the importance of small groups for relationship building and spiritual growth. There are about sixty small groups scattered throughout the city. These groups offer a sense of belonging for single young adults in a church of over 1,200. During our study of New Life in 2010, we interviewed twenty-five young adults at New Life between the ages of 21 and 35, with a median age of 29.

Why Do Evangelical Young Adults Come to (This) Church?

When we asked young adults at Consolidated and New Life how they chose their church, we heard something new compared with the responses from Catholic and Mainliner young adults: they talked about God guiding them to their church home. For example, we met 29-year-old Eva at New Life Fellowship. Eva is a college graduate who works in financial planning. Before joining New Life at age 25, Eva had always attended a Filipino Christian Church with her family. It was a very strict, charismatic church, which she found hard to reconcile with her life as she became a teenager. Dancing, in particular, was a problem since Eva liked to go clubbing. She heard about New Life from coworkers, and on her first visit she was "blown away" by Pastor Pete and amazed to see people dancing during worship. Although family and friends at her old church were upset when she joined New Life, she told them, "'I feel like God led me to this church,' and once you say that, you can't fight with God. Some people are very supportive and say 'wherever God leads you.' " Within a month of her first visit, Eva went through the new member class at New Life and joined a small group.

Malik from Consolidated Baptist also told us he was led to his church by God. Malik grew up attending small Baptist churches with his family, but in his 20s as he was taking classes at a community college and working, he stopped attending regularly. At age 29 Malik heard about the Monday night Real Talk meetings at Consolidated from a friend, and, wanting to make a change in his life, Malik checked it out. Here's how he described his first visit: "I was excited. I was amped because I committed myself to God. I'm like 'God, hey, I don't know about this church, but I'm going to check it out and if it's where you see fit for me to be, let me be.'" Just like Eva, Malik knew on his first visit that this is where God wanted him, and he quickly became a highly involved member. People told him he should visit several churches before joining Consolidated, but Malik was content because the Holy Spirit confirmed Consolidated was where he should be.

When asked what they like most about their churches, Evangelical young adults talked about the preaching and teaching offered by their pastors. Some encountered a pastor's books or heard him speak at a conference before deciding to make a personal visit to the church. Others encountered teaching that intrigued them on their first visit. This was case with 32-year-old Hector, who was born in Honduras and emigrated when he was 8. He had an eclectic religious journey with periods as a Roman Catholic, Jehovah's Witness, Seventh Day Adventist, Mormon, and Pentecostal. In his early 20s, Hector became addicted to drugs and alcohol but managed to become sober through Alcoholics Anonymous and lots of prayer. For many years, Hector resented churches, but a co-worker convinced him to try out New Life when he was 27. His first introduction to New Life was a small group meeting, which he found so welcoming that he started attending Sunday worship where he absorbed Pastor Pete's teaching about emotional health.

> There was something about emotional health that really attracted me because I realized I was a hardened person, pretty much damaged goods, and I wanted to heal, and I welcomed Jesus into my life, into my heart. Then I realized it was a map into my emotional being, and there were

> areas in my life that needed healing, and I was bitter and angry towards life and towards people, and how the teachings of emotional health meshed with spiritual health is what really kept me coming back.

Five years after his first visit, Hector spends roughly seven hours a week involved with New Life. He helps with the food pantry and co-leads a men's group. Thanks to Pastor Pete's teaching, Hector says he has stopped getting into unhealthy relationships and is working on healing his relationship with his mother. Hector would like to get married and have a family, but for now he's focused on becoming a healthy, whole person.

We met other young adults at New Life who told us the church's emphasis on slowing down was life-changing for them. Thirty-one-year-old Bruce is a good example. He grew up in a Chinese Christian Church with strict expectations and described his childhood church experience as "complex-good." In college, Bruce joined InterVarsity Christian Fellowship, and after graduating he joined InterVarsity staff full time. During a period of emotional and spiritual turmoil, which he called his "quarterlife crisis," a friend sent him Pastor Pete's *Emotionally Healthy Church* and *Emotionally Healthy Spirituality*, which were very helpful to him. When Bruce subsequently moved to New York, he started attending New Life, believing that "God had me at New Life as part of my healing process." He usually attends the smaller Sunday evening worship service, which is quieter and more meditative in tone. He embraces the Rule of Life with daily devotions that have helped him slow down: "The way I do life has completely changed. Yes, the contemplative, the meditative spiritual life is absolutely [. . .] for use of stronger word, is the *antidote* for my frenzied way of doing ministry and spiritual life." Bruce believes that New Life is especially attractive to Asian American twentysomethings who grew up as he did in strict homes attending immigrant churches. While these churches gave them a strong Christian foundation, they did not prepare them for the emotional challenges of emerging adulthood in New York City. Pastor Pete's preaching on emotional health addresses these challenges directly. But it is not for everyone; we heard of young adults who left New Life because they wanted a more Bible-centric church—like Consolidated.

Young adults at Consolidated Baptist rave about their pastors' "unapologetic preaching of the Word of God." At her first visit, 21-year-old Makayla was amazed by the preaching: "Sitting there listening to Pastor Gaines I was, like, 'Man, that is the Word. It isn't broken. That is the Word!' " Makayla is the youngest person we interviewed at Consolidated. She was working full time and going to school part time with hopes to go into nursing. Makayla grew up in a small Baptist church, which she left during her senior year in high school because there were few people her age and the preaching "was not relevant." When she found Consolidated, she quickly got involved and transferred her church membership. Makayla told us she prefers the 8:00 a.m. Sunday service because it helps her devotional life to praise God first thing in the morning, but she added that "the Word" is preached equally at all the services. Makayla thinks that the Bible-based teaching at Consolidated is exactly what young adults need to hear: "I feel like people our age are searching for something. So many things are thrown at us, it's confusing, and the Word of God, it's more simplistic than what the world would have us to think." In addition to Sunday mornings, Makayla attends the Monday night Real Talk Bible study for young adults.

Young adults at Consolidated raved about the teaching at Real Talk, and the 24-year-old young adult ministry pastor who leads it. Real Talk tackles difficult subjects relevant to twentysomethings, like negotiating romantic relationships. It is so popular it even draws young adults from other Black churches, like 27-year-old Joseph. Joseph is a college graduate working as a receptionist with plans to go to medical school to become a pediatrician. He spends a lot of time—over ten hours a week—in church-related activities between his home church, Real Talk at Consolidated, and volunteering with a regional para-church men's ministry group. What he likes most about Real Talk is the encouragement of the message:

> I guess it's "get real" basically with yourself. Don't allow your mask to—the mask that you put on—to become you or to absorb you. You have to

> break out of the mask [. . .]. We still have problems, however, we can go to him [i.e., God] for help and Real Talk reinforces that.

Joseph went on to explain that "getting real" means being authentic, and this is what Consolidated is all about: "Like I said, being authentic, just allowing God to use [us] for His glory, just the maturity there, the understanding of God's Word. It's very encouraging. It encourages me to just keep moving myself and keep being better."

Authenticity came up repeatedly in our interviews with Evangelicals. They told us that their churches enable them to be themselves, without fear of judgment, something that they did not find possible at other churches. Lee Chen, whom we profiled in Chapter 1, voiced this concern. Lee converted to Christianity in his early 20s and attended a Chinese Christian Church until he read Pastor Pete's book, which opened his eyes to the lack of authenticity in his church. It seemed that everyone was pretending to have a perfect Christian life and to have any kind of problems was seen as failure. At New Life, Lee found a small group in which people were honest about their problems and received empathy instead of judgment:

> Everyone in that group seems to be so willing to be so open with their lives, you know? With their weakness, with their vulnerabilities, which is so transparent . . . basically, exactly what Peter Scazzero wrote about [. . .]. Because everybody [else] was willing to let their guards down and share about their lives [. . .], it eventually led me to let my guard down and share about who I am, my weaknesses and the stuff that's going on in my family and the things that I'm working on.

Alicia, a 24-year-old college student we met at New Life, also talked to us about authenticity. Describing what she likes best about New Life, Alicia said, "There is very little judgment, and you can be yourself. You can talk about the problems that you have and be honest, and you can feel like it's a safe place for that [. . .]. People can be real, and people are free to have their own opinions or struggle with whatever they are struggling with." Alicia grew up in a Korean church, which was a positive experience for her, but after college she was ready for a more relaxed church, which she found in New Life: "If you are a little bit late or if you need to leave, you can leave the service. Or sometimes I feel like if you need to take a bathroom break during the service, it's okay, it's not so rigid." Alicia was one of a handful of young adults we interviewed who did not self-identify as Christian because of the judgmental views people have of that label. While her fear of judgment was unusually strong, we found concern about being judged was widespread among young adults.

One of the benefits of a church where young adults can "be real" without being judged is that they feel able to more fully experience the worship services. We heard this from young adults at New Life and Consolidated. At Consolidated, we met 24-year-old Aaron who described his first worship experience at Consolidated as awesome: "I felt that I can worship freely and not have people look at me or judge me because that's the environment that's set there." A similar idea was expressed by Scott, who also attends Consolidated: "I would say the feeling of just being able to worship and not feel like your worship has to be hindered however you choose to worship. If that's sitting down with your hands folded that's fine. If it's standing up with your hands in the air, that's fine. So it's not people rolling down on you for either way that you worship." Scott grew up in a nearby Baptist church, but he started going to Real Talk when he was 26 because he wanted a "more relevant" church. Scott likes this phrase he heard from the pastor: "We can't have an eight-track in an iPad generation." His previous church had an old-school pastor who required all women to wear skirts, whereas at Consolidated those dressed in T-shirts and jeans are not judged. In Scott's words, "All the other Black churches in Lexington are yesterday [. . .]. Those churches are putting people to sleep." After several months of attending Real Talk, Scott decided to make Consolidated Baptist his home church primarily for the freedom he felt to worship as he wished.

To authenticity and freedom in worship we need to acknowledge a final factor in church shopping: race and ethnicity are clearly important in attracting young adults to New Life and Consolidated. As a historically Black church, Consolidated draws Black young adults familiar with the Black Church. While some did not grow up attending church, all were exposed to the Black Church in their upbringing. When searching for a church, either because they moved or they were unhappy with their current church, they select from among the historically Black churches available in the Lexington area. On the other hand, young adults at New Life talked a lot about its racial and ethnic diversity. As we have already heard, New Life's diversity was especially important to those who grew up in immigrant churches. Coming from a Chinese church, Chapter 1's Lee Chen was initially shocked by the "mosh pit of people" at New Life. His parents had taught him to distrust anyone who is not Chinese, but the diversity at New Life, along with the church's racial reconciliation seminars, have made Lee less fearful of people of other ethnicities.

The ethnic and racial diversity of New Life was also the primary draw for Sarah Kim, whose previous churches were almost exclusively Korean:

> I immediately felt that it was a unique place, not like any church I had been to before. I looked around the room and saw that it was very diverse—not a token two people like I had witnessed before. And I felt that there was a freedom that people had, and I felt that I could be there and experience God and not worry about what I look like or what people thought about me [. . .]. People are very joyful in their worship and also very earnest, from what I gathered. I wasn't used to that worship environment, and I felt that it was encouraging in a way I never expected [. . .]. I realized that everyone was not the same as me, whereas in my old church, which was Korean-American, I felt that everyone was similar in upbringing and social economic background.

Sarah's sister first told her about New Life, and when she visited, Sarah was struck by what she calls its "multiethnicity." New Life is "different from [the mono-] ethnic churches that I have been to, which are [. . .] rigid and rule-based. In this church [i.e., New Life], we favor freedom." Sarah now leads a small group that meets three times a month sharing "the good and the bad and exploring what it's like to be a Christian in New York City as a single person." New Life's diversity and commitment to monastic practices have changed Sarah's life. She explains, "I am more aware when I am only with my Korean-American friends, and I find that to be odd [. . .] there's been a change in the diversity as far my friends go. And I have thought a lot about being contemplative in my walk with God, you know, pausing and resting and being aware that I have a lot of issues that God is working within me." What is really interesting is how Sarah links the increased diversity of her friendships with contemplative practices and spiritual growth. This is something we heard from other young adults at New Life whose parents immigrated to the United States. They were using New Life's "emotionally healthy" teaching and its encouragement of contemplative spiritual practices to help them navigate the often conflicting cultural norms they encountered among family, friends, work, and school.

Active Evangelicals Compared

When we compare our interviews of Active Evangelicals with those of Active Catholics and Active Mainliners, two things stand out. First, except for a few converts like Lee Chen, the Evangelicals we interviewed were born and raised in Evangelical churches. Moreover, they have not been away from churches for any extended period of time in late adolescence or young adulthood, when many Catholic and Mainliner young adults we interviewed took a "break" from churches. Because church life has been a consistent practice, they do not struggle with the question of whether to go to church. If they move to a new area, they do not ask *if* they should find a new church. Instead the question is *which* Evangelical church they will attend. Active Evangelicals seek out churches when they relocate. They also seek them out when they desire greater independence from their parents or when they are unhappy with their current church. And as they look for a church, they ask God to lead them to the place they should go for spiritual growth. While we encountered a similar commitment to institutional and communal expression of Christianity among Active Mainliners and Active

Catholics, we encountered this more selectively—among young adults at Methodist Clay Church in Indiana and among traditional Catholics in Washington, DC.

The second point that stands out is that Active Evangelicals have little difficulty finding a young-adult-friendly church, especially if they live in or near a city as large as Lexington, Kentucky. With the help of the internet and recommendations from friends, they can quickly locate Evangelical churches with a critical mass of young adults. Compared with the difficulty Mainliners and Catholics describe when trying to find a church that passes their critical-mass and shared-convictions tests, Evangelicals find church shopping to be a breeze.

Evangelical Twentysomethings in America

In Chapter 2, we learned that 3 out of 10 American twentysomethings identify with an Evangelical church or tradition, that 63% of Evangelicals report their faith is very or extremely important in their daily life, and that 66% of Evangelicals attend religious services at least twice monthly—far exceeding the second-highest rates of 33% and 42%, respectively, from twentysomething Mainliners and Catholics. That means Evangelicals edge out twentysomething Nones to be the single largest group of the four we examine in this book. It also means they are the most religiously fervent. Chapter 2 further revealed that Evangelical twentysomethings include the highest proportion of Black twentysomethings (26%), the fewest male twentysomethings (44%), and the fewest college graduates of those age 24 and over (26%). In this section, we examine different types of Evangelicals, from Active types (like Sarah Kim) to Nominal types (like Robert Rinaldi) to Estranged types—that is, twentysomethings who identify with an Evangelical church or denomination, but who indicate that their spiritual life is of little to no importance and report that they attend worship services never to at most once per year.

We deploy here the same typology of Active, Nominal, and Estranged as we did with Catholics and Mainliners (see Chapters 3 and 4), and immediately, we are struck by the lopsided proportions of our types: 47%

are Active Evangelicals, 50% are Nominal, and 3% are Estranged. The proportion of Active Evangelicals is *more than twice* the proportion of Active Mainliners or Active Catholics, while the proportion of Estranged Evangelicals is at least *six times smaller* than the proportion of Estranged Mainliners or Estranged Catholics. Indeed, out of the 560 Evangelicals in the National Study of American Twentysomethings (NSAT), just fifteen meet the Estranged criteria—which is too few to permit any further statistical analyses. We suspect, because of Evangelicalism's uncompromisingly binary categories of "saved" and "unsaved," there exists little cultural space where a twentysomething can identify with the religion and simultaneously maintain that spiritual life is unimportant and attendance at religious services is unnecessary.[4] An Estranged Evangelical is, apparently, a non-Evangelical.

With nearly equal numbers of Active and Nominal Evangelicals to analyze, we performed a discriminant analysis to see how demographic indicators differentiate Active and Nominal Evangelicals. Marital status, race, household income, and age—in declining order of effect—are important factors in distinguishing these two types (see Figures 5.1, 5.2, and 5.3). The difference marital status makes is striking: nearly 40% of Active Evangelicals are married, less than 3% are cohabiting, and none are divorced or separated. Among Nominal Evangelicals, less than 20% are married; the same proportion are cohabiting, and 2% are divorced or separated. The behavior of Evangelical twentysomethings shows that they clearly understand their faith's message about marital status—to marry is ideal, to divorce or separate is tragic, and to cohabit is sin. Marital status overlaps powerfully with Active or Nominal status among Evangelical twentysomethings.

Race and ethnicity also differentiate Active and Nominal twentysomethings (see Figure 5.2). Namely, Whites and Latinos are more likely to be Active Evangelicals, and Blacks are more likely to be Nominal. This is a different pattern from what we found among twentysomething Catholics and Mainliners. Whites were least likely to be Active Catholics, and Blacks were most likely to be Active Mainliners.[5] Why the difference? First, despite booming multiethnic churches like New Life Fellowship, most Evangelicals worship in segregated

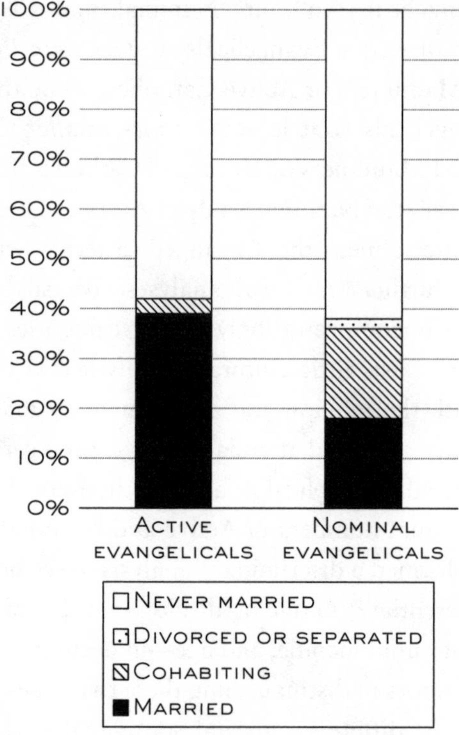

Figure 5.1

Marital Status of Active and Nominal Evangelical Twentysomethings

Source: NSAT 2013

churches.[6] We argue that the socially and politically conservative White ethos of White Evangelical churches attracts and affirms the worldviews of White Evangelicals, providing them with a weekly antidote to the more liberal and secular ethos that dominates mass media. This White ethos alienates many Asian, Latino, and Black Evangelicals, however, many of whom find that the non-English services and ethnic sensitivity offered by Asian and Latino churches, and the historic and distinctive worship traditions of the Black Church, provide an appealing respite from the minority experience that dominates the rest of their week. But many Black Evangelical twentysomethings, like Scott at Consolidated Baptist (see above), may find the "old school" traditionalism of the Black Church, and its strict dress codes in particular, leaves them

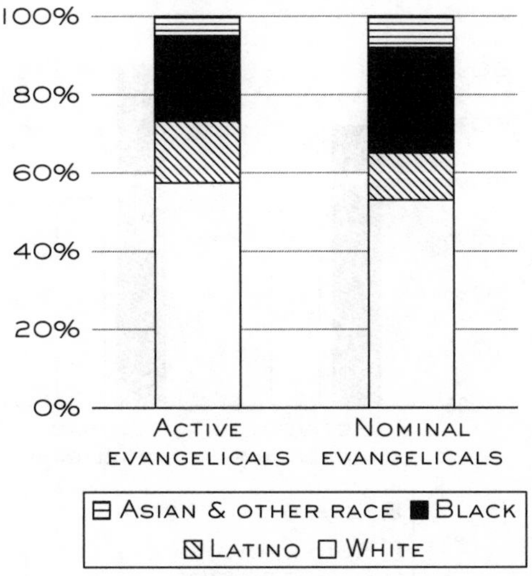

FIGURE 5.2

Race and Ethnicity of Active and Nominal Evangelical Twentysomethings

Source: NSAT 2013

without a church to call home. This possibility merits future scholarly investigation, as it may be a more recent phenomenon. About the considerable ethnic and political distance between Evangelicals of differing races and ethnicities we are quite certain, which their bifurcated vote for and against President Trump powerfully underscores.[7]

The second factor behind the race differential in Active Evangelical twentysomethings are differential rates of cohabitation. One out of 5 Black Evangelicals currently cohabit, which is twice the rate of White or Latino Evangelical twentysomethings, and cohabiting Evangelicals like to keep their distance from disapproving churches. This pattern, however, needs to be understood in context: Black Evangelical twentysomethings, though less Active than non-Black Evangelicals, are still twice as likely to be Active than twentysomething Catholics or Mainliners. Specifically, 43% of Black Evangelical twentysomethings are Active, which places them behind the 51% of White and 60% of Latino Evangelicals who are Active, but far ahead of the 22% of Catholic and 19% of Mainliner twentysomethings who are Active.

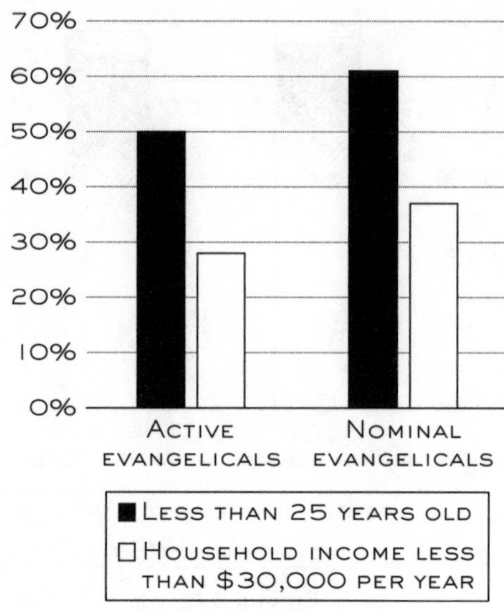

Figure 5.3
Age and Household Income of Active and Nominal Evangelical Twentysomethings
Source: NSAT 2013

The big story is that Evangelical twentysomethings—of any race—are at least twice as likely to be Active than their Catholic or Mainliner counterparts.

The final demographic factors that differentiate Active from Nominal Evangelical twentysomethings are income and age (see Figure 5.3). Active Evangelicals are more likely to be in their later 20s and Nominal Evangelicals are more likely to be from households that earn less than $30,000 per year. The underlying cause is likely the same for both factors—social stability. Older twentysomethings are more likely to have preferred work schedules, and more likely to have completed their educations, than their younger counterparts. The stability of older twentysomethings' lives facilitates their active pursuit of spiritual growth and congregational involvement. Lower income households are marked by more erratic work schedules, less reliable transportation options, and more frequent moves due to job loss or eviction, than middle- and upper-income households.[8] This instability makes it more difficult to attend church regularly or prioritize spiritual growth, even if Evangelical twentysomethings desire to do so.

Though marital status, race, income, and age differentiate Active from Nominal Evangelicals, there is much that these twentysomethings have in common. A solid majority of Active and Nominal types, for example, agree that "too many religious people in this country these days are negative, angry, and judgmental."[9] This is interesting, since it is Evangelicalism that produces so many of the negative, angry, and judgmental figures whose words are broadcasted in popular media (e.g., Jerry Falwell Jr., Franklin Graham, Pat Robertson). Clearly, twentysomething Evangelicals are unhappy with the image of religion that self-appointed spokespersons relay—a point that other observers of young American Evangelicals have made.[10] Active and Nominal Evangelical twentysomethings also agree on the importance of marrying and particularly on having children.[11] This follows the pattern we saw with Catholic and Mainliner types, though we note that Evangelical twentysomethings rank marriage the highest of all Christian twentysomethings. Finally, feelings of loneliness do not push Evangelical twentysomethings to, or from, Active engagement with their faith; equivalent proportions of Active and Nominal types (about 3 out of 10) say that they often feel lonely.

We expected Nominal Evangelicals to feel less "a part of a particular religion, denomination, or church" than their Active counterparts. That was, after all, the pattern among Catholic and Mainliner twentysomethings. Once again, the Evangelical pattern diverged: both Nominal and Active types report high levels of belonging (see Figure 5.4). We believe this may be a function of membership being less emphasized in Evangelical churches, since the overwhelming emphasis is on being saved. In fact, some Evangelical churches do not use the term "member," while others count anyone who views the congregation as "their church home" as an "adherent."[12] Simply professing that you are saved, and attending regularly, qualifies you as a part of a church in many Evangelical circles. And apparently, professing that you are saved is the more important of the two, given how strongly Nominal types feel they belong.

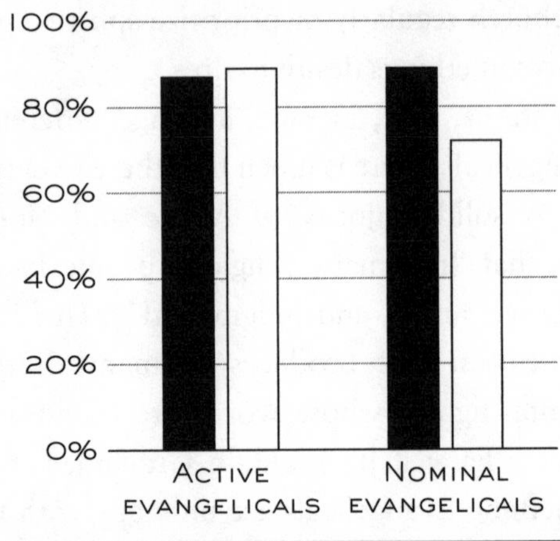

FIGURE 5.4

Religious Belonging, Helping Obligation by Active and Nominal Evangelical Twentysomethings

Source: NSAT 2013

Feeling equally a part of Evangelical Christianity does not mean that Active and Nominal twentysomethings draw the same implications about their faith. For example, Nominal types agree less often than their Active counterparts that "we have an obligation to help others, even if it means personal sacrifice" (see Figure 5.4). Nominal types also report fewer friends who do volunteer work regularly (see Figure 5.5). This is to be expected, since friendships shape values and shared values foster close friendships. Social reciprocity is a powerful force, even though it is rarely acknowledged in America's individualistic culture. Reciprocity extends even to Evangelicals' feelings about the divine: Active Evangelical twentysomethings overwhelmingly (84%) indicate they "have a lot of friends who attend church regularly," and a large majority (61%) report they feel "very" or "extremely close" to God most of the time (see Figure 5.6). Coincidence? We think not; the respective figures for Nominal Evangelicals are 63% and 22%. What

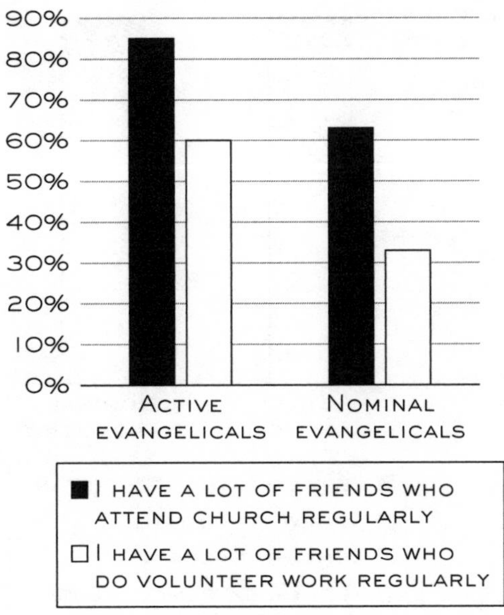

FIGURE 5.5

Church-Attending, Volunteering Friends of Active and Nominal Evangelical Twentysomethings

Source: NSAT 2013

Evangelicals' friends do, in other words, is highly related to how close Evangelicals feel to God. And there's a 99.999% probability that the proportion of Evangelicals' friends who attend church regularly is connected to the proportion of Evangelicals who feel close to God.[13]

Perhaps churchgoing friends inspire Evangelical twentysomethings to pray more often or meditate more frequently. Active Evangelicals, who report the most churchgoing friends, pray more often than their Nominal counterparts (see Figure 5.7): 2 out of 3 Active Evangelicals pray daily, about twice the rate of Nominal Evangelicals. Prayer, as we said in Chapter 2, is America's most frequent religious activity. But among Active Evangelicals, weekly meditation is also popular: 1 out of 3 Active Evangelicals meditates at least weekly. This places them behind their Active Catholic counterparts (46% meditate weekly, see Figure 3.7), ahead of Active Mainliners (23%, see Figure 4.7), and far ahead of Nominal Evangelicals (10%). The bottom line is this: daily

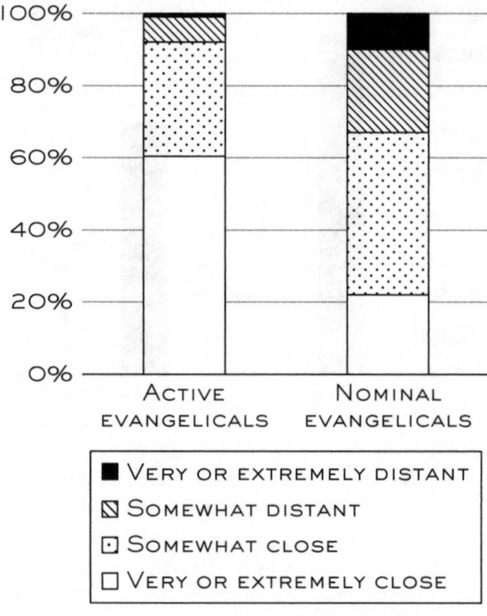

Figure 5.6

Feelings of Closeness to God Most of the Time Among Active and Nominal Evangelical Twentysomethings

Source: NSAT 2013

prayer, occasional meditation, having a lot of churchgoing friends, and feeling close to God are four phenomena that cluster together, as do less-than-daily prayer, infrequent meditation, having fewer churchgoing friends, and feeling "somewhat close" to or even "somewhat distant" from God.

One statistic captures the difference between Active and Nominal Evangelicals: 90% of Active types indicate that their religious faith is "extremely" or "very important" in "shaping how I live my daily life," while only 36% of Nominal types indicate the same (see Figure 5.8). But does this difference make a difference? We saw above that it affects marital status: Active Evangelicals are more likely to be married or never married while Nominal Evangelicals are more likely to be divorced, separated, or cohabiting. It also appears to affect ethics and certainty about life's purpose. Active Evangelicals are less likely to endorse privatized and materialistic ethics and more likely to affirm

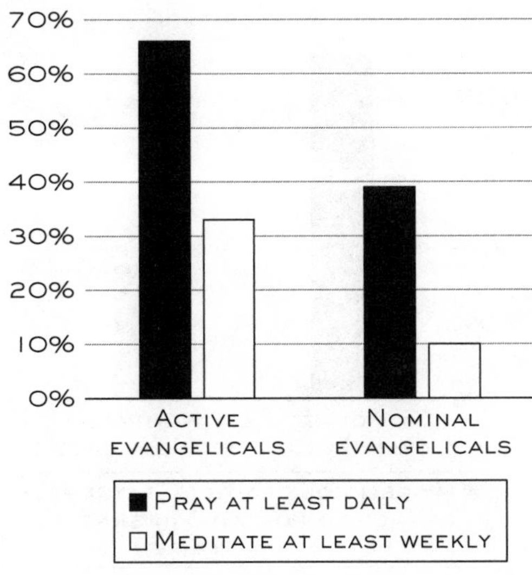

Figure 5.7

Prayer and Meditation of Active and Nominal Evangelical Twentysomethings

Source: NSAT 2013

that their life has purpose and meaning (see Figures 5.9 and 5.10). It does not affect pro-social values, however, such as indicating one's "deep passion is social justice," which 2 out of 5 Active and Nominal Evangelicals affirm.[14]

American Evangelicalism, at least based on the responses of twentysomething Evangelicals, seems well poised to maintain its population in the United States during the next couple of decades. Over 70% of Nominal Evangelical twentysomethings and over 80% of Active Evangelicals plan to join churches when they have children (see Figure 5.11). Given national religious retention rates of 60%,[15] the high proportion of Active and Nominal types vis-à-vis Estranged types, and Evangelicalism's emphasis on conversion, we expect this branch of American Christianity will maintain its 30% share of the young adult population. And given the higher rates at which Evangelical twentysomethings marry and have children, their intentions to join churches when they become parents have the highest likelihoods of

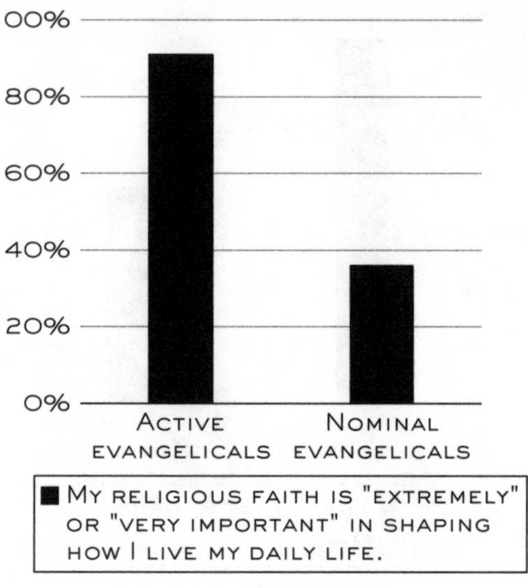

Figure 5.8

Importance of Religious Faith in Daily Life of Active and Nominal Evangelical Twentysomethings

Source: NSAT 2013

implementation. The importance that Active and Nominal Evangelicals assigned to their childhood faith will, save for some exceptional future event, be carried to the next generation.

Contrasting Christians

There are abundant differences among Catholic, Mainliner, and Evangelical twentysomethings, in beliefs, practices, and even demographics. Yet as important as these differences are, we argue that *Active* Catholics, Mainliners, and Evangelicals have more in common with each other than they do with their Nominal and Estranged counterparts who occasionally join them in worship. As Active types, they choose to participate in religious communities because the spiritual experiences and social connections found through these organizations are important, if not essential, to their lives. Though they may experience instability in their personal and professional lives, they seek to be rooted

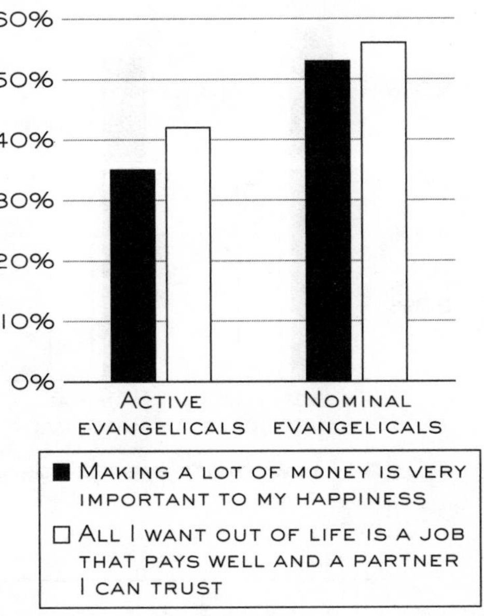

Figure 5.9
Individualistic Ethics of Active and Nominal Evangelical Twentysomethings
Source: NSAT 2013

in a religious community with other young adults who share their convictions. In other words, they want a religious community that passes the critical mass and shared convictions tests. This makes Active types the opposite of religiously unaffiliated twentysomethings, who, as we demonstrate in the next chapter, are a churning aggregate of skeptics, spiritual eclectics, and unaffiliated believers, and who have in common only a rejection of "organized religion." But we are getting a bit ahead of ourselves.

In this and the preceding two chapters, we identified patterns among the 169 Active Christian young adults that we personally interviewed who were involved in congregations. Some patterns are distinct to their branch of Christianity. Evangelicals and Mainliners, for example, expect great preaching and well-planned worship, while Catholics can be content with less-than-superb liturgy. Catholics and Mainliners meanwhile pay close attention to social teachings of their pastors

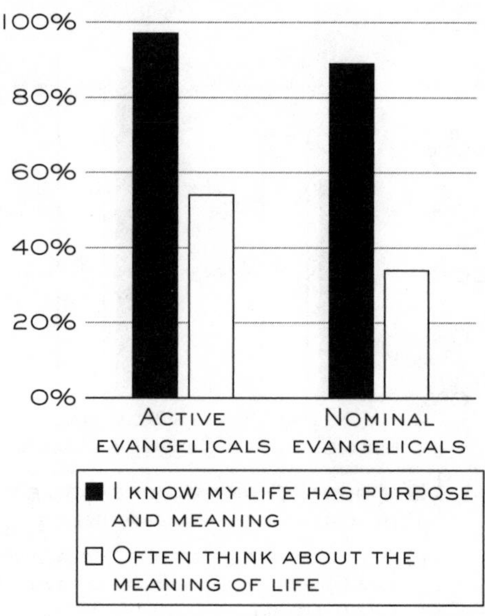

Figure 5.10

Life's Purpose and Meaning by Active and Nominal Evangelical Twentysomethings

Source: NSAT 2013

while Evangelicals evaluate pastors for their adherence "to the Word." And when first visiting a congregation, Catholics do not expect to be warmly greeted and invited to join a small group, Mainliners prefer an understated approach, but an outpouring of invitations is expected by Evangelicals.

How these Active Christian twentysomethings find churches also differs. Catholics can turn to diocesan young adult ministries to help them connect with peers, Evangelicals pray for guidance as they Google search, while some Mainliners resist invitations for years before joining a friend for worship. All three, though, seek recommendations from peers and use social media to find a young-adult-friendly church that is a good fit. That job is relatively easy for Evangelicals, due to the preponderance of conservative Protestant churches in most regions, but it requires more effort from Catholics and Mainliners—especially if they reside far from a metropolitan center. Finding support for one's religious

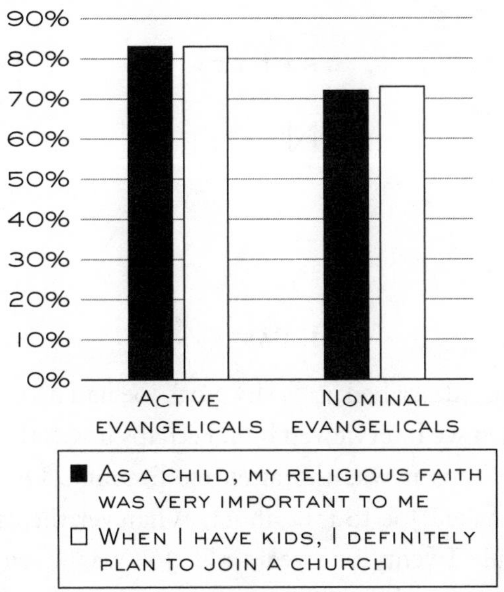

Figure 5.11

Faith Past and Future of Active and Nominal Evangelical Twentysomethings

Source: NSAT 2013

commitments is something that Active Christian twentysomethings seem to understand, and when they find it, their religious and spiritual lives appear to soar.

All of which makes their contrast with religiously unaffiliated twentysomethings so striking. There are no congregations of the unaffiliated—no places where a critical mass of young adults gathers and affirms their non-affiliation. Except, perhaps, at colleges and universities, which is where we began our interviews with unaffiliated twentysomethings. But non-affiliation with religion needs social support as much as affiliation does, as the next chapter, as well as the varied paths of unaffiliated twentysomethings, demonstrates.

CHAPTER 6
NONES

JOE PASTERNAK

For someone self-described as "a shy guy," Joe had no trouble talking—at length—when we interviewed him. Perhaps it was the promised confidentiality. Perhaps it was the attentive listening. Or perhaps it was the topics we asked Joe to talk about. Whatever the cause, Joe had a lot to say to us. Twenty-one years old, Joe was a senior kinesiology major attending a public university in the Northeast when we first interviewed him and 24 when we re-interviewed him. Originally a microbiology major, Joe switched to kinesiology after he injured his knee playing rugby his freshman year. In explaining why, Joe moves from high school popularity to physiology to social reflection to science to religion:

> My freshman year I [tore] my ACL, I really just went into a shell [. . .] I didn't party at all. Basically, I studied my stress levels, and what caused them [. . .]. I would try to correlate things, like my emotional state or my physiological state with the causes of it and how I could lessen or greaten the effect, or the feeling, that I had. And I think that [. . .] when I started to question why my leg was messed up, why I couldn't walk, or why these people are making fun of me when they don't even know me, I started to question why people say things: [it's because] there's huge differences in what they believe to be true. I think there are general truths, in the study of sciences [. . .]. I think when you start to lessen the effect the ego has on somebody, you're more apt to experience [. . .] logical and rational [thought]. I think if more people thought like that there would be more peace and understanding. I think that a lot of wars and injustice today are the result of religion and as interesting as religion

> may be, I think that people get offended if you insult their religion, they take it personally. It is the direct result of ego.

Joe's answer takes us on quite a journey—from freshman to senior year, from popularity to withdrawal, from unkindness to irrationality, and from war to religion. Joe must have seen our puzzlement at his lengthy explanation, so he tried to clear the haze: "I feel that a lot of the conclusions I've made have been a result of consciousness-altering substances." Ah, now we understood: not all of Joe's answer, but a whole lot more about Joe!

Sensing this, Joe offered qualifications, unprompted. "Basically pot or mushrooms. I haven't done anything else besides those two." These substances, Joe explained, "induce a different kind of awareness." They dissolve one's "ego filter" and eliminate "biases and irrational judgment," of which religion is primary. And Joe is not inexperienced when it comes to religion. "Raised Christian," Joe "went to church every single Sunday, from pre-school to high school." But Joe stopped attending church and ceased identifying as a Christian when he began college. "I don't practice now. I don't go to church. I go to church if my mom asks me to for Christmas and stuff like that . . . but other than that I don't go to church." We asked if Joe had any religious beliefs; he had none. "I don't believe in a god. I believe that it's arrogant for humans to believe that somebody would create the universe and would take the shape of a human." Expanding, Joe said "basically, all religions are about people who had great influence at the time, like Jesus, or Buddha, or the prophets; they're all very ascetic people." Joe offers some appreciation for the "peace and coexistence" that select elements of the Bible and other religious scriptures promote, but most of these texts "can be disproven" and "serve no purpose in terms of establishing moral value."

Shifting gears, we asked Joe if the word "spirituality" had meaning for him. "I don't know. A lot of people say that I'm very spiritual. But I don't really think much about it [. . .]. I don't think a spirit exists." Next, we asked if Joe ever prayed or meditated, and he said once, when a friend was in a coma, he focused his thoughts on "her body's strength to recover, but I question how effective my thoughts would be." As for meditation, "the closest thing [. . .] would be yoga; it relaxes me." Aside from that, Joe did not do any "organized meditation." Finally, we asked Joe if his present life or future hopes were guided by any sense of purpose or direction. Joe did not hesitate: "Yeah!" Explaining, Joe spoke about reading Spinoza, and how he agreed with Spinoza that "fame, sensual pleasure, or money" are "fleeting," and "that true good is the spread of knowledge." Hence Joe, following Spinoza, wanted to have only "as much money as you need to be able to live," and since "knowledge exists infinitely [. . .] the more knowledge you acquire" the "greater happiness" of one's own and others' lives. Reading Spinoza, Joe explains, has made him "more open-minded," and eager "to try to talk to people and find out what causes them pleasure, what causes them pain, and to maybe show them there's another perspective."

When we re-interviewed Joe, he was 24, had graduated from college, worked a couple years as an assistant athletic trainer, and then stumbled into a good paying job as a research laboratory technician, where he had been promoted recently to lab manager. Living at home to save money, Joe also took advantage of his employer's tuition benefit to enroll in college courses. "I've actually taken a few classes, undergrad classes in public health, so I'm still, I guess, into natural healing and natural well-being." Joe had also become involved in weekly volunteering—at his mother's church. "It's called the [Care Ministry, it's] for families that lose their job or have their house burn down." He also joined the church's team for a trip to New Orleans after Hurricane Katrina to assist with rebuilding efforts. Yet Joe was clear that although he *was* a member of the church, he was "not really practicing," and he remained a follower of Spinoza, citing the importance he places on "the acquisition of knowledge," making "only enough money to promote health," and speaking "to people in a way that they understand and that allows you to promote your ideals of health and knowledge."

Joe's re-involvement with religion, then, was not based on a re-adherence to its religious claims. Rather, he framed it within his understanding of Spinoza, seeing "Christianity" and "the Bible [as] suitable mediums through which to propose just certain things in how you should live your life." His church offered convenient opportunities to help others, which he participated in, "but I think that all religions do that as well." In other words, Joe was still neither a Christian nor a theist, but he found value in the church community working together to help others. This second interview uncovered two other changes since his first interview: he now described himself as "very spiritual," and he was adamant about the importance of maintaining good health. Joe had come to accept the "spiritual" label that friends had long applied to him: that is, because he often thought about and talked about "universal truth and universal ways to live," he was a spiritual person. Based on his reflections on existential questions, Joe made a commitment to healthy living: he now practiced moderation in consumption of alcohol and had ceased all use of consciousness-altering substances. An early work schedule, combined with his employer's random drug-testing policy, helped underscore Joe's commitment to healthy living. Across both interviews, Joe maintained that he had abandoned his childhood affiliation with Christianity specifically and with religion in general; Joe's changes lie in how he now expresses his beliefs: by volunteering (through a convenient and familiar religious program), and by framing his reflectiveness and commitment to health as spiritual.

Types of Nones

Over the past thirty years the United States has seen a sizable increase in the number of religiously unaffiliated Americans. According to the 2016 General Social Survey (GSS), 21.7% of American adults have no religious affiliation.[1] The rise of the Nones, especially among Americans under age 30, has been a popular news headline,[2] but this label is widely misunderstood. Though Nones indicate no religious affiliation, it does not mean they have *no* religious beliefs or practices. Religion is a complex phenomenon with individual and social dimensions, including affiliation, belief, and practices. While some Nones are ardent secularists, a solid majority of Nones hold beliefs in a supernatural or transcendent reality, and some appear quite conventional in their beliefs. According to the 2016 GSS, 20% of Nones "know God really exists," 11% "believe in God" though they have some doubts, 4% believe in God "some of the time," and 30% "believe in a Higher Power of some kind." Just 14% of Nones "do not believe in God," and another 21% "don't know whether there is a God and . . . do not believe there is any way to find out." Looking at other religious beliefs and practices, we see 38% of Nones affirming that the Bible is the inspired or literal "Word of God," 28% attending religious services at least annually, and 35% reporting prayer on a daily or weekly basis. A more apt label for such Nones is "Unaffiliated Believers." They have much in common with the majority of Americans who are Christian but choose not to identify as Christian or with any other religion. Rather than rejecting religion, they are rejecting affiliation with *organized* religion. Between one-third and one-half of American Nones are Unaffiliated Believers.[3]

Besides Unaffiliated Believers, there are Nones with less conventional beliefs and practices. They may, for example, believe in a universal spirit but not a personal God, and they may practice yoga or meditation. Within the American context, such beliefs and practices may be considered alternative or spiritual, but it is not at all clear where the boundary is between the religious and the spiritual, or religion and spirituality.[4] For example, vipassana meditation is a conventional religious practice in Thailand, just as hatha yoga is in India, but in the United States, meditation and yoga are presented as religious, secular, or spiritual practices depending on the context.[5] Surveys regularly show that most Americans see themselves as religious *and* spiritual: 78% claim a religious affiliation, and 90% describe themselves as at least "slightly" spiritual in the 2016 GSS. Still, as we heard from Abby in Chapter 1 and Joe in this chapter, some Nones insist they are spiritual but not religious. We call them "Spiritual Eclectics." In her study of unaffiliated American parents, religious studies scholar Christel Manning explains that spiritual Nones embrace a pluralistic orientation combining beliefs—such as belief in a higher power or life force, with spiritual practices from various traditions.[6] Between one-quarter and one-third of American Nones fall into this category.

In addition to Unaffiliated Believers and Spiritual Eclectics, there are Nones who reject religion or spirituality in any form. Earlier in this book we referred to them as secularists, but Manning makes a helpful and important distinction between "Philosophical Secularists" and those who are "Indifferent Secularists."[7] Philosophical Secularists replace a religious worldview with an equivalent non-religious belief system, asserting that our existence is shaped by forces we can rationally and empirically explain. The remaining secularists fall into a category of indifference, as they express no interest in any type of worldview—be it religious, spiritual, or secular. Between one-sixth and one-fifth of American Nones are secularists.[8]

Using this typology of Nones—Unaffiliated Believers, Spiritual Eclectics, Philosophical Secularists, and Indifferent Secularists—helps us interpret our interview and survey data from twentysomething Nones. Abby, for example, initially presents as a pensive atheist, making her a Philosophical Secularist in this typology. By her senior year, however, Abby moved to being a Spiritual Eclectic. She still does not believe in God, but she does believe in spiritual energy and supernatural phenomena. Joe makes a similar shift. When we interviewed him as a college student enthralled with Spinoza, he was a Philosophical Secularist, but by his mid-20s Joe accepted the label "very spiritual" and volunteered in humanitarian efforts organized by his childhood church, making him a Spiritual Eclectic. Why the shift? In short, Abby's and Joe's stories illustrate that identities can be quite fluid, and especially so in the less institutionally supported arena occupied by the unaffiliated.

Change in religious, spiritual, and secular identities appears common. The 2014 Pew Religious Landscape Survey reports that "almost half" of those raised with no religious affiliation end up identifying with a religion as adults.[9] Long-standing lines of research on religious switching also support a considerable amount of churn in individual religious identities: more than 40% of Americans change religious affiliations during their lifetimes, with moving and marriage being the two most common causes.[10] Indeed, studies show individuals shifting back and forth among categories and even occupying "liminal" spaces between categories.[11] Joe's changes, for instance, may be far from over. When we last spoke he was saving money to "move out" of his parent's home, and his long-time girlfriend was starting to pressure him about making their relationship a priority. Were we to interview Joe a third time, we would not find any answer he gave surprising: he could tell us he switched his volunteer work from his mother's church to a secular organization, he could say he is engaged to marry and is exploring his fiancée's Buddhism, or he could explain how moving out of state left him feeling lonely, and on a lark, he stopped in at a church near his condo and now volunteers there. There's nothing Joe might say that would surprise us; individuals have the capacity for extraordinary change over time.

Much as we would like to, we do not have sufficient longitudinal data to devise a typology of change among twentysomething Nones. But we do want to draw attention to the role that context plays in shaping these changes. Universities, where our first interviews with religiously unaffiliated twentysomethings occurred, are on the whole more welcoming settings for Nones than other settings—such as family homes, neighborhoods, community organizations, and workplaces, and these latter contexts can foster exploration of religious and spiritual resources by post-college Nones. This is what happened to Joe: (1) he returned from his public university to live at home, rent free, with his church-attending mother, (2) he also was separated from the time demands of coursework as well as expansive opportunities for campus involvement, and (3) he found himself with time on his hands and fewer ways to spend it. To be sure, Joe retained his basic secularism, but he now combined it with a friendlier view of religion and of his mother's church in particular, and accepted a label of "very spiritual." Our point is this: when Joe's context changed from secular-and-spiritual-friendly to religious-and-spiritual-friendly, Joe changed with it.

Understanding the lives of twentysomething Nones thus requires recognition of larger social contexts and their potential effects. Religious grandparents, for example, exist in abundance (see Chapter 2), and many unaffiliated young adult interviewees said their grandparents' high religiosity led them to silence their own views and even attend religious services for the sake of family harmony. Geography is similarly influential. While belief in God is widespread in America, one encounters significant regional variations. The Northeast and Northwest, and their metropolitan regions in particular, foster neutrality if not animosity toward conventional religion, while rural and Southern regions encourage it and harbor prejudice toward religious skeptics and Spiritual Eclectics. Even workplaces can vary in their receptivity to religious or spiritual expression—the "God and Country" and "Make America Great Again" ethos of blue-collar, male-dominated industries would alienate many secularists, as would hospitals' employment of pastoral counselors who encourage spiritual practices during the healing process.[12] In short, many contexts in the United States are friendly to conventional religion and traditional forms of spirituality, leaving Nones to swim against strong cultural currents.

Appreciating these contexts makes the uncertainty so often voiced by unaffiliated interviewees understandable. Some stated that their present views of religion were not "final," and "in the future" they would take more time to consider their views. Others described, like Abby in Chapter 1, how they were "moving away" or "recovering" from childhood religious experiences, and though they closed the door on their childhood religion, they did not close it on all religious ideas or practices. Still others voiced a "personal" disdain for "organized religion," but they emphasized acceptance and tolerance toward those who were religious. Since anti-religious views are often judged as intolerant (e.g., the outcry following Donald Trump's statements about Muslims[13]), we recognize some of this uncertainty may be a product of interviewees' desire to appear tolerant—an important value among twentysomethings. But much of this uncertainty is genuine, as unaffiliated interviewees do not attend weekly meetings that affirm their developing worldview, while the Active Christians interviewed in the previous three chapters do. Without social support, it is a Herculean effort to maintain and express an unconventional worldview. Or to put it more formally, secularism and spirituality are as much social constructions as religion, and their adherents need social support to remain committed.

Shifting Contexts, Changing Identities

Our interviews with Amy and Sahil really drove home the role that supportive and unsupportive contexts play. Amy, like Joe, spoke about graduate school when we first interviewed her during her junior year of college. An enthusiastic student of Spanish literature at an exclusive liberal arts college, Amy wanted to pursue a PhD in Spanish literature. But a "weird," mononucleosis-like infection hit her hard during her senior year, and unable to shake it for months, Amy put the limited energy she had left into completing her senior year classes. Moving home after graduation, she sought employment related to her Spanish skills but found nothing. Under pressure from her mother, Amy took a job in retail. When we re-interviewed Amy, a little over a year since she had graduated from college, she was unhappy. She disliked her job, struggled with living at home, and was frustrated by the inability to find work related to Spanish. Amy said she was "done with" studying Spanish. Instead, she had begun researching graduate programs in social work, believing that her Spanish-speaking proficiency combined with her experience of extended illness would serve her well in a "helping career."

During our first interview, Amy explained that she had attended Catholic schools from preschool through high school. But her family was not Catholic, and she never attended any religious services except those required during her schooling. "I feel like I should have gotten more out of Catholic school than just 'Wow, Catholicism sucks' . . . but I don't think I did." When we asked Amy about her own religious beliefs and practices, she explained that she did not "affiliate with a religion," that she despised religions that oppress women, and that no religion had the right to restrict people's expressions of their sexuality. Given Amy's unequivocal views and her disappointing first year out of college, we expected Amy to be unmoved in her rejection of religion at the time of our second interview, and we were partly correct. Amy told us: "I don't really believe in anything religion-wise." But she also recounted a story of a "real" spiritual experience when she was 13 (at a Catholic shrine), and she summed up her less-than-ideal experiences over the past two years with "I feel that things happen for a reason." Explaining, she said that her present job "kind of fell into my lap [. . . and] I feel like there is some sort of purpose that I'm there. And by the same token, I feel like there's a reason that this [social work] thing happened, and I feel very good about it and very confident about what I'm going to be doing. I just haven't figured out all the reasons yet." This was quite unlike what Amy said while in college; now one year beyond residence on a liberal arts campus, and Amy was voicing openness to spiritual experiences and the idea of destiny.

Sahil was waiting to hear back on his medical school applications when we first interviewed him, during his last semester at an Ivy League university. His mother, a physician, and his father, a retired engineer, had emigrated from India in their 20s. Sahil was their only child. But Sahil emphasized that his parents did not pressure him to be a doctor, nor did they pressure him to keep the Hindu faith. The only thing they insisted on, Sahil said, is that he marry an Indian physician. Currently dating a pre-med Indian, Sahil was certain his parents would approve—even though he had not yet told them about her. Sahil's parents were also proud of his decision to pursue medicine and were "perfectly fine" with his rejection of the Hindu religion. Sahil was very careful when speaking about religion: he described himself as an atheist who is "culturally Hindu" but admitted he did not know if God exists (making him an agnostic, not an atheist) nor did he understand religion. His carefulness was likely rooted in his membership in a Jewish fraternity. "There's a lot of very religious people in my fraternity . . . and they keep kosher, they go to Hillel, they fast it seems very often [. . .]. I don't really know the religion well enough to question it." Sahil then emphasized, "I'm actually very open to learning about it, as long as no one imposes their beliefs on me." Openness to learning about religion is not uncommon among skeptics: as the Pew Forum study on religious knowledge documented, atheists know more on average about religion than most believers do.[14]

A little more than a year after Sahil had graduated from college, on the morning of Memorial Day, we caught up with him again. The date and time was Sahil's choice: now a busy medical student,

Sahil planned to celebrate his successful completion of his first year by taking the holiday off. Sahil was attending medical school in the same state to which his parents recently relocated, qualifying him for in-state tuition and making his parents—who are footing Sahil's bills—particularly thankful. Sahil recognized that this arrangement enables him to remain within the "bubble" of higher education and admitted that medical school—while far from easy—was nonetheless not like "the real world" that many of his fraternity brothers entered. Checking in with Sahil about his religious and spiritual life, he had little to say: "I'm not religious." When asked about any changes with regard to religion or spirituality since we last spoke with him, he answered "no." Yet we noticed how the carefulness of Sahil's words when speaking about religion, and the explanatory possibility he granted to religion, so evident in his first interview, were now gone. With a thousand miles and twelve months separating Sahil from his devout Jewish fraternity brothers, matters of religion and spirituality ceased to register with Sahil. Life was medical school, plain and simple. Even Sahil's Indian pre-med girlfriend from college, with whom he had envisioned marriage, was out of the picture. Sahil had grown indifferent to seemingly everything that was not part of his professional education.

To Amy and Sahil we could add dozens more whose post-college contexts played a role in their religious and spiritual identities. We limit ourselves to three. (1) Billy Johnson was an award-winning actor at his Methodist university, who now paid bills by bartending in New York City while acting in unpaid student films. As an undergraduate, he enjoyed conversations about truth and meaning and relished deconstructing conventional answers (especially those provided by religion). One year after graduating with honors, Billy ended our conversation with this: "I do wish I had more direction, religiously and spiritually; I mean, I just can't stress that enough." (2) Charity Jean-Louis, by contrast, graduated from an East Coast university and completed her first year of law school at a public Midwestern university. Charity's indifference to all things religious or spiritual did not alter during this time. And (3) Judith Cohen, a classmate of Sahil's, completed her pre-med undergraduate degree along with a master's degree in medical anthropology in just four years. An atheist who appreciates Judaism as a "fun" way to bond with her family, Judith acknowledged it would be "nice" to believe in God, but she could not "assent" to that concept as an undergraduate or graduate student.

There were exceptions to this pattern of shifting contexts and changing identity, however. One young adult, a Philosophical Secularist, ranted about religious zealots as an undergraduate, and one year later, though living at home and working full time, continued to declare religion as "unnecessary" for a moral life. Another twentysomething, a Spiritual Eclectic who enjoyed "feminist and eastern spiritual practices," was engaged to marry a "pastor's kid" when we first interviewed her and had expected to re-affiliate with religion. But the sudden death of her father-in-law pushed her new husband away from religion, and she remained unaffiliated two years later. Exceptions like these are expected in any social pattern, as the complexity and unpredictability of human life can touch anyone. It was important, therefore, that we triangulate these qualitative interview findings with analyses of our national survey.

Nones in the Nation

In Chapter 2, we learned 3 out of 10 American twentysomethings are Nones, 4 out of 5 of these Nones agree that "too many religious people are negative, angry, and judgmental," and 3 out of 4 say their childhood faith, if any, was not important to them. We also learned that twentysomething Nones do not differ from their peers in gender, education, or employment, but they are more likely to be White and to cohabit, and less likely to marry or be parents. In this section, we look first at Nones' social context, to see if the pattern of context-shaping identity observed among our interviewees is at all generalizable. We then examine what Nones believe, value, and do, comparing Nones, where appropriate, with a single, collapsed category of religiously affiliated twentysomethings.

Let us start with Nones and religion. Our National Study of American Twentysomethings (NSAT) included an indicator of social context: Did respondents have "a lot of friends who attend church regularly?" Twentysomething Nones whose friends attended church regularly were themselves more likely to believe in God (37% compared to 24% of Nones without such friends; see Figure 6.1) and less likely to be uncertain or disbelieve in God. In other words, Nones whose social context included religiously active peers were more likely to believe in God; but only 1 in 5 Nones had such friends. This may explain why 3 out of 4 Nones responding to the NSAT reported "no doubts" about being nonreligious "in the last year," why 9 out of 10 did not "think of [themselves] as part of a particular religion, denomination, or church," and why 9 out of 10 had no plans to "join a church" when they "have kids." These responses make clear that Nones' disaffiliation with religion is intentional and part of a larger approach that keeps actively religious peers at a distance, and they harbor no plans to join a religion in the future.

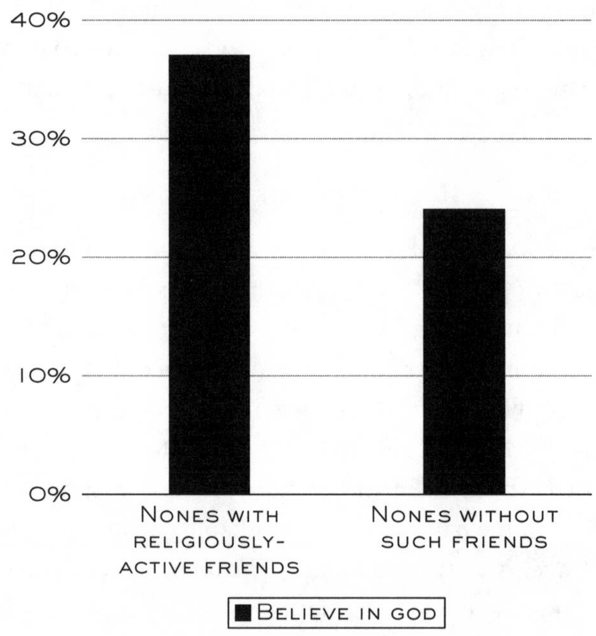

Figure 6.1

Friends' Religiosity and Belief in God Among Unaffiliated Twentysomethings (Nones)

Source: NSAT 2013

What about Nones' family context? Does having religiously active parents influence Nones' beliefs? The 2008 General Social Survey (GSS) asked about the religious service attendance of respondents' mothers and fathers. Of the 322 twentysomethings who participated in the survey, 91 identified as religiously unaffiliated (i.e., 28% Nones).[15] We then examined two indicators: confidence in the existence of God, and belief in heaven. There were six response options to the God item—one for atheists, one for agnostics, and four indicating levels of belief, and there were four response options for the heaven item—definitely yes or probably yes, and definitely no or probably no.[16] Nones whose mothers and fathers did *not* attend religious services regularly were more likely to affirm atheist or agnostic views than Nones whose mothers and fathers did attend regularly (see Figure 6.2). And Nones whose mothers and fathers did *not* attend religious services regularly were

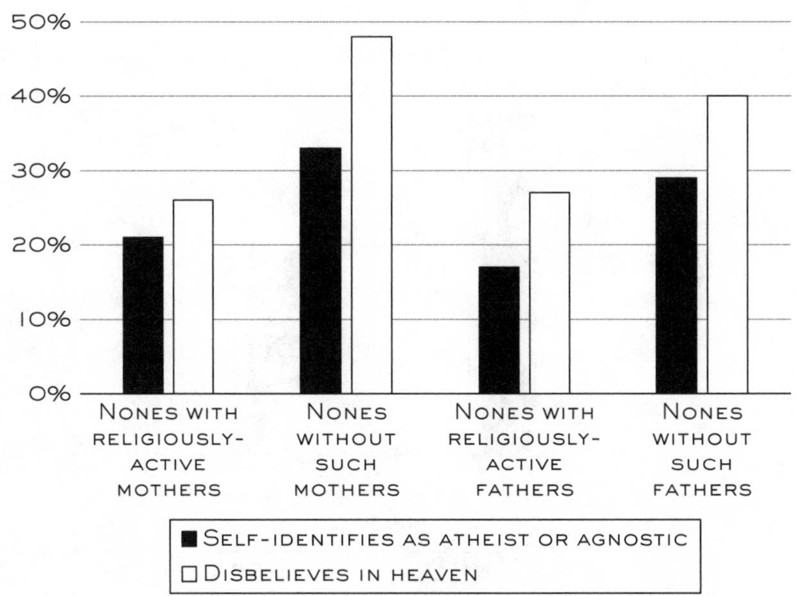

Figure 6.2

Parents' Religiosity, Identification as Atheist or Agnostic, and Disbelief in Heaven Among Unaffiliated Twentysomethings (Nones)

Source: GSS 2008

Note: There were 91 unaffiliated twentysomething respondents in the 2008 GSS.

also more likely to disbelieve in heaven than Nones whose mothers and fathers *did* attend religious services regularly. In short, religiously active parents, like religiously active friends, make a difference: Nones with religiously active parents were more likely to express belief in God and heaven than Nones with religiously inactive parents.

We see, then, that twentysomethings' social context can support or undermine their secular and spiritual identities. This is an important finding about the social construction of secularity and eclectic spirituality. But we also see something else: age strengthens confidence. Dividing NSAT respondents into two age groups, 20–24 and 25–29 years old, we see older twentysomethings expressing a bit more certainty about their views than younger twentysomethings (see Figure 6.3). Older Nones are more likely to have "no doubts" about "being non-religious," and less likely to believe in God, than younger Nones. Since our in-depth interviewees were under 25 years

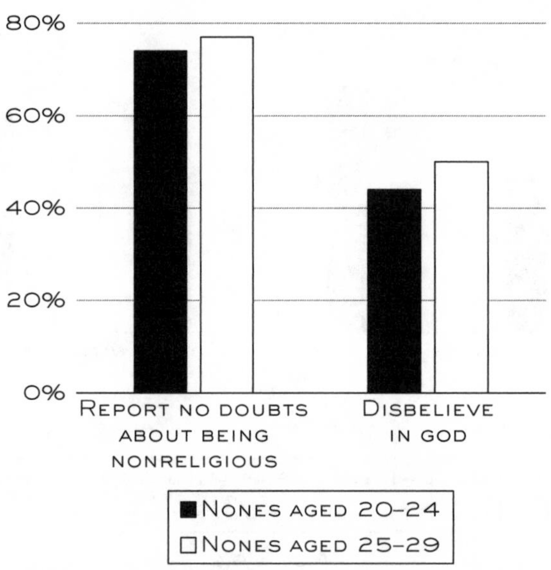

Figure 6.3

Certainty of Nonreligious Identity and Disbelief in God by Age Among Unaffiliated Twentysomethings (Nones)

Source: NSAT 2013

old, these survey analyses suggest uncertainty among Nones declines with age. This could be attributed to the increased settledness of older twentysomething's contexts or a function of general maturation. We lack data to evaluate these possibilities, but research on political views indicates "attitude stability" increases throughout early adulthood,[17] and we suspect religious, spiritual, and secular views act similarly.

As with Nones of all ages (above), less than half of twentysomething Nones say they do not believe in God, with 1 out of 4 believing in God, and another 1 out of 4 "unsure."[18] When asked if they view God "as a spiritual force," 1 out of 3 Nones agreed.[19] And 1 out of 3 Nones said they occasionally pray, the same proportion occasionally meditate, and 1 out of 6 pray or meditate at least weekly (see Figure 2.5). How we worded questions made a lot of difference: just 9% of Nones agreed "spiritual growth is very or extremely important" (see Figure 2.8).

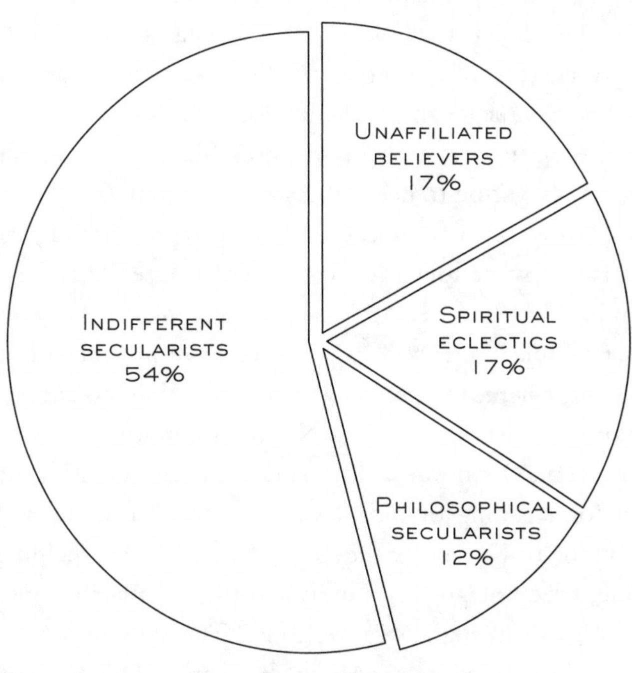

Figure 6.4
Types of Unaffiliated Twentysomethings (Nones)
Source: NSAT 2013

The terms "spiritual" or "spirituality" did not appeal to most Nones, a finding that runs counter to characterizations of today's young adults, especially Nones, as a "spiritual but not religious" generation.[20] Using the NSAT, we classified 17% of twentysomething Nones as Unaffiliated Believers—because they believe "God is a personal being involved in the lives of people today," another 17% as Spiritual Eclectics—because they regard spiritual growth as adults to be fairly to extremely important, still another 12% as Philosophical Secularists—because they thought "about the meaning of life" fairly to very often, and the rest (54%) as Indifferent Secularists—because they did not meet any of the other group's criteria (see Figure 6.4).[21] We think it noteworthy that the majority of American twentysomething Nones are Indifferent Secularists, opting to occupy a space that is somewhat parallel to that of Nominal Christian twentysomethings (see Chapters 3–5). In other words, most twentysomething Nones are as ambivalent about their secularism as most Christian twentysomethings are about their religious affiliation.

Though Nones as a whole reject religious affiliation, they overwhelmingly agree (70%) that their "life has purpose and meaning" and that "to have a meaningful life, you need to help other people" (see Figure 6.5). In fact, nearly two-thirds (63%) of Nones agree that "we have an obligation to help others—even if it means personal sacrifice." While these rates are not as high as those reported by religiously affiliated twentysomethings (of whom 90% agree "life has purpose and meaning," 85% agree "to have a meaningful life, you need to help other people," and 77% agree "we have an obligation to help others—even if it means personal sacrifice"), they nonetheless reveal strongly pro-social norms among Nones despite their rejection of organized religion. Or to put it differently, religious identification is not necessary for meaning or moral values. Consider, for example, that nearly 1 out of 10 Nones say they spent "a lot" of time helping "homeless people, needy neighbors, family friends, or other people in need, directly and not through organizations." The rate among religiously affiliated twentysomethings? About the same. One-half of Nones, moreover, agree that "my deep passion is greater social justice"; among religiously affiliated twentysomethings, the rate falls by 5%.

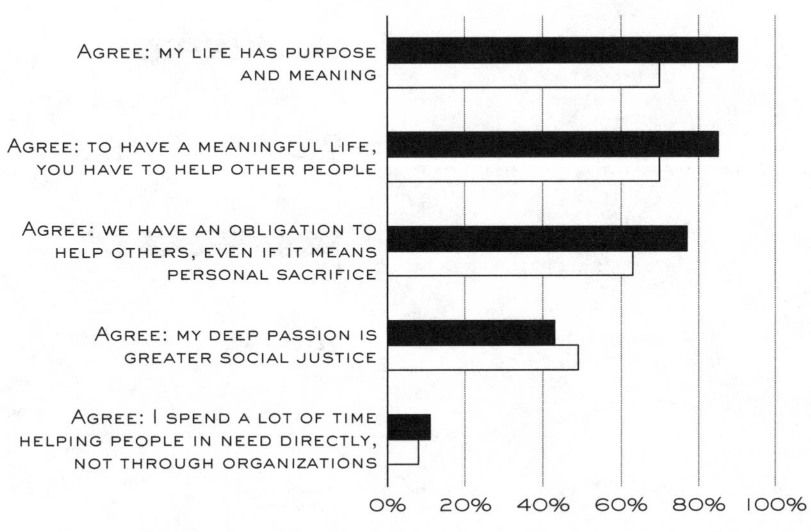

Figure 6.5

Pro-Social Values and Behavior of Religiously Affiliated and Unaffiliated Twentysomethings (Nones)

Source: NSAT 2013

This is important, because there is a long tradition in America that views religious affiliation as necessary for a healthy and strong democracy. President Dwight Eisenhower famously remarked, "Our form of government has no sense unless it is founded in a deeply felt religious faith, and I don't care what it is."[22] Alexis de Tocqueville, the French aristocrat and observer of 1830s America, similarly cited the importance of religious participation in tempering withdrawal from public life by its highly individualistic citizens.[23] A moral and engaged citizenry, to be sure, is necessary for a robust republic. But we know all too well how immoral some have been who wear religion on their sleeve, and we recognize that kindness and compassion abound in people of all sorts. For this reason, we compare the values and civic engagement of religiously affiliated and religiously unaffiliated twentysomethings. As the reader can plainly see, there are pro-social and civically engaged

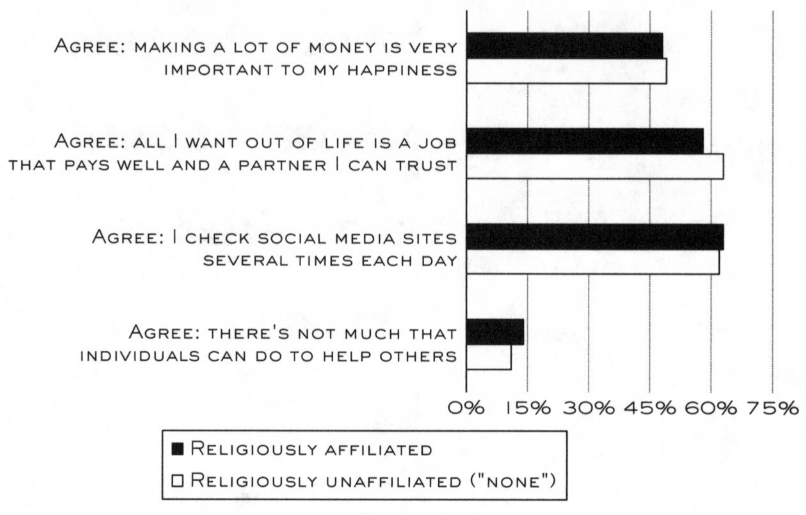

FIGURE 6.6

Shared Values Among Religiously Affiliated and Unaffiliated Twentysomethings (Nones)

Source: NSAT 2013

twentysomethings on both sides of the religious divide, just as there are withdrawn individualists on both sides of the divide.

Twentysomething Nones and their religiously affiliated peers agree on several things (see Figure 6.6). Just under half of both groups agree that "making a lot of money is very important to my happiness," and just over half disagree. About 3 out of 5 religiously affiliated and unaffiliated twentysomethings agree that "all I want out of life is a job that pays well and a partner I can trust." Similar proportions use social media several times daily, and only 1 out of 8 subscribe to the bleak view that "there's not much that individuals can do to help others." Where Nones and their religiously affiliated peers part ways lies in values that religions traditionally affirm (see Figure 6.7). Nones are less likely to agree that one's own or another's "gender identity" is important, less likely to agree that "having children" is very important to them, and less likely to say that they "would be very unhappy if [they] never marr[ied]" than their religiously affiliated peers. Twentysomething Nones are also less likely to think "about the meaning of life" and less

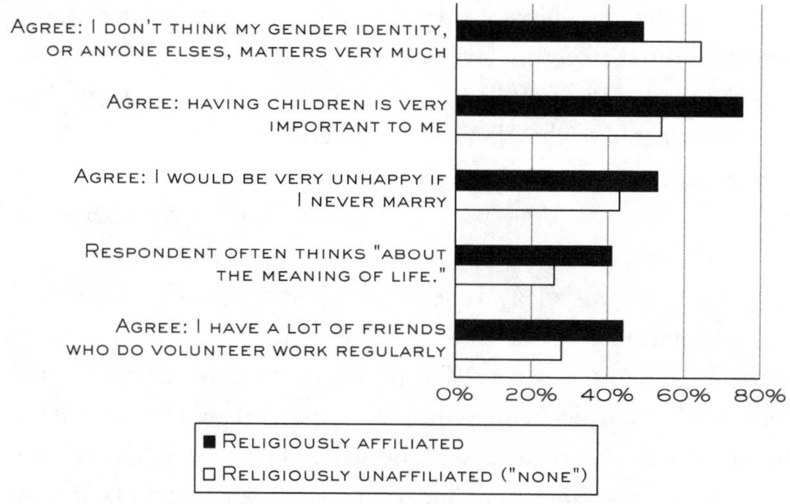

Figure 6.7

Value Differences Between Religiously Affiliated and Unaffiliated Twentysomethings (Nones)

Source: NSAT 2013

likely to have "a lot of friends who do volunteer work regularly," both of which are facilitated by involvement in a religious organization.

Switching to civic engagement, twentysomething Nones are as likely to participate in service clubs, veteran's organizations, senior citizen organizations, and women's organizations as religiously affiliated twentysomethings.[24] Nones are also as likely to be involved in special issue political organizations, neighborhood or community organizations, and race organizations as their religiously affiliated peers are.[25] Religiously affiliated twentysomethings, not surprisingly, are more likely to be active in religious organizations, and in "hobby clubs, sport organizations, or youth groups," and "school associations or clubs."[26] Youth groups are, of course, frequently organized by houses of worship, as are some sport organizations. And the higher fertility of religiously affiliated twentysomethings would be a significant factor in their involvement in school organizations. In short, twentysomething Nones are as civically engaged (and disengaged) as their religiously affiliated peers, with one exception: voting. This merits a closer look.

Twentysomething Nones revealed they are less likely to be registered to vote, and less likely to have voted in the 2012 presidential election, than their religiously affiliated peers. Seventy-two percent of Nones who participated in the NSAT are registered and 67% voted in 2012. The respective figures among their religiously affiliated counterparts are 80% and 81%. And by all indicators, this pattern persisted in 2016: 15% of voters were religiously unaffiliated, though their population percentage was 23%, while 75% of voters were Christian, though their population percentage was 71%.[27] Why are Nones consistently less likely to register or vote? The reasons are surely many, and among them may be a suspicion not only of organized religion but also of social institutions in general. We tested this using the 2008 GSS, which asked respondents about their "confidence in" various institutions, including the military, Congress, executive branch of government, education, and banks and financial institutions. On all five of these institutions, about 8% to 12% more twentysomething Nones indicated they had "hardly any" confidence (the lowest category) in these institutions compared with their religiously affiliated peers (see Figure 6.8). A sizable proportion of twentysomething Nones express little confidence in a variety of social institutions; their disaffiliation with organized religion is thus part of a larger constellation of institutional suspicion and distrust.

We have arrived, therefore, at an interesting place. On the one hand, twentysomething Nones express pro-social values, describe equal (un-) involvement in civic and community life, and indicate that their lives are meaningful and purposeful. On the other hand, they voice less concern about marrying or having children and are less likely to be registered or to have voted than their religious counterparts. The underlying factor, we argue, is that twentysomething Nones are more privatized in their outlook and behavior than religiously affiliated twentysomethings. That is, they live meaningful lives, they value helping others, and they in fact do give help to people in need, but they accomplish these privately and individually, not as a shared undertaking with institutions and their affiliated members. Twentysomething Nones appear to tolerate institutions rather than seek them out and join them. Though they do marry and become parents, forming a family is less central

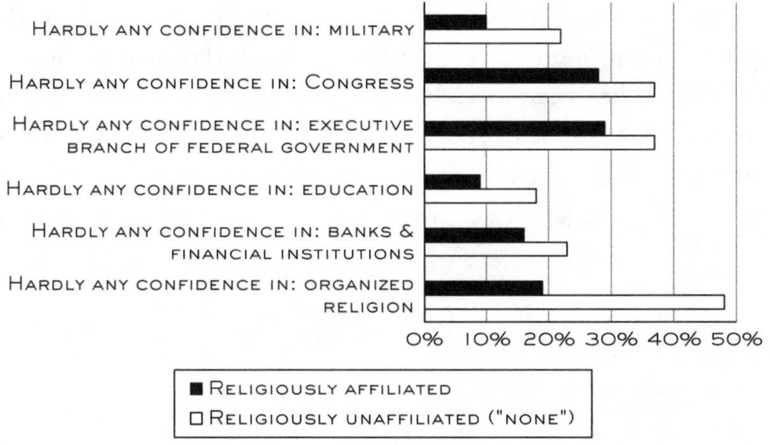

Figure 6.8

Confidence in Institutions Between Religiously Affiliated and Unaffiliated Twentysomethings (Nones)

Source: GSS 2008

to their lives than it is among religiously affiliated twentysomethings. About a sixth of twentysomething Nones even believe in a personal and involved God but reject formal affiliation with religion. And while the majority of twentysomething Nones do vote, their wariness about national politics leads them to do so at significantly lower rates than religiously affiliated twentysomethings.

If twentysomething Nones were to gather under any banner, it is the Gadsden flag: "Don't Tread on Me." They are America's freethinkers, and they stand in a line that includes luminaries like Thomas Paine and Benjamin Franklin; few twentysomethings Nones, however, appear to know this. They keep politics and social institutions at an arm's length, preferring the periphery of American public life. Not only is our republic the worse for these citizens' disengagement, life at the periphery is challenging and marked by frequent turnover. It is one thing to camp for a week in a national park, and quite another to live on the frontier year-round. Social institutions meet important social needs, and while we understand the frustration with admittedly flawed institutions, ignoring them does not make the needs they serve disappear. This is why the uncertainty and switching we observed in Joe,

Amy, and twentysomething Nones like them are so prevalent. (It is also why the proportion of twentysomethings classified as Active in their religion has been as stable as it is.) As the next chapter makes clear, the desire for settledness and lasting connection shapes today's twentysomethings as much as it shaped yesterday's twentysomethings. And we have no doubt it will shape tomorrow's twentysomethings too.

CHAPTER 7

PRACTICAL POSTMODERNS

BIGGER THAN TEXAS

America's second-most populated state could be comprised exclusively of her Protestant and Catholic twentysomethings. That is not a misprint: there are more American *twentysomethings* affiliated with Protestant and Catholic faith than there are persons *of any age* residing in the State of Texas (see Table 7.1). And if we built a capital in this Christian State and assigned only those young adults who attend church regularly and prioritize spiritual growth to live there—relocating Chapter 1's Jeremy Harris and Lee Chen from New York City to join Texan Maria Martinez—that Committed City would have a population of 11.3 million twentysomethings, surpassing New York City's population (8.5 million) by 2.8 million (see Table 7.2).

Life would be far from harmonious in this Christian State or even its Committed City, however. The progressivism of Mainliners like Jeremy would clash with the conservative theologies of their co-resident Catholic and Evangelical peers like Maria and Lee, while relations between the latter two would devolve over views of the Eucharist, Mary, interpretation of the Bible, and more. Separate states, then, might be wiser. We could let Evangelical twentysomethings like Lee replace the population of Pennsylvania, Catholic twentysomethings like Maria replace the population of Washington State, and Mainliner twentysomethings like Jeremy replace the population of Missouri (see Table 7.1). And to leave no twentysomething without a home state, we could assign religiously unaffiliated twentysomethings like Abby Newton to Ohio, where they would need to build an additional city of 800,000 in order to house their population, and resettle twentysomethings affiliated with all other religions to a now extraordinarily diverse Oklahoma.

Table 7.1 Population Rank and Estimates of Select U.S. States and Twentysomething Affiliations, 2013

U.S. State or *Twentysomething Affiliation*	Population (in millions)
1. California	38.3
Twentysomething Christian Affiliates	*26.5*
2. Texas	26.4
5. Illinois	12.9
Twentysomething Evangelical Protestant Affiliates	*12.8*
6. Pennsylvania	12.8
Twentysomething Religiously Unaffiliated (Nones)	*12.4*
7. Ohio	11.6
12. Virginia	8.3
Twentysomething Roman Catholic Affiliates	*7.7*
13. Washington	7.0
17. Tennessee	6.5
Twentysomething Mainline Protestant Affiliates	*6.0*
18. Missouri	6.0
28. Oklahoma	3.8
Twentysomething Other Religion Affiliates	*3.8*
29. Connecticut	3.6
50. Wyoming	0.6

Source: U.S. Census Bureau Population Estimates Program, 2013 for States; the 2013 U.S. Census Bureau Estimate of American Population Aged 20–29 (42.7 million) apportioned by the authors using religious affiliation from the NSAT 2013.

Our point here is simple: affiliation with religion is widespread among American twentysomethings. This is important to understand. But twentysomethings who indicate no affiliation with religion are a sizable population too, and this is also important to understand. Most important of all, though, is to look beyond affiliation to learn what religion means to twentysomethings who are affiliated, and what having no religious affiliation means to those who are not affiliated. Doing this in Chapters 3, 4, and 5 made it clear that Christian twentysomethings varied from Active to Nominal to Estranged in their overall religiousness, and in Chapter 6 helped

Table 7.2 Population Rank and Estimates of Select U.S. Cities and Active or Deliberate Twentysomething Affiliates, 2013

U.S. City or *Active/Deliberate Twentysomething Affiliates*	Population (in millions)
Active Christian Twentysomethings	*11.3*
1. New York City, New York	8.5
Deliberately Unaffiliated Twentysomethings (Nones)	*6.7*
Active Evangelical Protestant Twentysomethings	*6.0*
2. Los Angeles, California	3.9
Active Roman Catholic Twentysomethings	*3.2*
3. Chicago, Illinois	2.7
4. Houston, Texas	2.2
Active Mainline Protestant Twentysomethings	*2.1*
5. Philadelphia, Pennsylvania	1.6
6. Phoenix, Arizona	1.5
7. San Antonio, Texas	1.4
8. San Diego, California	1.4
Active Other Religion Twentysomethings	*1.3*
9. Dallas, Texas	1.2

Source: U.S. Census Bureau Population Estimates Program, 2013 for Cities; the 2013 U.S. Census Bureau Estimate of American Population Aged 20–29 (42.7 million) apportioned by the authors using the NSAT 2013.

sort twentysomething Nones into Unaffiliated Believers, Spiritual Eclectics, Philosophical Secularists, and Indifferent Secularists. For Active Christian twentysomethings theology and ethics really matter, with the Eucharist being central to Catholics, Bible teaching to Evangelicals, and social justice to Mainliners, as does attending worship with a critical mass of other young adults, while nostalgia and family life play the primary role in the continued religious affiliation of Nominal and Estranged Christian twentysomethings. For twentysomething Nones, context and time reveal secularism, spiritual eclecticism, and theistic belief to vary in their appeal and expression.

When we extrapolate our results from the National Study of American Twentysomethings (NSAT) to the U.S. population of Americans age 20 to 29, four large patterns become apparent (see Figure 7.1).

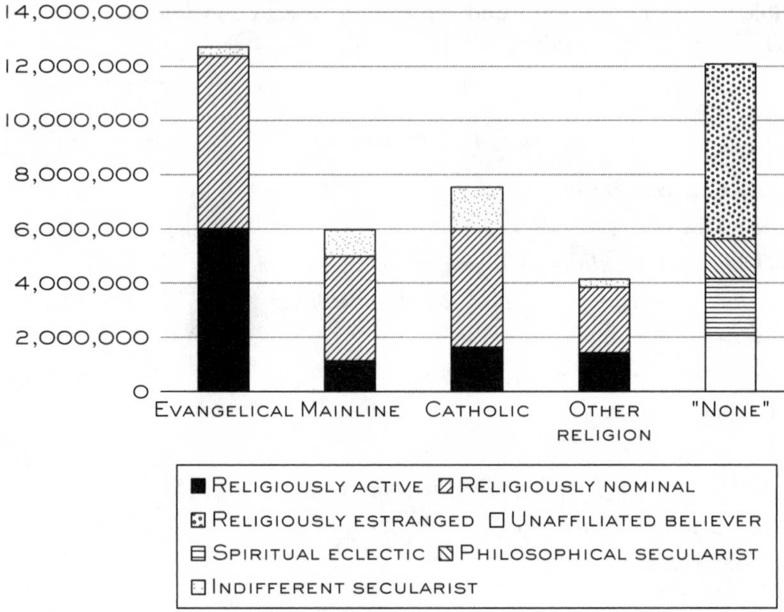

Figure 7.1

Population Estimates for the Religious Affiliations of American Twentysomethings

Source: NSAT 2013

Note: The 2013 U.S. Census Bureau Estimate of American Population Aged 20–29 (42.7 million) apportioned by the authors using religious affiliation from the NSAT.

- First, religiously affiliated twentysomethings prefer nominal levels of affiliation. Seventeen million out of 30.4 million religiously affiliated twentysomethings see faith as a valued part of their childhood, an intended factor in their settled futures, but only an occasional element in their lives presently.
- Second, religiously unaffiliated twentysomethings are mostly Indifferent Secularists. More than half of America's 12.3 million twentysomethings who indicate a religious affiliation of None also indicate little to no interest in spiritual growth as an adult and rarely to never think "about the meaning of life."
- Third, about 1 out of 4 American twentysomethings make religion a priority in their lives. More than 10 million out of 42.7 million American twentysomethings attend worship regularly (twice

monthly to more than weekly) *and* indicate that growing in their spiritual lives as adults is "very" or "extremely important."

- Fourth, 1 in 8 twentysomethings opt for the periphery of their stated affiliation. More than 3 million religiously affiliated twentysomethings are estranged from their religious affiliation—rarely attending worship and assigning a low value to their spiritual lives, while 2 million Nones believe in a personal, involved God and pray to that divine being with considerable regularity.

In other words, the modal patterns among American twentysomethings are to sideline their religion or be indifferent about their secularism, with exceptions for one-quarter who prioritize their faith and one-eighth who are uncertain about their affiliation or non-affiliation with religion.

These patterns, which we have described in detail in Chapters 3–6, raise two issues that we tackle in this closing chapter. First, how does twentysomething religiosity compare with adolescent religiosity? Does twentysomething religiosity represent a carryover, a cooling out, or a careful sifting of adolescent patterns? And does twentysomething religiosity help illuminate the ways young adults interact with other social institutions during their third decade? Second, how do American twentysomethings make sense of spirituality and organize their spiritual lives? Does spiritual life become more important during one's 20s? Is spiritual life associated with key life statuses, like parenthood or completing college? And how does spiritual life compare to religion with respect to these life statuses? We examine these issues next, before closing this chapter with reflections on how emerging adulthood has shaped the religious, spiritual, and secular lives of today's twentysomethings and is producing the most pluralist generation in American history.

From Adolescence to Emerging Adulthood

There is little about the religious, spiritual, and secular lives of American teens that scholars have not examined at this point. Because of the National Study of Youth and Religion, underwritten by the

Lilly Endowment, Inc. and incorporating interviews and surveys with American adolescents in four waves between 2003 and 2013, there is an abundance of published and forthcoming scholarly publications.[1] Of particular value for our purposes is Lisa Pearce and Melinda Lundquist Denton's book *A Faith of Their Own* (2011), because in it they generated five profiles of religiosity using eight measures of religious belief, practice, and importance.[2] These five profiles were Abiders—teens who affirm and are active in a traditional religion; Adapters—teens who respect all religions and express individualized beliefs; Assenters—teens who affirm but do not prioritize a traditional religion; Avoiders—teens who claim a religious affiliation but demonstrate no interest in religion; and "Atheists"—teens who do not claim a religious affiliation or believe in God (for the sake of alliteration, Pearce and Denton apply the Atheist label to this profile; because of its stigma, this is not a label claimed by most in this profile).[3] Pearce and Denton note that 75% of American teens give "incongruent" (i.e., logically inconsistent) answers to questions about religious beliefs, practices, and importance, and fall into the Adapters, Assenters, and Avoiders profiles. Twenty-five percent of American teens give logically consistent answers about religion—the 22% who are Abiders and the 3% who are Atheists (see Table 7.3).

We were fortunate to have Pearce and Denton as advisors to this project, and they recreated their five profiles using items in our NSAT. We can therefore compare their analysis of adolescents in 2003 and 2005 with our survey of twentysomethings in 2013, and identify changes as well as continuities in the religious, spiritual, and secular lives of American twentysomethings since adolescence (see Table 7.3). Specifically, we identify three key findings:

- First, the proportions of Abiders and Assenters remain stable (i.e., statistically equivalent) between middle adolescence (13–17) and the late 20s (25–29). Most American adolescents and twentysomethings affirm a traditional religion, with 1 out of 5 actively involved.
- Second, there is a sharp decline in the proportions of Adapters and Avoiders—from 44% of late adolescents to 22% of those in their

Table 7.3 Adolescent and Twentysomething Religious Types Compared

	National Surveys of Youth and Religion (2002, 2005)		National Study of American Twentysomethings (2013)	
	Ages 13–17 (Wave 1)	Ages 16–21 (Wave 2)	Ages 20–24	Ages 25–29
Pearce and Denton's five religious profiles				
Abiders—affirm and actively involved in a traditional religion	22%	20%	18%	20%
Adapters—accept all religions and express individualized beliefs	28%	20%	9%	7%
Assenters—affirm but do not prioritize involvement in a traditional religion	30%	31%	36%	33%
Avoiders—claim a religious affiliation but indicate no interest or involvement in religion	17%	24%	17%	15%
Atheists—do not believe in God or religion	3%	5%	20%	24%

Source: Pearce and Denton, *A Faith of Their Own*, p. 34; NSAT 2013.

Note: Percentages may not total 100 due to rounding.

late 20s. These incongruent profiles lose popularity as Americans mature.

- Third, there is a substantial increase in the popularity of the Atheist profile. Rejection of religious affiliation and disbelief in God rises from 1 out of 33 middle adolescents to 1 out of 4 late twentysomethings.

These patterns confirm much of what we found in Chapter 2 in our analyses of the General Social Survey. That is, as Americans move through their 20s, many who are uncertain about religion choose to "fish or cut bait." And cutting bait is the most frequent choice.

But there's one exception to this fish or cut bait pattern, and it is fairly big: 1 out of 3 twentysomethings postpone any decision about religion and sideline its present role. Assenters to religion, these twentysomethings affirm their affiliation but relegate anything more than occasional involvement to the future. We suspect two things are happening here. First, American young adults, like American adolescents, do not view religion as important in this period of their lives, though they accept that some choose to prioritize it.[4] Second, the structural constraints of attaining adult independence require a flexibility that conflicts with participation expectations of local congregations. Employers, for example, expect newer employees to demonstrate commitment by working weekends, holidays, or graveyard shifts, while friends and partners often demand a twentysomething's Saturday nights or Sundays. Assenters could, given these constraints, opt to fish or cut bait with respect to religion. But because these twentysomethings enjoyed fishing as children, they refuse to surrender their fishing gear even as they go fishing only on holidays and important family gatherings. During those special events, they may think about a future moment when their lives settle down, when they will have time to learn all about fishing, and either make fishing their own passion or give it up permanently. But with career paths to find, partners to consider, and a social life to tend—that time is not now.

We can actually see evidence of this sorting out of religion during one's 20s: 20–24-year-olds comprise the highest proportion of the three incongruent profiles, while 25–29-year-olds make up the majority of the two congruent profiles (see Figure 7.2). As twentysomethings age, it appears that they more and more settle the religion question—answering it (20% are Abiders and 24% are Atheists) or sidelining it (33% are Assenters). Those who have not settled it by their late 20s are mainly those who have not settled other areas of their lives. Late twentysomething Avoiders and Adapters, for example, are the least likely to be married or have children of the

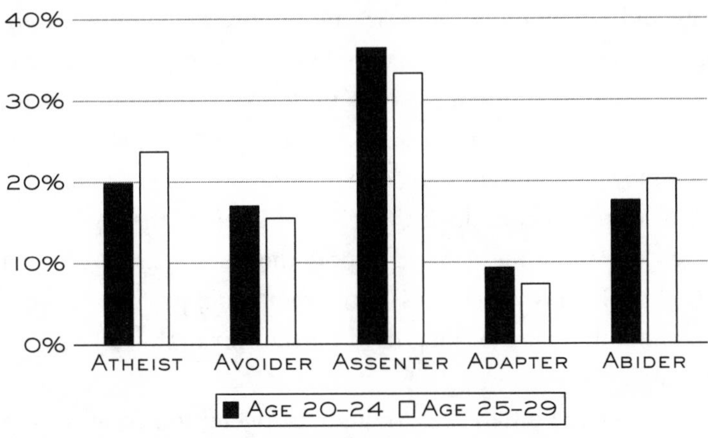

Figure 7.2
Religious Profiles of Early and Late Twentysomethings
Source: NSAT 2013

five profiles. Adapters in their late 20s are also least likely to have graduated from college and most likely to be female, while Avoiders in their late 20s are most likely to have graduated from college and most likely to be male. Since 95% of American twentysomethings are cisgender heterosexuals, and 90% hope to find a lifetime monogamous partner,[5] we suspect these older Adapters and Avoiders are keeping their religious options open until their romantic partnerships solidify. Finding a long-term partner has become difficult enough, to take a firm stance on religion would seriously narrow one's pool of potential partners.[6] It certainly did for Chapter 4's Gillian Muller, who broke up with her boyfriend of four months when she realized his opposition to raising children in the church conflicted with her conviction to do so.

On Purpose and Social Engagement

It is interesting to see when and how Pearce and Denton's religious profiles connect with other behaviors and views of American twentysomethings. There is no obvious pattern between religious profiles and rates of college completion, for example. Looking at twentysomethings over

24 years old, we see Avoiders are the most likely to have graduated from college (43%), followed by Abiders (41%), Assenters (34%), Atheists (32%), and Adapters (29%). Nor is there a discernible pattern in rates of employment (all five profiles fall between 60% and 65% employed) or unemployment (between 10% and 16% of all five profiles have received benefits). But we do see that Abiders report the highest rates of marriage (38%), while Atheists report the highest rates of cohabitation (24%). Twentysomethings in the remaining profiles, however, report comparable rates of long-term partnerships (30–36% married or cohabiting).

There are large differences, though, in twentysomethings' certainty about the purpose and meaning of their lives, and in several pro-social indicators. Abiders express overwhelming certainty about their lives' purpose and meaning, for example, with Adapters close behind (see Figure 7.3). One in three Atheists, however, is uncertain about their life's purpose. This could be an indicator of existential honesty were it not clustered with Atheists' greater resistance to helping others, lower rates of voting, and community disengagement (see Figures 7.3 and 7.4). When viewed as a cluster, it becomes apparent that the more distant twentysomethings are from religious affiliation or belief in God, the more they lose the pro-social benefits that accompany involvement in organized religion.

Twentysomethings certainly have the right to reject religious beliefs and practices. We are not making a judgment about twentysomethings who reject religion. This is rather a *sociological* observation about what happens when withdrawal from one societal institution, in this case religion, is not compensated by involvement in other institutions, such as voluntary or civic organizations. Traditionally, societies look to religion to explain life's purpose, provide scripts to guide family formation, and supply opportunities for engagement with others. Psychologists, moreover, have demonstrated that identifying a larger purpose and possessing positive relationships with others are essential to human flourishing.[7] We have seen that many twentysomethings find purpose and positive relationships within religious affiliation, and many find these beyond organized religion. But 1 out of 6 twentysomethings do

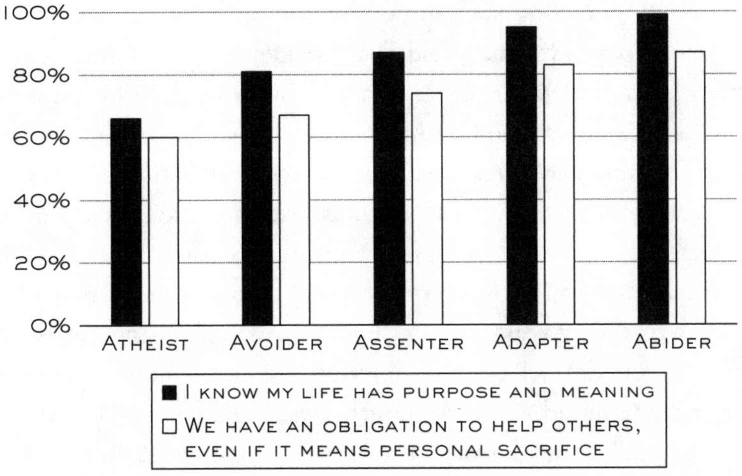

Figure 7.3

Purpose and Helping Obligation Across Religious Profiles of American Twentysomethings

Source: NSAT 2013

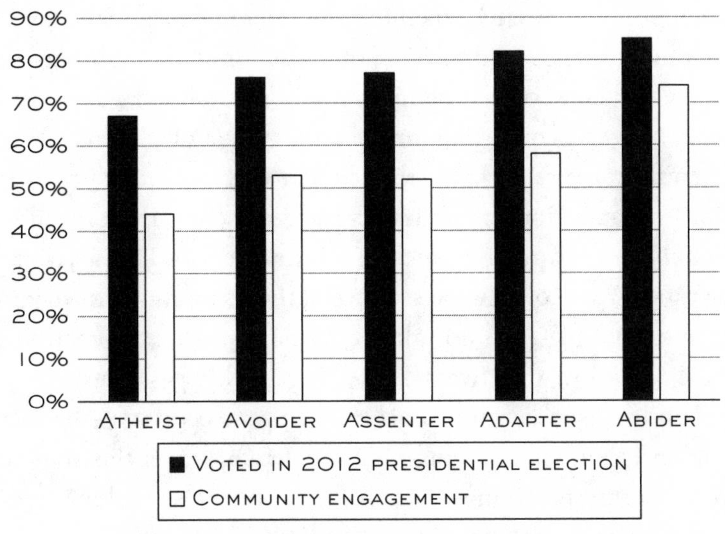

Figure 7.4

Voting and Community Engagement Across Religious Profiles of American Twentysomethings

Source: NSAT 2013

not report a sense of meaning or purpose for their lives, and 1 out of 6 are disengaged from all voluntary and civic activities or even informal assistance to family, friends, or other people in need. This is not good for these young adults. Indeed, it is not good for America as a whole.

This sobering news must be balanced, however, with the encouraging news that 5 out of 6 American twentysomethings have a clear sense of life's purpose, and the same proportion report formal involvement in their local communities or informal assistance to persons in need. Despite troubling reports of young adults' high rates of anxiety and short-sighted decisions,[8] and the lack of cultural scripts to guide young adults through emerging adulthood, most American twentysomethings are finding a path—a positive, pro-social path—through their third decade. To our eyes, they are doing so in the pragmatic manner long characteristic of Americans, using culture less for guiding scripts and more as a toolkit from which they pick and choose affiliations, involvements, values, and action sequences.[9] If there is anything new happening, it is the solidly postmodern approach twentysomethings take to their young adult pilgrimage. American twentysomethings consider religious institutions (and likely voluntary, civic, and political organizations too) less as custodians of society and conservators of cultural wisdom and more as nodes on a crowded network, competing for their attention and allegiance.[10]

Given this, it is remarkable that so many twentysomethings include religious organizations as nodes on their personal network and keep religious beliefs and practices in their cultural toolkits. That is a testament to the timelessness of religion's answers, the adaptability of religion to contemporary times, the nostalgia of American twentysomethings, or all three. We know that twentysomethings will bypass nodes they find useless and jettison cultural tools they find unnecessary—the increase in religiously unaffiliated young adults demonstrates this. But this is not most twentysomethings. The 1 out of 4 twentysomethings who are religiously active prioritize religious nodes and keep religious beliefs and practices at the top of their cultural toolboxes. The nominally affiliated majority, however, are content to keep religion as an occasional node in their personal network, stowing beliefs and practices in their toolboxes for possible regular use in the future.

The Spiritual Lives of American Twentysomethings

We asked the 1,880 twentysomethings who participated in the NSAT a set of nine items that touched on their spiritual life and their views of spirituality. These included queries about (1) prayer, (2) meditation, (3) spiritual growth as an adult, (4) thinking about the meaning of life, (5) feeling a "spiritual or emotional connection to all the people around me," (6) including other religious traditions in one's own spirituality, (7) feeling "so connected to nature that everything seems to be part of one living organism," (8) regarding any art or music as "a way to communicate one's spirituality," and (9) thinking of God not as a personal but "as a spiritual force." Previous chapters cited results with most of these items as we examined Catholic, Mainline Protestant, Evangelical, and religiously unaffiliated twentysomethings. Here, we focus on these items as a group to understand the relative importance of, and variation in, American twentysomethings' spiritual lives.

Our first step, using a statistical procedure called factor analysis, revealed that twentysomethings subdivide these nine items into two clusters.[11] The first cluster included frequency of prayer, frequency of meditation, the importance of growing spiritually as an adult, thinking about the meaning of life, and feeling a strong spiritual or emotional connection to "all the people around me." The second cluster included thinking of God not as personal but "as a spiritual force," regarding *any* art or music as "a way to communicate one's spirituality," including other religious traditions in one's own spirituality, feeling "so connected to nature that everything seems to be part of one living organism," and again, feeling a strong spiritual or emotional connection to "all the people around me." The first cluster we labeled "traditional spirituality," as it includes practices and values that many American churches encourage. The second cluster we labeled "nontraditional spirituality," as it includes practices, experiences, and opinions that fewer Evangelical, Mainline Protestant, or Catholic congregations encourage.

We used factor analysis to generate respondent scores for traditional and nontraditional spirituality, then we compared twentysomethings' scores across demographic and religious categories. This is where we encountered both expected and unexpected patterns. First, the expected patterns: traditional spirituality was higher among female twentysomethings than it was among males, among Black and Latino twentysomethings than among Whites, among married twentysomethings than among other marital statuses, among parents than among non-parents, and among younger twentysomethings than among their older counterparts. It was also higher among those who attended religious services more frequently, among Active Christians, and among Abiders. In short, traditional spirituality is highest among those groups that are highest in traditional religiosity. One can view these indicators of traditional spirituality, in short, as one more measure of traditional religiosity.

What we did not expect were our results for nontraditional spirituality: this cluster of spiritual life measures was highest among the *most* theologically conservative and religiously active twentysomethings, second highest among religiously unaffiliated twentysomethings, and lowest among theologically liberal, religiously Nominal, and religiously Estranged twentysomethings. Twentysomethings who attend religious services weekly or more often, for example, had the highest scores for nontraditional spirituality, followed by twentysomethings who never attend religious services, followed by monthly and less than monthly attending twentysomethings. Similarly, Abiders had the highest scores for nontraditional spirituality, Atheists had the second highest, Assenters took third place, while Avoiders and Adapters tied for last place. Nontraditional spirituality was even higher than traditional spirituality among married twentysomethings and among twentysomethings with children, two subsets of twentysomethings who otherwise score high on adherence to traditional religiosity.

So what is going on here? First, we must note that traditional spirituality is the more robust measure of the two—its variation is wider and it uncovers the largest differences among twentysomethings. Second, the chief anomaly in nontraditional spirituality is its high levels among the most actively religious twentysomethings; that twentysomething Nones rank second highest comports with their subpopulations of

Unaffiliated Believers and Spiritual Eclectics, and that Nominal and Estranged twentysomethings rank lowest comports with their sidelining of religion. On reflection, we realized that the high level of nontraditional spirituality among Active twentysomethings' reflects their high engagement with all things religious and spiritual. To religiously committed twentysomethings, all of life communicates spiritual truth, including nature, art, and music. Even other religions feature practices that can be co-opted, which is what religiously Active twentysomethings have arguably done with meditation. The agreement on these items is so high among Active twentysomethings that it offsets their low agreement that God is an impersonal "spiritual force."[12] In other words, Active twentysomethings possess a broad and encompassing view of religion and spirituality, Nominal and Estranged twentysomethings constrain religion and spirituality to the sideline of their everyday lives, while a sizable proportion (though far from a majority), of twentysomething Nones are open to nontraditional spirituality.

Do twentysomethings become more spiritual as they age? On the surface, it appeared that older twentysomethings scored higher in nontraditional spirituality and lower in traditional spirituality than their younger counterparts. But age lost its predictive relationship with both types of spirituality once we controlled for religious affiliation.[13] We also looked to see if twentysomethings were more spiritually inclined than adolescents but could not find any evidence for this. Pearce and Denton did analyze how often teens ponder "the meaning of life," which is one of the nine items we asked in the NSAT, and they found no variation from middle to late adolescence. But they did find variation across religious profiles: about 2 in 5 of their adolescent Adapters reported pondering the meaning of life "very often," as do 1 in 4 of their Abiders and 1 in 7 of their Assenters, Avoiders, and Atheists. Our Adapter, Abider, and Assenter twentysomethings reported equivalent rates of pondering the meaning of life, while Avoider and Atheist twentysomethings reported slightly lower rates.[14] In short, this one measure of spiritual/existential reflection appears stable between adolescence and young adulthood, and if anything, declines slightly among young adults who are most distant from religion.

This brings us to our final and most important analyses of twentysomething spirituality—whether spirituality is associated with important statuses in the lives of American twentysomethings, and its importance relative to that of religion. Since our data are not longitudinal, we cannot make claims about causation. But we can assess whether spirituality factor scores, religious attendance, and religious affiliations have significant associations with marriage, cohabitation, parenthood, employment, completion of bachelor's degrees, voting, social connectedness, and community engagement—and we can do so controlling for race, gender, household income, and age (see Table 7.4).[15] These analyses reveal:

- traditional spirituality is negatively associated with cohabiting and being in the labor force, but positively associated with being engaged in one's community;
- nontraditional spirituality is positively associated with being married, being a parent, and feeling socially connected, and negatively associated with cohabiting and voting;
- frequent attendance at worship is positively associated with marriage, employment, college completion, voting, and community engagement, and negatively associated with cohabiting;
- Evangelical twentysomethings are less likely to complete bachelor's degrees, less likely to be engaged in their communities, and more likely to be parents than Nones (the reference category);
- Mainline Protestant and other religiously affiliated twentysomethings are less likely to complete bachelor's degrees than Nones; and
- Roman Catholic twentysomethings are more likely to feel socially connected to others than Nones.

These are remarkable findings because they demonstrate that spirituality and organized religion are both robustly associated with eight important statuses, even after controlling for age, race, gender, and household income.

Twentysomethings' religious, spiritual, and secular lives are inextricably linked to statuses that are consequential for individuals and

Table 7.4 Summary Table for Logistic Regressions of Twentysomething Statuses on Spirituality Scores, Religious Attendance, and Religious Affiliations

	Binary Dependent Variables							
	Married	Cohabiting	Parent	Employed	College graduate[1]	Voted 2012	Socially Connected	Community Engaged
	(N = 1746)	(N = 1746)	(N = 1720)	(N = 1746)	(N = 1154)	(N = 1746)	(N = 1739)	(N = 1746)
Spirituality Factor Scores								
Traditional		–		–				+
Nontraditional	+	–	+			–	+	
Frequency of Attendance at Religious Services	+	–		+	+	+		+
Religious Affiliation[2]								
Evangelical			+		–			–
Mainline Protestant					–			

(continued)

Table 7.4 Continued

	Binary Dependent Variables							
	Married	Cohabiting	Parent	Employed	College graduate[1]	Voted 2012	Socially Connected	Community Engaged
	(N = 1746)	(N = 1746)	(N = 1720)	(N = 1746)	(N = 1154)	(N = 1746)	(N = 1739)	(N = 1746)
Roman Catholic							+	
Other Religion					–			
Nagelkerke R Square	.318	.108	.278	.093	.212	.112	.096	.174

+ = significant positive association ($p < .05$)

– = significant negative association ($p < .05$)

All analyses include controls (not shown) for age in years, gender, household income in dollars, and race/ethnicity.

[1] Of respondents 24–29 years old only.

[2] Reference category is religiously unaffiliated (Nones).

societal institutions. For example, becoming a parent, which is more frequent among Evangelicals and those high in nontraditional spirituality, is a joyous event when young adults are ready and able to rear the child. When they are unprepared for parenthood, however, care for a child can derail a parent's career and burden communities with that child's unmet needs. Similarly, when twentysomethings vote and get involved in their communities, as those high in traditional spirituality and frequent in worship attendance do, it benefits neighborhoods and governments. But when twentysomethings do not vote, as is common among those who endorse a nontraditional spirituality, or refuse to engage with their communities, as is common among Estranged Evangelicals, democratic institutions are undermined. How American twentysomethings understand and express their religious, spiritual, and secular lives is connected to diverse and important life statuses.

These findings are remarkable for a second reason. They demonstrate that spirituality and attendance at worship have more direct relevance to these eight life statuses than religious affiliation does. Catholic affiliation is associated with just one of eight life statuses, feeling socially connected, once spirituality and worship attendance are held constant in our statistical models. Mainline Protestant affiliation is similarly associated with just one life status, having a lower rate of college completion than Nones, again with spirituality and worship attendance rates held constant. Evangelical affiliation has the broadest showing in these analyses, being associated with higher likelihoods of its affiliates being parents and lower likelihoods of them completing college or being engaged in their communities than Nones. We need to counterbalance, to be sure, the lower likelihoods of Protestant twentysomethings completing college compared to Nones with the higher likelihoods of college completion by frequent worship attenders. The lower college completion rates of Protestant twentysomethings are concentrated among infrequently attending Evangelicals and Mainliners. As seen above and earlier in this book, religious affiliation plays an outsized role in twentysomethings' spirituality and their frequency of attendance at worship. Its direct association with these eight statuses, however, is more limited.

Adulthood and the Soul

Front and center, sidelined, banned from the playing field, or generating a game of one's own? With 47 million twentysomethings in America, we expected to encounter more than four strategies with respect to religious and spiritual life. But just as emerging adulthood is relentless in its demands on American twentysomethings, so is the apparent pressure to settle into one of these strategies. There is no escape from the lengthening process of preparing for work, establishing a career, attaining financial independence, maintaining a social life, and forming a long-term partnership—we saw that in Chapter 1's stories of Maria, Jeremy, Lee, and Abby, and understood why from Chapter 2's discussion of emerging adulthood. There also appears to be little escape from the social pressure to prioritize, sideline, reject, or innovate religious and spiritual life. Two things impressed us about this: how serious and persistent our interviewees were in responding to the demands of emerging adulthood, and how much twentysomethings flocked together with likeminded friends.

Some of the seriousness we encountered among our interviewees is a selection effect—twentysomethings who avoid responsibility likely avoid interviews with researchers. Some of this seriousness is also a reflexive effect—researchers who ask twentysomethings serious questions are likely to hear serious answers. But even with these caveats, we encountered scores of responsible adults in their 20s, who were quite serious about their education, their work lives, their finances, their friendships, and their partners. This is good news, and it needs a wide telling, as too many broadcast twentysomething caricatures based on interactions with a handful of unrepresentative exceptions. Plenty of twentysomethings demonstrate remarkable maturity, while plenty of Americans over 30 fail to do so; it is time we let go of the view that irresponsibility is the unique province of the young.

We also encountered a high level of social encapsulation among twentysomethings in our ethnographic observations and in our analyses of the NSAT. Twentysomethings who prioritize their religious and spiritual lives are friends with other prioritizers, twentysomethings who reject organized religion (or reject and innovate spiritually) are friends with other rejectors, and twentysomethings who sideline religion and spirituality are friends with other sideliners.[16] This is not a claim about causality—a twentysomething's friends are as likely to determine an individual's prioritizing, rejecting, sidelining, or innovating of their religious and spiritual life as that twentysomething's a priori decision. What we *are* claiming is that these four strategies represent commitments of consequence for twentysomething identity and relationships. These strategies define religious, spiritual, and secular identities, constrain friendship circles, and influence long-term partnerships.

And yes, we used the word *commitment* with respect to American twentysomething behaviors. It is a fitting descriptor, and opting to prioritize, reject, sideline, or innovate religion is not the only commitment twentysomethings make. Our respondents committed themselves to jobs, to schooling, to relationships, to marriage, to parenthood, and to community engagement. Commitment is still a requirement of adulthood, and today's twentysomethings approach adulthood with the same American pragmatism that generations before them employed. Today's young adults, like all adults, have bills and need money, get sick and need health care, have or overwhelmingly desire to have children, and enjoy friendship and romance as much as anyone. So even if young adults make their money through the "gig" economy or patch together education from online providers, they still have to eat, arrange housing, manage expenses, and fulfill obligations to partners, family, and children. Commitments may be less to a specific employer or school, and more to working for or gaining credentials from a menu of providers, but they are commitments nonetheless.

Successfully navigating emerging adulthood demands commitment, and today's young adults are rising to the challenge. It is high time that grumpy pundits let go of the view that twentysomethings resist commitment and avoid responsibility—and direct their ire to the way that schooling, work, relationships, communities, and governments have changed during the past half-century—often for the worse. Schooling costs have soared while returns to education have declined, corporations dismiss faithful employees with years of experience, the contingency of American community and the prevalence of social media offers scores of acquaintances but produces few enduring relationships, affluent communities mobilize against affordable housing and regard the crumbling infrastructure of poorer communities as "not my problem," while governments raid pension funds and ignore long-term planning. It is far from a welcoming world out there, and the 47 million American twentysomethings trying to stand on their own two feet deserve support, not blame.

We reach, then, the end of this journey to understand the religious, spiritual, and secular lives of American twentysomethings. And contrary to many, we interpret twentysomethings not through the lens of religious decline and secular triumph but rather as America's most truly pluralist generation of adults. The 1950s view that good Americans were *religious* Americans led scores to affiliate with religion to avoid their neighbor's or co-worker's disapproval.[17] That view holds no currency among today's American twentysomethings, who feel freer than any previous American generation to embrace religious, spiritual, and secular lives as they see fit. We see American twentysomethings as postmodern pilgrims, freely selecting religious, spiritual, or secular tools from their cultural toolkits, and using them as much or as little as they please as they travel the spokes and nodes of our vast American social network. Many twentysomethings prioritize their religious and spiritual lives, many others do not, many postpone these matters until they reach a more settled time in their lives, and some fill their spiritual basket with anything they like. Our closing hope is simply this: that all would respect twentysomethings for the pilgrimage to adulthood they are on but did not choose, recognizing the advantages of those who came of age in earlier eras, and supporting young adults' efforts to find a forward pathway in our changing and increasingly uncertain world.

METHODOLOGICAL APPENDIX

The Changing SEA Project

On July 23, 2008, authors Clydesdale and Garces-Foley met for the first time at the Life Cycle Institute at Catholic University of America (CUA), to plan a national study on "the spiritual hunger of young adult Americans." This project was begun by sociologist Dean R. Hoge who, along with colleagues James Youniss, professor of psychology at CUA, and Joseph Tamney, emeritus professor of sociology at Ball State University, received a planning grant from the Lilly Endowment in January 2008. As Hoge described it,

> For many Americans the twenties are being defined as years for exploration, training, and tentative (not long-term) commitments. This phase of the life cycle is being called "Emerging Adulthood," and it has received widespread attention lately. It is bewildering to leaders to America's churches.[1]

Hoge, Youniss, and Tamney held conversations with an advisory board of CUA faculty and Garces-Foley, from nearby Marymount University, to create a research plan. First, we would commission authors to produce papers on aspects of emerging adults' values, commitments, and search for meaning and share these with the public online and, second, we would commission researchers to study churches successful in engaging young adults and produce a book on Catholic churches and another on Protestant churches.[2]

To everyone's shock, Hoge was diagnosed with stomach cancer in early 2008. Despite his illness, Hoge was intent on seeing the research project move forward, and his colleagues ensured that it did. Over the summer the team held focus groups with local pastors and consulted with researchers. These conversations were wide-ranging, about existing datasets to be mined, scholars to be recruited to write synthesizing articles, ethnographic research in congregations with broad young adult involvement, and commissioning a possible survey of young adults in America.

We had every hope that Hoge would recover and lead the project. In the interim, Youniss submitted a three-year grant proposal to Lilly and agreed to serve as our temporary principal investigator (PI). Clydesdale and Garces-Foley agreed to take charge of the first two components of the project: commissioning and posting syntheses of emerging adult research on a minister-friendly website, and recruiting ethnographers and overseeing their studies of Protestant and Catholic congregations. Tragically, Hoge died on September 13, 2008, a loss to all who knew him, and to the Life Cycle Institute, CUA, and the sociology of religion. The Life Cycle Institute asked Father Anthony Pogorelc, who had been part of the advisory board and helped lead the focus groups, to step into Hoge's role as the grant PI. At that point, the four of us—Youniss, Garces-Foley, Clydesdale, and Pogorelc, committed to bringing this final project of Hoge's to completion, in honor and memory of this fine scholar and dedicated churchman.

In late 2008, the Lilly Endowment notified Youniss and the Life Cycle Institute of its award, which made 2009 a year of much research activity. We adopted the name "The Changing Spirituality of Emerging Adults Project," partly for its catchy "ChangingSEA" abbreviation, and created a website to disseminate our initial products. We issued two requests for proposals, for the synthesizing essay project and the ethnographic studies, and worked to select essayists and ethnographers. Within a year we began sharing the results. By 2011 the website included fifteen synthesizing essays by outstanding social scientists, four essays on ministry implications authored by Protestant and Catholic leaders, and nine summaries from our ethnographic studies. The original website went dark in 2013, but its articles remain available in CUA's archives: http://archives.lib.cua.edu/findingaid/changspir.cfm.

Throughout the first two parts of this project, we would meet regularly to discuss our findings and plan our next steps, and we ultimately opted to commission a national survey of American twentysomethings. That survey's findings, combined with the rich data from our congregational and ministry ethnographies, convinced us that we needed to write a scholarly yet reader-friendly book that would convey our project's results. A practical book for ministry leaders was beyond our expertise, as we are scholars of religion and not ministers. Moreover, there is no shortage of "how-to" writings on ministry—complete with overgeneralizations and thin evidence. What ministers need, we believe, is the same thing that anyone interested in the religious, spiritual, and secular lives of young adults needs: robust, data-driven analysis with well-informed interpretation. Once we began writing, we realized something else: a book focused on Protestant and Catholic young adults was too analytically limited. Since we had survey data on all American twentysomethings, and since both authors had separate research projects that included scores of interviews with young adults, including religiously unaffiliated young adults, we decided to pool these interviews and expand the book's scope to include twentysomething Nones. Adding in these interviews, we now had qualitative and quantitative data on four types of twentysomethings accounting for 91% of Americans between the ages of 20 and 29: Evangelical Protestant, Mainline Protestant, Roman Catholic, and religiously unaffiliated (i.e., Nones).

In the remainder of this appendix, we describe the congregational ethnographies, the National Study of American Twentysomethings (NSAT, i.e., the survey), and the in-depth interviews with Nones that are the basis for this volume's claims. At the very end, we include the NSAT Questionnaire and Congregational Studies Interview Schedule.

Congregational Studies

In response to the call for proposals issued in April 2009, we received twenty-seven applications from ethnographic researchers around the country. Each applicant proposed a local congregation with a robust young adult population to study. Looking for excellent researchers in different regions of the country studying different types of churches, we selected six individuals to be research fellows: Walt Bower, Tricia C. Bruce, Richard Cimino, Justin Farrell, Ashley Palmer, Grace Yukich. Bruce and Palmer studied Catholics, Cimino and Bower studied Evangelical Protestants, and Farrell and Yukich studied Mainline Protestants. In addition, Garces-Foley conducted a study of Catholic dioceses and parishes in the Washington, DC region. Gerardo Marti was also hired as a research fellow, but instead of a congregational study, he studied the national emerging church movement. We gathered the fellows for an orientation at the 2009 Society for the Scientific Study of Religion meeting in Denver and were fortunate to have Nancy Ammerman and Steve Warner join us for several hours to discuss best practices in congregational studies.

The congregational studies began in earnest in fall of 2009. Each researcher was expected to develop a comprehensive profile of the church through extensive archival research, to observe seven to eight worship services and ten to twelve other church functions (e.g., new member classes, Bible study, potluck, social event), conduct a congregational survey and thirty to forty in-depth interviews with young adults and staff. Garces-Foley did observations at diocesan events and four selected parishes in the DC region. In 2010 Hilary Kaell joined the team to conduct a smaller scale study of an emergent Episcopal congregation. All researchers followed protocols for observations and reporting and a common interview guide with variations for young adults, staff, Protestants and Catholics. Interviewees were recruited, with permission of the pastor, by advertising the study on e-mail lists and bulletin announcements. In a conversational format lasting about an hour, the interviewees answered questions about their family background, religious worldview, finding the church, getting involved in the church, worship services, leadership, moral teachings, and social issues.

By the end of 2010, the data collection was complete. Each fellow produced hundreds of pages: church histories, observation reports, interview reports, interview audios files, and extensive analysis of websites, podcasts, and bulletins. Fellows also authored essays summarizing findings from their own study, which were published on the Changing SEA website and are now available in the CUA archives (see above). All together the congregation studies team completed 144 observations and 234 interviews; 169 of the interviewees were 18–35 years old. The interviews were transcribed and coded in Atlas.ti with the help of student assistants at Marymount University, especially Karen Nevin, Nana Marfo, and Mollie Kennedy. The interview questions are listed at the end of this appendix.

National Study of American Twentysomethings

William V. D'Antonio, former president of the American Sociological Association and senior fellow at the Life Cycle Institute (now the Institute for Policy Research & Catholic Studies) at CUA, spoke highly about the cost and quality of survey research he commissioned from William C. McCready of Knowledge Networks, Inc (now owned by The GfK Group, a global information analytics corporation). McCready's four decades of survey research experience began at the National Opinion Research Center at the University of Chicago, continued at the Public Opinion Lab at Northern Illinois University, included survey projects funded by the Centers for Disease Control and Prevention, the National Institutes of Health, and the National Science Foundation, before he assumed the vice presidency of Knowledge Networks in Palo Alto, California. McCready, like other survey research experts, observed the alarming erosion of survey response rates and worked with Knowledge Networks, Inc. to use random-digit dialing (initially) to recruit a statistically representative panel of American adults who would be eligible for award points, redeemable from their online marketplace, in exchange for completing online surveys. Interested individuals without internet access are provided a free computer and internet service in exchange for completing weekly surveys.[3] This panel, now trademarked as KnowledgePanel®, has grown to include more than 55,000 members, including hard to reach populations and special subgroups. Since formed, new panelists are recruited by telephone and postal mail invitations to a national random sample. KnowledgePanel methodology and samples have been rigorously evaluated and since 2003 been presented to scholars in the American Association for Public Opinion Research and attending the Joint Statistical Meetings of the American Statistical Association. There is also a series of white papers and peer-reviewed journal articles about the generation and maintenance of this nationally representative online survey panel.[4] Our KnowledgePanel survey was also reasonably priced—less than half the cost of a telephone survey and a fifth the price of an in-person, door-to-door survey. This made KnowledgePanel an economical option for mixed-method researchers like us.

Once we decided to field a national survey, we reviewed surveys of American religion, particularly those conducted with adolescents, identifying useful and previously deployed questions. To these we added Likert items of our own, and after winnowing the pool to forty-seven items, not including demographic items (GfK supplies these to clients), we contracted with The GfK Group to invite a probability-selected subpopulation of its KnowledgePanel members in their 20s to complete our survey (panelists are not required to participate in any given survey). GfK invited 3,594 panelists to complete the survey between on May 16, 2013, following up with nonrespondents on day three and day six to encourage their participation, and closing the survey on May 28, 2013, with a final sample of 1,880 American twentysomethings and a response rate of 52.3%. Our forty-seven survey items are listed at the end of this appendix.

Shortly after receiving our survey data file, we realized there was a miscommunication about what it would include. Panelists' voting, political, civic, and voluntary data were not included, but we were able to purchase these for a reasonable fee. We also realized, after the fact, that KnowledgePanel uses atypical response options in its religious preference question (see item wording below), which made identification of Evangelical and Mainline Protestants more challenging. To be fair, we did not anticipate subdividing Protestants when we fielded the survey but came to realize its importance a few years later. Evangelicals, who regard correct belief a matter of eternal life or damnation, were defined as follows: (1) all who indicated their religion was Pentecostal, (2) Baptists who believe that God is personal and involved in the world, and that only one religion is true, (3) "Other" Christians who believe that God is personal and involved in the world, and that only one religion is true, and (4) "Protestants" who believe that God is personal and involved in the world, that only one religion is true, and who indicate that they do not incorporate practices of other religions in their own spirituality. We did this because (1) a small percentage of Baptists are members of the American Baptist Churches USA, which is a Mainline Protestant denomination, (2) Evangelicals attending nondenominational churches would most likely select "Other Christian," and (3) there are splinter denominations of "Methodists, Lutherans, Presbyterians, and Episcopalians" that identify with the larger, neo-Evangelical movement. Mainliners, whose commitment to good deeds far exceeds their concern for doctrinal conformity, includes everyone else who is a "Protestant," "Baptist," or "Other Christian" and not identified as an Evangelical. Thankfully, Catholics and the religiously unaffiliated, "Nones," were easy to identify, and "Other Religion" became the catchall for those responding Mormon, Jewish, Muslim, Hindu, Buddhist, Eastern Orthodox, or "Other non-Christian, please specify."

Additional In-Depth Interviews

In order to hear from Nones, as well as Nominal and Estranged Christians, we relied on qualitative interviews from separate research projects with young adults. Clydesdale's interviews were conducted between 2006 and 2010 with 125 young adults, interviewed in person during their junior or senior year of college, then re-interviewed by phone more than a year after they had graduated from college. Twenty-five of these young adults were religiously unaffiliated (Nones). Fully 98% (123) of these young adults were retained for the second-wave interviews, including all twenty-five Nones. Sixty interviewees attended campuses that had received grants from the Lilly Endowment to foster exploration of vocation among undergraduates. Sixty-five interviewees attended campuses that had not received such grants but were in many ways comparable to the campuses that had received these grants. These wide-ranging interviews were part of the data collected and reported in Clydesdale's *The Purposeful Graduate: Why Colleges Must Talk to Students About Vocation*. Those seeking further information on these interviews, including the questions asked, are directed to that book's methodological appendix.[5]

Garces-Foley's study of religiously unaffiliated students at Marymount University began in 2014. She recruited twenty-four students—primarily undergraduates—via fliers and social networks to participate in one-to-two-hour interviews conducted by her research assistant, April Westmark.

Clydesdale and Garces-Foley used Atlas.ti to code interview transcripts. Chapter 6 draws from interviews with forty-nine Nones from both data sets.

NSAT Questionnaire

The first 29 items required Likert agree/disagree responses (Strongly Agree, Agree, Disagree, Strongly Disagree). These items were placed on a grid, and their order was randomized.

1. I have a lot of friends who do volunteer work regularly.
2. I have a lot of friends who attend church regularly.
3. I have friends, but no really close friends.
4. I often feel lonely.
5. There's not much that individuals can do to help others.

6. I check social media sites (like Facebook) several times each day.
7. We have an obligation to help others—even if it means personal sacrifice.
8. I would be very unhappy if I never marry.
9. Having children is very important to me.
10. Most churches and synagogues today are not concerned enough with social justice.
11. Most churches and synagogues today are effective in helping people find meaning in life.
12. An individual should arrive at his or her own religious beliefs independent of any churches or synagogues.
13. Most mainstream religion is irrelevant to the needs and concerns of most people my age.
14. When I have kids, I definitely plan to join a church.
15. Too many religious people in this country these days are negative, angry, and judgmental.
16. As a child, my religious faith was very important to me.
17. I try to include practices from other religious traditions in my own spirituality.
18. In the last two years I have been invited by others to attend religious services with them.
19. Regardless of whether or not I now attend any religious services, I think of myself as part of a particular religion, denomination, or church.
20. I sometimes feel so connected to nature that everything seems to be part of one living organism.
21. I often feel a strong spiritual or emotional connection with all the people around me.
22. I used to believe in a personal God, but now I think of God as a spiritual force.
23. Any art or music can be a way to communicate one's spirituality.
24. All I want out of life is a job that pays well and a partner I can trust.
25. My deep passion is greater social justice.
26. I don't think my gender identity, or anyone else's, matters very much.
27. Making a lot of money is very important to my happiness.
28. To have a meaningful life, you need to help other people.
29. I know my life has purpose and meaning.

Remaining items had varying response options, and some were restricted to those giving specific answers to previous items.

30. Over the past three years, have you become:
    1) More religious
    2) Less religious
    3) Stayed about the same
    4) I am not religious
31. In the last year, how much, if at all, have you had doubts about whether your religious beliefs are true?
    1) Many doubts
    2) Some doubts
    3) A few doubts
    4) No doubts
32. In the last year, how much, if at all, have you had doubts about being nonreligious?
    1) Many doubts
    2) Some doubts
    3) A few doubts
    4) No doubts
33. How important has it been to you as an adult to grow in your spiritual life? Would you say
    1) Extremely important
    2) Very important
    3) Fairly important
    4) Not very important
    5) Not at all important
34. How often, if ever, do you meditate?
    1) Never
    2) Less than once a month
    3) One or two times a month
    4) About once a week
    5) A few times a week
    6) About once a day
    7) Many times a day
35. How often do you attend religious services?
    1) More than once a week
    2) Once a week

3) Once or twice a month
4) A few times a year
5) Once a year or less
6) Never

36. In the last year, how much, if at all, did you help homeless people, needy neighbors, family, friends, or other people in need, directly not through organizations (includes giving money)
    1) A lot
    2) Some
    3) A little
    4) None
37. Do you believe in God or not or are you unsure?
    1) Yes
    2) No
    3) Unsure
38. Which of the following comes closest to your own view of God?
    1) God is a personal being involved in the lives of people today
    2) God created the world, but is NOT involved in the world now
    3) God is not personal, but something like a cosmic life force
39. Which of the following comes closest to your own views about religion?
    1) Only one religion is true
    2) Many religions may be true
    3) There is very little truth in any religion
40. Some people think that it is OK to pick and choose their religious beliefs without having to accept the teachings of their religious faith as a whole.
    1) Agree
    2) Disagree
41. How important or unimportant is religious faith in shaping how you live your daily life?
    1) Extremely important
    2) Very
    3) Somewhat
    4) Not very
    5) Not important at all

42. How distant or close to God do you feel most of the time?
    1) Extremely distant
    2) Very distant
    3) Somewhat distant
    4) Somewhat close
    5) Very close
    6) Extremely close
43. How often, if ever, do you pray by yourself alone?
    1) Never
    2) Less than once a month
    3) One or two times a month
    4) About once a week
    5) A few times a week
    6) About once a day
    7) Many times a day
44. How often if at all do you think about the meaning of life?
    1) Very often
    2) Fairly often
    3) Sometimes
    4) Rarely
    5) Never
45. In what year did you receive your highest educational degree? [write in year]
46. Have you ever received unemployment benefits?
    1) Yes
    2) No
47. Which was the primary or most important place of your education?
    1) Public
    2) Secular Private
    3) Religious Private
    4) Stopped going to school/dropped out
    5) Magnet or charter school
    6) Home schooled
    7) Other

The GfK Group also provided us with responses to their religion question, which in addition to GfK-supplied demographic indicators and the proprietary data we purchased about our respondent's voting and involvement in political, voluntary, and civic activities, played a crucial role in our analyses:

What is your religion?

1) Baptist—any denomination
2) Protestant (e.g., Methodist, Lutheran, Presbyterian, Episcopal)
3) Catholic
4) Mormon
5) Jewish
6) Muslim
7) Hindu
8) Buddhist
9) Pentecostal
10) Eastern Orthodox
11) Other Christian
12) Other non-Christian, please specify
13) None

Congregational Studies Interview Schedule

1. Participant Data Form
   a. I see that your primary occupation is ______. How do you like it?
   b. What are your plans and goals for the future?
   c. [If in a committed relationship] How did you meet your ______?
      i. What is her/his religious background?
2. On Religion
   a. What religious influences did you have growing up? Did you experience these things as positive or negative as a child?
   b. Have you ever been involved with a religious group other than this church?
      i. [If yes] Who/what/when/how long? Why did you leave the group?
      ii. [If no] Why not?
   c. If someone asks you what religion you are now—how would you respond?

3. This Church
   a. When did you first visit this church?
   b. How did you learn about it and decide to come?
   c. Was there anything going on in your life at that time that prompted you to check it out?
   d. Tell me about that first visit—what were your first impressions?
   e. What drew you to keep coming back?
   f. What makes this church different from other churches you've been involved with?
   g. What's your relationship to the church now—are you a member?
      i. [If a member] How did you decide to make that commitment?
      ii. What were the preparation steps?
   h. [For long-time member]: I'd like to learn more about the church history. Can you tell me about some of the changes you've witnessed since _____? How do you feel about those changes?
   i. How did your friends and family outside the church respond to your coming?
   j. Are you involved with any other religious groups in addition to this church? Describe.
   k. Have you made any changes in your life as a result of being involved with this church?
      i. [If yes] Could you describe a few of these for me?
4. Worship
   a. How often do you attend worship services here?
   b. How would you describe the worship service to someone who's never been here?
   c. How would you characterize the different worship services?
      i. Which service do you usually attend and why?
   d. [For long-time members] In what ways has the style of worship changed since you started coming?
      i. Any idea what led to those changes?
      ii. How do you feel about these changes?
   e. What do you enjoy most about the worship services?
   f. What would you change if you could?
   g. Do you think the worship service appeals broadly to young adults 18–29?
      i. [If no] What changes need to be made for that to happen?

h. Many congregations have disagreements about the style of music used in worship services: has that happened here?
  i. [If yes] Can you tell me about those disagreements and how they were resolved?
i. Have there been conflicts over the use of technology or other aspects of the worship service?
  i. [If yes] Can you tell me about those disagreements and how they were resolved?

5. Church Teachings and Ministries
  a. Of all the ministries it offers, which do you think is the most important?
  b. What is the most important message/teaching offered by the minister(s)?
  c. Do you think this message would resonate with young adults in particular? How so/why not?
  d. In terms of your faith journey, in what ways have the church's teachings been helpful to you?
  e. Have any of the church's teachings been challenging for you to accept? Please explain.
    i. [If yes] How does that affect your relationship to the church?
  f. Do the ministers ever preach about issues of gender?
    i. [If yes] Who? When? What did they say about it?
    ii. [If yes] Do you agree with what was said about it?
      a) [If no] How does that affect your relationship to the church?
  g. Does the topic of gender come up outside of worship services in other church contexts?
    i. [If yes] Who? When? What did they say about it?
    ii. [If yes] Do you agree with what was said about it?
      a) [If no] Did you or others feel comfortable expressing disagreement?
        1. [If yes] Can you describe what happened?
        2. How does that affect your relationship to the church?
  h. What do you think about having certain roles/groups open only to men?
    i. [if disagree] How does that affect your relationship to the church?

- i. Do the ministers ever preach about issues of sexual morality?
  - i. [If yes] What do they say about it?
    - a) Can you remember a specific sermon? Who? When? What?
  - ii. [If yes] Do you agree with what the ministers are saying?
    - a) [If no] How does that affect your relationship to the church?
- j. Does the topic of sexual morality come up outside of sermons in other church contexts?
  - i. [If yes] What do they say about it?
    - a) Can you remember a specific example? Who? When? What?
  - ii. [If yes] Do you agree with what was said about it?
    - a) [If no] Did you or others feel comfortable expressing disagreement?
      1. [If yes] Can you describe what happened?
      2. How does that affect your relationship to the church?
- k. Are you aware of any church ministries that address any of these issues?
  - i. [If yes] What do you think of those efforts?
  - ii. [If no] Do you think church members should be involved in addressing social issues?
    - a) How?
- l. Do the ministers ever preach about any social issues?
  - i. [If yes] Who? When? What did they say about it?
  - ii. [If yes] Do you agree with what was said about it?
    - a) [If no] How have you dealt with your disagreement on that?
- m. Do these kinds of issues come up outside of sermons in other church contexts?
  - i. [If yes] Who? When? What did they say about it?
  - ii. [If yes] Do you agree with what was said about it? Did you or others feel comfortable expressing disagreement? Describe what happened.
- n. Do the ministers ever address political issues from the pulpit?
  - i. [If yes] Who? When? What did they say about it?
  - ii. [If yes] How did you feel about what was said?
    - a) [If disagreed] How have you dealt with your disagreement on that?

i. Do these kinds of issues come up outside of sermons in other church contexts? [If yes] Who? When? What did they say about it?
ii. [If yes] Do you agree with what was said about it? Did you or others feel comfortable expressing disagreement? Describe what happened.

o. Do you know anyone who has left because they disagreed with anything about the church's ministry or teaching?
   i. [If yes] Please tell me about why they left.
p. Do you think any of the church teachings or ministries are especially challenging for young adults?

6. Fellowship and Activities
   a. What kinds of things are you involved with?
   b. How did you get involved in ___________? What appeals to you about it?
   c. Are you in any leadership roles?
      i. [If yes] Please tell me how that came about and how that has been going.
      ii. [If no] Would you like to be?
   d. How many hours per week are you typically active in church related activities?
   e. Do you support the church financially?
   f. Would you like to be more involved in the church?
      i. [If yes] In what ways? What keeps you from getting involved more?
   g. How much have you learned about the way the church works?
   h. Please tell me about your friendships at the church: how many close friends do you have here?
      i. Are they similar in age to you, older or younger?
   i. Many Americans like to volunteer in their local community, I'm wondering how you think it is different when people volunteer to help the local community through a church group?
   j. How much interaction is there between the 18–29 group and those who are older than them?
      i. [If not much] What could be done to encourage more interaction between age groups?

k. How many young adults do you think are in leadership roles in the church?
    i. Which roles are they in?
l. In terms of attracting young adults to the church, do you think it makes a difference to have young adults in leadership roles? Explain.
m. Are there any obstacles in this church that keep young adults from getting more involved in the church especially as leaders?

7. Overall

    a. What makes you most proud of your church?
    b. If you knew a young adult who you thought might be interested in a church, how would you talk up this church to him or her?
    c. What could the church do to attract more young adults?
    d. Are there any obstacles that keep the church from moving forward to reach its mission?
    e. What do church leaders need to know about young adults in order to better reach and engage this demographic?

NOTES

CHAPTER 1

1. Nancy Tatom Ammerman, *Sacred Stories, Spiritual Tribes: Finding Religion in Everyday Life* (New York: Oxford University Press, 2013).
2. Pew Forum, *"Nones" on the Rise: One-in-Five Adults Have No Religious Affiliation* (Washington, DC: Religion and Public Life Report, October 9, 2012), http://www.pewforum.org/Unaffiliated/nones-on-the-rise.aspx.
3. For an introduction to this diverse scholarly literature, see: Patricia Herzog, ed., *The Sociology of Emerging Adulthood: Studying Youth in the Context of Public Issues* (San Diego, CA: Cognella Academic, 2017); Jeffrey Jensen Arnett and Jennifer Lynn Tanner, eds., *Emerging Adults in America: Coming of Age in the 21st Century* (Washington, DC: American Psychological Association, 2006); Christian Smith et al., *Lost in Transition: The Dark Side of Emerging Adulthood* (New York: Oxford University Press, 2011); Christian Smith with Patricia Snell, *Souls in Transition: The Religious and Spiritual Lives of Emerging Adults* (New York: Oxford University Press, 2009); Richard Arum and Josipa Roksa, *Aspiring Adults Adrift: Tentative Transitions of College Graduates* (Chicago: University of Chicago Press, 2014).
4. See, for example, Sally Koslow, *Slouching Toward Adulthood: Observations for the Not-So-Empty Nest* (New York: Viking, 2012); Jean M. Twenge, *Generation Me: Why Today's Young Americans Are More Confident, Assertive, Entitled—and More Miserable Than Ever Before*, rev. ed. (New York: Atria, 2014) and *iGen: Why Today's Super-Connected Kids Are Growing Up Less Rebellious, More Tolerant, Less Happy —and Completely Unprepared for Adulthood* (New York: Atria, 2017); Gail Gross, "Millennials: The Lost Generation?" *Huffington Post*, November 15, 2016, https://www.huffingtonpost.com/entry/millennials-the-lost-generation_us_582aaabde4b0852d9ec21ca9.

5. Robin Marantz Henig, "What Is It About 20-Somethings? Why Are So Many People in their 20s Taking So Long to Grow Up?" *New York Times Magazine*, August 18, 2010.
6. The NSAT included responses from forty-seven Mormons, thirty-one Jews, seven Muslims, nine Hindus, fourteen Buddhists, five Eastern Orthodox, and forty-seven "Other non-Christian religion" twentysomethings (see the Methodological Appendix for more information about the NSAT and its available religion questions). Alas, there are too few respondents for any one religion to produce generalizable analyses, but we do report findings from these "other religion" twentysomethings as whole, in Chapters 2 and 7.
7. See the Methodological Appendix for more information about our research methods.
8. Alexis de Tocqueville, *Democracy in America*, trans. and ed. Harvey C. Mansfield and Delba Winthrop (Chicago: University of Chicago Press, 2000). See also Robert N. Bellah, Richard Madsen, William M. Sullivan, Ann Swidler, and Steven M. Tipton, *Habits of the Heart: Individualism and Commitment in American Life* (Berkeley: University of California Press, 1985).
9. Kim Parker, "The Boomerang Generation: Feeling OK about Living with Mom and Dad," Pew Research Center Social & Demographic Trends, March 15, 2012, http://www.pewsocialtrends.org/2012/03/15/the-boomerang-generation/. See also Richard Settersten and Barbara E. Ray, *Not Quite Adults: Why 20-Somethings Are Choosing a Slower Path to Adulthood, and Why It's Good for Everyone* (New York: Bantam Books Trade Paperback, 2010).
10. Barry Schwartz and Ken Kliban, *The Paradox of Choice: Why More Is Less* (New York: Harper Collins, 2004).
11. Frank F. Furstenberg Jr., Sheela Kennedy, Vonnie C. McLoyd, Ruben G. Rumbaut, and Richard A. Settersen Jr., "Growing Up Is Harder to Do," *Contexts* 3, no. 3 (Aug. 2004): 33–41.
12. Tim Clydesdale, *The Purposeful Graduate: Why Colleges Must Talk to Students about Vocation* (Chicago: University of Chicago Press, 2015), 202.
13. We are indebted to the work of Manuel Castells, Robert Wuthnow, Wade Clark Roof, and Ann Swidler for this claim. Manuel Castells, *The Rise of the Network Society*, vol. 1 of *The Information Age: Economy, Society, and Culture* (Malden, MA: Blackwell, 1996); Robert Wuthnow, *After Heaven: Spirituality in America Since the 1950s* (Berkeley: University of California Press, 1998); Wade Clark Roof, *Spiritual Marketplace: Baby Boomers and the Remaking of American Religion* (Princeton, NJ: Princeton University Press, 1999); Ann Swidler, "Culture in Action: Symbols and Strategies," *American Sociological Review* 51, no. 2 (1986): 273–286.

14. Katherine S. Newman. "Ties that Bind: Cultural Interpretations of Delayed Adulthood in Western Europe and Japan," *Sociological Forum* 23, no. 4 (Dec. 2008): 645–669.

CHAPTER 2

1. The term "emerging adulthood" was coined by psychologist Jeffrey Jensen Arnett in his book of the same title (Oxford University Press, 2004). Arnett argues that emerging adulthood is a new developmental stage that follows adolescence, precedes young adulthood, and is completed by most by age 25 though it can extend into the late 20s. Scholars since Arnett widely agree that emerging adulthood extends to age 29, and developmental psychologists have debated whether this is a new developmental stage and whether it is a global phenomenon or restricted to First World nations. We are not psychologists and remain agnostic about emerging adulthood's status as a distinct developmental stage, but we agree with Arnett that the transition to adulthood has steadily transformed and use his term, emerging adulthood, and young adulthood interchangeably. For an introduction to the sociological literature on emerging adulthood, see Richard A. Settersten Jr., Frank F. Furstenberg, and Ruben G. Rumbaut, eds., *On the Frontier of Adulthood: Theory, Research, and Public Policy* (Chicago: University of Chicago Press, 2005). And for a glimpse into the breadth of this phenomenon across the First World, see Katherine S. Newman, "Ties That Bind: Cultural Interpretations of Delayed Adulthood in Western Europe and Japan," *Sociological Forum* 23, no. 4 (Dec. 2008): 645–669.
2. See the Methodological Appendix for details about the NSAT. The GSS is a publicly available dataset, funded chiefly by the National Science Foundation and administered annually or biannually since 1972 by NORC. All statistical analyses are by the authors. See Tom W. Smith, Michael Davern, Jeremy Freese, and Michael Hout, General Social Surveys, 1972–2016 [machine-readable data file]/Principal Investigator, Smith, Tom W.; Co-Principal Investigators, Peter V. Marsden and Michael Hout; Sponsored by National Science Foundation. NORC ed. Chicago: NORC, 2017. 1 data file (62,466 logical records) + 1 codebook (3,689 pp.).—(National Data Program for the Social Sciences, no. 24).
3. See Chapter 1, note 4.
4. For a quick overview of this phenomena, see Penny Edgell, "Work and Careers" essay, originally written for our Changing Spirituality of Emerging Adults project, and now archived at Catholic University of America: "The Changing Spirituality of Emerging Adults Project Collection." An inventory of the Changing Spirituality of Emerging Adults Project Collection at the

American Catholic History Research Center and University Archives, https://cuislandora.wrlc.org/islandora/object/achc-cseapc:11. See also Jacob S. Hacker, *The Great Risk Shift: The Assault on American Jobs, Families, Health Care, and Retirement—and How You Can Fight Back* (New York: Oxford University Press, 2006).

5. "The aspiration to attain a college degree has become nearly universal among high school students," report Jenny Nagaoka, Melissa Roderick, and Vanessa Coca, "Barriers to College Attainment: Lessons from Chicago," Consortium on Chicago School Research at the University of Chicago, 2009, https://consortium.uchicago.edu/sites/default/files/publications/CAP_ChicagoSchools-1.pdf. And fully 75% of recent high school graduates are enrolled in post-secondary education according to Joel McFarland et al., *Condition of Education 2017*, National Center of Education Statistics, 2017, https://nces.ed.gov/pubs2017/2017144.pdf.
6. The overall completion rate for first-time seekers of four-year degrees who began at four-year institutions, from the entering cohort of 2011, was 66.7%. For first-time seekers of two-year degrees who began at two-year institutions, from the same cohort, the completion rate was 37.7%, with a continuation to four-year degree completion rate of 14.7%. Doug Shapiro et al., *Completing College: A National View of Student Completion Rates—Fall 2011 Cohort*, Signature Report No. 14, Herndon, VA: National Student Clearinghouse Research Center, December, 2017, https://nscresearchcenter.org/wp-content/uploads/SignatureReport14_Final.pdf. We know, however, that "over 75 percent of full-time community college freshmen claim that they plan on earning a baccalaureate or higher degree," ERIC Clearinghouse for Junior Colleges, Los Angeles, CA, "Assessing Student Degree Aspirations," ERIC Digest, https://www.ericdigests.org/pre-922/degree.htm. If we take 75% of the 766,297 first-time entering cohort of 2011 at two-year institutions that likely aspired to a four-year degree as our denominator, their four-year degree completion rate becomes 19.6%, and the overall four-year degree completion rate for the entering cohort of 2011 becomes 53.6%. In short, 46% of those who aspire to a four-year degree and who enroll in a two- or four-year degree program do not attain a four-year degree within six years of matriculation. That is approximately 959,344 individuals from the entering cohort of 2011 alone (authors' estimate).
7. The U.S. median annual earnings for bachelor's degree holders was $48,130 in 1995 and $49,940 in 2014 (using 2015 dollars); see Table 502.30, "Median annual earnings of full-time year-round workers 25 to 34 years old and full-time year-round workers as a percentage of the labor force, by sex, race/ethnicity, and educational attainment: Selected years, 1995 through 2015," National Center for Education Statistics, https://nces.ed.gov/programs/digest/d16/tables/dt16_502.30.asp. For rental housing prices

during recessions, see Jann Swanson, "Rental Market Is Clear Winner in Recession Aftermath," *Mortgage News Daily*, July 13, 2015, http://www.mortgagenewsdaily.com/07132015_rental_market.asp. For further insight into the lives of university graduates and the intense competition to find work, see Liz Alderman, "Young and Educated in Europe, but Desperate for Jobs," *New York Times*, Nov. 15, 2013, http://www.nytimes.com/2013/11/16/world/europe/youth-unemployement-in-europe.html.

8. See Christian Smith et al., *Lost in Transition: The Dark Side of Emerging Adulthood* (New York: Oxford University Press, 2011); Jean M. Twenge, *iGen: Why Today's Super-Connected Kids Are Growing Up Less Rebellious, More Tolerant, Less Happy—and Completely Unprepared for Adulthood* (New York: Atria, 2017); Donna Freitas, *Sex and the Soul: Juggling Sexuality, Spirituality, Romance, and Religion on America's College Campuses* (New York: Oxford University Press, 2008); Claire Cain Miller, "The Divorce Surge Is Over, but the Myth Lives On," *New York Times*, December 2, 2014, https://www.nytimes.com/2014/12/02/upshot/the-divorce-surge-is-over-but-the-myth-lives-on.html.
9. This is still the case, even ten years after this claim was originally made, according to Jeffrey Jensen Arnett, *Emerging Adulthood: The Winding Road from the Late Teens Through the Twenties*, 2nd ed. (New York: Oxford University Press, 2014).
10. Joseph O. Baker and Buster G. Smith, *American Secularism: Cultural Contours of Nonreligious Belief Systems* (New York: New York University Press, 2015) use the term "cosmic belief system" to signify a continuum that runs from zealous religiosity to thorough secularity, on which one can locate various belief systems concerned with "basic facts about the nature of the universe and 'how the world works' " (p. 8). While this approach has many merits, the term is not widely known and our use of it would introduce confusion rather than clarity.
11. We created our categories of Evangelical and Mainline Protestants using multiple factors, as denomination alone is an insufficient indicator. There are, for example, Presbyterians who affirm Calvin's theology as originally penned in the early sixteenth century, and Baptists who affirm many religions as true. For details, see the methodological appendix.
12. In the NSAT, 36% of twentysomething respondents age 24 and over had completed their bachelor's degree.
13. See Andrew M. Greeley, *The Catholic Myth: The Behavior and Beliefs of American Catholics* (New York: Touchstone, 1997); Christian Smith with Patricia Snell, *Souls in Transition: The Religious and Spiritual Lives of Emerging Adults* (New York: Oxford University Press, 2009); Jeremy Uecker, Mark Regnerus, and Margaret Vaaler, "Losing My Religion: The Social Sources of Religious Decline Among Emerging Adults," *Social Forces* 85, no.

4 (2007): 1–26; Perry Glanzer, Jonathan P. Hill, and Todd Ream, "Changing Souls: Higher Education's Influence upon the Religious Lives of Emerging Adults," in *Emerging Adults' Religiousness and Spirituality: Meaning-Making in an Age of Transition*, ed. Carolyn McNamara Barry and Mona M. Abo-Zena, 152–170 (New York: Oxford University Press, 2014).

14. See, for example, Ed Stetzer, "The Real Reason Young Adults Drop Out of Church," *Christianity Today*. December 1, 2014, http://www.christianitytoday.com/edstetzer/2014/december/real-reasons-young-adults-drop-out-of-church.html; Rachel Held Evans, "Want Millennials Back in the Pews? Stop Trying to Make Church 'Cool,'" *Washington Post*, April 30, 2015, https://www.washingtonpost.com/opinions/jesus-doesnt-tweet/2015/04/30/fb07ef1a-ed01-11e4-8666-a1d756d0218e_story.html?utm_term=.8af89b252430; Zac David, "Can the Catholic Church Keep Millennials from Passing It By?," *America Magazine*, October 19, 2017, https://www.americamagazine.org/faith/2017/10/19/can-catholic-church-keep-millennials-passing-it); Julie Bourbon, "Study Asks: Why Are Young Catholics Going, Going, Gone?," *National Catholic Reporter*, January 22, 2018, https://www.ncronline.org/news/parish/study-asks-why-are-young-catholics-going-going-gone.

15. See C. Kirk Hadaway, Penny Long Marler, and Mark Chaves, "Overreporting Church Attendance in America: Evidence That Demands the Same Verdict," *American Sociological Review* 63, no. 1 (Feb. 1998): 122–130; "Perception," in *International Encyclopedia of the Social Sciences*, ed. David L. Sills. vol. 11 (New York: Macmillan, 1968), 527–581.

16. See Baker and Smith, *American Secularism*.

17. See Kristine Crane, "8 Ways Meditation Can Improve Your Life," *Huffington Post*, updated December 6, 2017, https://www.huffingtonpost.com/2014/09/19/meditation-benefits_n_5842870.html.

18. Sixty-three percent of Evangelical participants in the NSAT indicated their religion was "very" or "extremely important in their "daily life." Some 33% of Catholic, 30% of Mainline Protestant, and 5% of unaffiliated twentysomethings reported the same.

19. See Smith with Snell, *Souls in Transition* and Robert Wuthnow, *After the Baby Boomers: How Twenty- and Thirty-Somethings Are Shaping the Future of American Religion* (Princeton, NJ: Princeton University Press, 2010).

20. Sixty-three percent of Evangelical, 8% of Mainline, 23% of Catholic, and 34% of other religion twentysomethings affirmed "only one religion is true." Sixty-one percent of Evangelical, 46% of Mainline Protestant, and 44% of Catholic twentysomethings said they had "no doubts in the last year about the truth of my religious beliefs" (authors' analysis of NSAT 2013).

21. Seventy-one percent of Evangelical and Mainline Protestants alike agreed that "as a child, my religious faith was very important." Sixty-six percent

of Catholic and 24% of unaffiliated twentysomethings agreed to the same statement (authors' analysis of NSAT 2013).

22. Sixty-eight percent of Evangelical twentysomethings disagreed that "most mainstream religion is irrelevant to people my age"; respective percentages for Mainline, Catholic, other religion, and unaffiliated twentysomethings were 61%, 63%, 50%, and 39%. Sixty-nine percent of Evangelical twentysomethings disagreed that "most churches are not concerned enough with social justice"; respective percentages for Mainline, Catholic, other religion, and unaffiliated twentysomethings were 73%, 68%, 64%, and 46% (authors' analyses of NSAT 2013).
23. See Rachel Held Evans, *Searching for Sunday: Loving, Leaving, and Finding the Church* (Nashville, TN: Thomas Nelson, 2015); David Kinnaman and Gabe Lyons *Unchristian: What a New Generation Really Thinks About Christianity . . . and Why It Matters* (Grand Rapids, MI: Baker Books, 2012).
24. Fifty-six percent of Evangelical, 49% of Mainline Protestant, 51% of Catholic, 56% of other religion, and 29% of unaffiliated twentysomethings agreed "I often feel a strong spiritual or emotional connection with all the people around me" (authors' analysis of NSAT).
25. There is scholarly precedent for this view. Lynn Schofield Clark's *From Angels to Aliens: Teenagers, the Media, and the Supernatural* (New York: Oxford University Press 2003) makes the claim that television shows about supernatural phenomena seeded teen interests in the same.
26. Many scholars include Reconstructionist as the fourth denomination, but at 1% Pew considers them too small: "Most Jews by religion identify with either Reform (40%), Conservative (22%) or Orthodox Judaism (12%), with just 19% saying they belong to no particular denomination," *A Portrait of Jewish Americans: Findings from a Pew Research Center Survey of U.S. Jews* (Washington, DC: Pew Research Center's Religion and Public Life Project, 2013), http://www.pewforum.org/2013/10/01/jewish-american-beliefs-attitudes-culture-survey/.
27. See note 1 this chapter.
28. See Ed Stetzer, "No, American Christianity Is Not Dead," CNN, May 16, 2015, http://www.cnn.com/2015/05/16/living/christianity-american-dead/index.html. Alas, we cannot separate Evangelical and Mainline Protestants in all years of the GSS, nor match our Protestant categories with GSS's Protestant category, so we treat them here as a single (but heterogeneous) category.
29. See Gaston Espinosa, "Demographic and Religious Changes Among Hispanics of the United States," *Social Compass* 51, no. 3 (2004): 303–320; Marilynn Johnson, "'The Quiet Revival': New Immigrants and the Transformation of Christianity in Greater Boston," *Religion and American Culture* 24, no. 2 (Summer 2014): 231.

30. Benjamin Franklin and Albert H. Smyth, "Letter to Jean-Baptiste Leroy on November 13, 1789," *The Writings of Benjamin Franklin*, vol. 10 (New York: Macmillan, 1905–1907), 69, http://www.worldcat.org/title/writings-of-benjamin-franklin/oclc/123578841.
31. See Merril Silverstein and Vern L. Bengtson, "Return to Religion? Predictors of Religious Change Among Baby-Boomers in Their Transition to Later Life," *Journal of Population Ageing* (Dec. 2017): 1–15; James R. Peacock and Margaret M. Poloma, "Religiosity and Life Satisfaction Across the Life Course," *Social Indicators Research* 48, no. 3 (Nov. 1999): 321–345.

CHAPTER 3

1. Michael exemplifies a view that Christian Smith and Melinda Denton call religion "as a very nice thing" in *Soul Searching: The Religious and Spiritual Lives of American Teenagers* (New York: Oxford University Press, 2005), 124, and author Tim Clydesdale has likened to bland "vegetables" on the buffet table of life after high school in *The First Year Out: Understanding American Teens After High School* (Chicago: University of Chicago Press, 2007), 57.
2. Jerome P. Baggett, *Sense of the Faithful: How American Catholics Live their Faith* (New York: Oxford University Press, 2009).
3. See Christian Smith et al., *Young Catholic America: Emerging Adults In, Out of, and Gone from the Church* (New York: Oxford University Press, 2014); Christian Smith with Patricia Snell, *Souls in Transition: The Religious and Spiritual Lives of Emerging Adults* (New York: Oxford University Press, 2009).
4. We derived this estimate as follows: the 2010 U.S. Census reported 42.7M twentysomethings, of which 7.6M would be Roman Catholic (18% of respondents to the NSAT), of which 3.2M would report attending Mass at least monthly (42% of Catholics in the NSAT).
5. For further information about our research methods, see the Methodological Appendix.
6. Lisa Ferguson, "Defining Dynamic Orthodoxy," *Franciscan Way Magazine*, Autumn 2005, 14.
7. We interviewed nineteen young adults at St. Ann's ranging from 20 to 35 years of age (median age 25).
8. Donna Freitas, *Sex and the Soul: Juggling Sexuality, Spirituality, Romance and Religion on America's College Campuses*, rev. ed. (New York: Oxford University Press, 2015).
9. At St. Peter's we interviewed twenty-five young adults between 20 and 35 years of age (median age 22).

10. FOCUS is an acronym for "Fellowship of Catholic University Students," and it is a missional outreach on 125 American college and university campuses. See https://www.focus.org/.
11. See Kathleen Garces-Foley, "Parishes as Homes and Hubs for Young Adult Catholics," in *American Parishes: Remaking Local Catholicism*, ed. Gary Adler, Tricia Bruce, and Brian Stark (New York City: Fordham University Press, 2019).
12. We interviewed twenty-four young adults in the two DC-area dioceses including eighteen who belong to one of these four parishes (age range 23–35; median age 29).
13. Those seeking a comprehensive analysis of Catholic young adults are directed to Smith et al., *Young Catholic America*, from which we adopted our "Nominal" and "Estranged" labels—though we applied different criteria to create these types.
14. We group Catholic twentysomethings, then, from the perspective of their religious affiliation (acknowledging that individual Catholics may, and some surely will, have a different view of their religiosity). Attendance at religious service and importance of adult spiritual growth have a Chronbach's alpha of .78, indicating substantial overlap in their variation.
15. See Baggett, *Sense of the Faithful*; Smith et al., *Young Catholic America*.
16. Cross-tabulations of the NSAT revealed no significant differences (via Chi-square or gamma statistics) among Active, Nominal, and Estranged Catholic twentysomethings in often feeling lonely (c. 22%), daily use of social media (c. 62% "check social media sites several times each day"), sense of one's life having purpose and meaning (c. 88% report knowing "my life has purpose and meaning"), being "very unhappy" if they never marry (c. 50%), agreeing "I don't think my gender identity, or anyone else's, matters very much" (c. 59%), reporting feelings of spiritual connectedness (c. 51% "often feel a strong spiritual or emotional connection with all the people around me"), seeing art and music as similarly valid means of spiritual expression (c. 82%), and incorporating practices from other religious traditions into their own spirituality (c. 33%). There is not space sufficient to relay all results in figures; hence some NSAT results are reported in the text or notes only.
17. See also discussion of American individualism in Chapter 1.
18. According to Smith et al., *Young Catholic America*, 152, about 9% of the U.S. emerging adult population are "family Catholics" or "raised Catholic" but do not themselves identify as Catholic.

CHAPTER 4

1. See, for example, James Davison Hunter, *Evangelicalism: The Coming Generation* (Chicago: University of Chicago Press, 1987), or Wade Clark

Roof and William McKinney, *American Mainline Religion: Its Changing Shape and Future* (New Brunswick, NJ: Rutgers University Press, 1987).

2. See Christian Smith with Patricia Snell, *Souls in Transition: The Religious and Spiritual Lives of Emerging Adults* (New York: Oxford University Press, 2009).
3. Nancy T. Ammerman, "Golden Rule Christianity: Lived Religion in the American Mainstream," in *Lived Religion in America: Toward a History of Practice*, ed. David D. Hall (Princeton, NJ: Princeton University Press, 1997), 196–216. See also Roof and McKinney, *American Mainline Religion*.
4. David A. Roozen, "Oldline Protestantism: Pockets of Vitality Within a Continuing Stream of Decline," Hartford Institute for Religion Research Working Paper 1104.1, Hartford, CT: Hartford Seminary, 2004, http://hirr.hartsem.edu/bookshelf/roozen_article5.html.
5. We derived this estimate as follows: the 2010 U.S. Census reported 42.7M twentysomethings, of which 5.978M would be Mainline Protestant (14% according to the NSAT), of which 2.092M would report attending worship at least twice monthly (35% of Mainline Protestants according to the NSAT).
6. There are, to be sure, Evangelical splinter groups of Methodists, Lutherans, Presbyterians, and Episcopalians. We applied a couple of filters to make sure Mainliners in the NSAT were truly Mainline Protestant. See the Methodological Appendix for more information.
7. To be precise, 84% of twentysomething Mainliners agree with this view. The freedom to follow one's own conscience theologically is a distinctively Mainline Protestant view (see Roof and McKinney, *American Mainline Religion*), and its broad embrace by Active, Nominal, and Estranged Mainliners confirms their identity as affiliates of Mainline Protestantism.
8. Sixty-four percent of twentysomething Mainliners, on average, "check social media sites (like Facebook) several times each day."
9. Thirty-eight percent of Active Mainliners, 21% of Nominal Mainliners, and 22% of Estranged Mainliners agree "I have friends, but no really close friends" (Chi-square = 5.231, p = .073); 48% of Active Mainliners, 43% of Nominal Mainliners, and 29% of Estranged Mainliners agree "I often feel lonely" (Chi-square = 2.679, p = .262).
10. Forty-eight percent Active Mainliners, 64% of Nominal Mainliners, and 74% of Estranged Mainliners agree "I don't think my gender identity, or anyone else's, matters very much" (Chi-square = 5.458, p = .065).
11. Ninety percent of Active Mainliners, 92% of Nominal Mainliners, and 79% of Estranged Mainliners agree "any art or music can be a way to communicate one's spirituality" (Chi-square = 4.139, p = .126).
12. Thirty-four percent of Active Mainliners, 24% of Nominal Mainliners, and 14% of Estranged Mainliners agree "most churches and synagogues

today are not concerned enough with social justice" (Chi-square = 3.556, p = .168).

13. Terrell L. Strayhorn, *College Students' Sense of Belonging: A Key to Educational Success for All Students* (New York: Routledge, 2012); Alan Seidman, ed., *College Student Retention: Formula for Student Success*, ACE Series on Higher Education, 2nd ed. (Lanham, MD: Rowman and Littlefield, 2012).
14. See Ammerman, "Golden Rule Christianity."
15. Émile Durkheim, *The Elementary Forms of the Religious Life, a Study in Religious Sociology* (London: G. Allen and Unwin, 1915).
16. Though 71% of current Mainliners intend to join churches when then have children, we do not expect 100% follow-through. Some Mainliners will not have kids, some will join churches that are not Mainline, and some will not join at all. There are conversions to Mainline churches (usually switching to these churches from other Christian traditions), but we see no reason to anticipate these would rise for Mainline churches only (which would be necessary for a proportion increase in Mainline affiliation). Realistically, we should halve the stated plans of current Mainliners, given the well-known gap between intentions and actual behavior, and estimate a 65% decline in affiliated population. But given the stability overall of twentysomething religiosity during the past four decades (see Chapter 2), and the 60% intergenerational retention rate found by Vern L. Bengtson with Norella M. Putney and Susan Harris, *Families and Faith: How Religion Is Passed Down Across Generations* (New York: Oxford University Press, 2013), we make a conservative prediction that 60% of the current proportion of twentysomethings will be retained.

CHAPTER 5

1. We derive this estimate as follows. The American Community Survey of the U.S. Census Bureau estimates 42.7 million Americans between the ages of 20 and 29 in 2013. The NSAT, also conducted in 2013, reported 30% of its representative panel affiliated with Evangelical churches and denominations, which would equate to 12.81M American Evangelical twentysomethings. Of Evangelical twentysomethings overall, 47% were Active—which equates to 6M Active Evangelical twentysomethings.
2. Scholars diverge in how they organize the diverse set of American Christians. Christian Smith groups all Protestants under four labels: Evangelical, Fundamentalist, Mainline, and Liberal, then adds a fifth label for Catholics in *American Evangelicalism: Embattled and Thriving* (Chicago: University of Chicago Press, 1998); we collapse the first two into Evangelical and

the second two into Mainline. Corwin E. Smidt, by contrast, groups American Christians using four labels: Evangelical Protestant, Mainline Protestant, Black Protestant, and Roman Catholic in *American Evangelicals Today* (Lanham, MD: Rowman and Littlefield, 2013); we apportion all Protestants into Evangelical or Mainline categories. There are virtues of using more than two categories—especially in book-length analyses of American Protestantism. But our goal is broader and our audience includes non-specialists, so we opt for parsimony and memorability—applying the Evangelical label to all theologically conservative Protestants and the Mainline label to all theologically moderate and liberal Protestants. For a more fine-grained analysis, we recommend the Smith and Smidt volumes.

3. For example, see James Bielo, *Emerging Evangelicals: Faith, Modernity, and the Desire for Authenticity* (New York: New York University Press, 2011), and Josh Packard, *The Emerging Church: Religion at the Margins* (Boulder, CO: Lynne Rienner, 2012).
4. See Benton Johnson, Dean R. Hoge, and Donald A. Luidens, "Mainline Churches: The Real Reason for Decline," *First Things* 31 (Mar. 1993): 13–18.
5. Our sample size of twentysomething Mainliners was proportional to the population, and therefore the smallest. Thirty-six (i.e., 14%) of our 262 Mainline respondents were Black, which is a higher rate than the 1–10% rate that Pew Research Center found among Mainline denominations in its 2014 Religious Landscape Survey. The Pew dataset includes all ages, so it is not exactly comparable to our sample. Our 14% rate could, therefore, be too high. See Michael Lipka, "The Most and Least Racially Diverse U.S. Religious Groups," Pew Research Center, July 27, 2015, http://www.pewresearch.org/fact-tank/2015/07/27/the-most-and-least-racially-diverse-u-s-religious-groups/.
6. The Southern Baptist Convention, for example, is 85% White; the Church of the Nazarene is 88% White; the Presbyterian Church in America is 80% White; and the Lutheran Church-Missouri Synod is 95% White. The African Methodist Episcopal Church, by contrast, is 94% Black, and the National Baptist Convention is 99% Black. See Lipka, "Most and Least Racially Diverse."
7. Eighty-one percent of White, born-again/Evangelical Christians voted for Donald Trump in 2016 (see Gregory A. Smith and Jessica Martinez, "How the Faithful Voted: A Preliminary 2016 Analysis," Pew Research Center, November 9, 2016, http://www.pewresearch.org/fact-tank/2016/11/09/how-the-faithful-voted-a-preliminary-2016-analysis/). By contrast, 89% of Blacks, 66% of Latino, 65% of Asian, and 56% of other race Americans voted for Hillary Clinton (http://www.cnn.com/election/2016/results/exit-polls/national/president).

8. Matthew Desmond, *Evicted: Poverty and Profit in the American City* (New York: Crown, 2016).
9. Specifically, 61% of Active Evangelical and 56% of Nominal Evangelical twentysomethings agree with this statement—but the 5% difference is not statistically significant (Chi-square = 3.779, p = .151; Gamma = .032, approximate significance = .70).
10. Ross Douthat, "Is There an Evangelical Crisis?," *New York Times*, November 25, 2017, https://www.nytimes.com/2017/11/25/opinion/sunday/trump-evangelical-crisis.html; Jared C. Wilson, "This Theologically Orphaned Generation," The Gospel Coalition, November 14, 2017, https://www.thegospelcoalition.org/blogs/jared-c-wilson/theologically-orphaned-generation/.
11. Fifty-three percent of all Evangelical twentysomethings agree "I would be very unhappy if I never marry," and 76% agree "having children is very important to me" (authors' analysis of NSAT 2013).
12. Willow Creek Community Church, which launched the Evangelical "seeker sensitive" movement, with an attendance of over 25,000 each weekend, invites attendees to "join the 2:42 community," https://www.willowcreek.org/en/about/ways-to-belong. The Assemblies of God emphasizes "adherents" over "members," with twice as many of the former than latter. Adherents are "all persons who consider an Assembly of God church to be their church home," "Assemblies of God Statistics, USA," n.d., http://agchurches.org/Sitefiles/Default/RSS/Assemblies%20of%20God%20Statistics.pdf.
13. Gamma = -.279, p < .001
14. Forty percent of Active Evangelical twentysomethings and 37% of Nominal Evangelical twentysomethings indicate their "deep passion is social justice" (NSAT 2013).
15. See Vern Bengston with Norella M. Putney and Susan Harris, *Families and Faith: How Religion Is Passed Down Across Generations* (Oxford: Oxford University Press, 2013).

CHAPTER 6

1. Authors' analyses of the 2016 GSS. See Chapter 2, note 2.
2. See, for example, Steve McSwain, "'NONES!' Are Now 'DONES.' Is the Church Dying?," *Huffington Post*, November 17, 2014, https://www.huffingtonpost.com/entry/nones-and-now-the-dones-t_b_6164112.html.
3. Christel Manning refers to this group as "unchurched believers" and estimates they may be as many as one-half of all religiously unaffiliated Americans in *Losing Our Religion: How Unaffiliated Parents Are Raising Their Children* (New York: New York University Press, 2015), 34.

4. Nancy Tatom Ammerman, *Sacred Stories, Spiritual Tribes: Finding Religion in Everyday Life* (Oxford: Oxford University Press, 2014).
5. Courtney Bender, *The New Metaphysicals: Spirituality and the American Religious Imagination* (Chicago: University of Chicago Press, 2010).
6. Manning, *Losing our Religion*, 39, uses the term "spiritual seekers," while we use "Spiritual Eclectics," as the former suggests an intentionality to the seeking that we find infrequent, while the latter captures the haphazard assembly of beliefs and practices that we find predominant.
7. Manning, *Losing our Religion*, 34, estimates that roughly one-fifth of American Nones are philosophical secularists. Her discussion of secular indifferents, though, is rooted in her qualitative analyses, and she does not propose a magnitude for this group. Our NSAT analyses below, do so.
8. We get this estimate using the 2016 GSS. Specifically, 61% of Nones who indicate they do not believe in God also indicate they are "not spiritual," and 43% of Nones who indicate they "don't know whether there is a God and . . . don't believe there is a way to find out" also indicate they are "not spiritual." This works out to 50.2% of the 35% of Nones who indicate these views about God, or 17.5%. That means about one out of six Americans in 2016 are unaffiliated, nonspiritual nontheists.
9. See "America's Changing Religious Landscape," Pew Research Center, May 12, 2015, http://assets.pewresearch.org/wp-content/uploads/sites/11/2015/05/RLS-08-26-full-report.pdf, 9.
10. Marc Musick and John Wilson, "Religious Switching for Marriage Reasons," *Sociology of Religion* 56, no. 3 (Oct. 1995): 257–270. Matthew T. Loveland, "Religious Switching: Preference Development, Maintenance, and Change," *Journal for the Scientific Study of Religion* 42, no. 1 (Mar. 2003): 147–157.
11. See Manning, *Losing our Religion*, 35.
12. Wendy Cadge, *Paging God: Religion in the Halls of Medicine* (Chicago: University of Chicago Press, 2012).
13. For an overview of Trump's statements, see Gregory Krieg, "Trump's History of Anti-Muslim Rhetoric Hits Dangerous New Low," CNN, November 30, 2017, https://www.cnn.com/2017/11/29/politics/donald-trump-muslim-attacks/index.html.
14. "U.S. Religious Knowledge Survey," Pew Forum on Religion & Public Life, September 28, 2010, http://assets.pewresearch.org/wp-content/uploads/sites/11/2010/09/religious-knowledge-full-report.pdf.
15. That the proportion of GSS Nones matches other survey estimates gives us confidence in the GSS's validity, but we note that 91 Nones is a small sample and that these analyses are suggestive, not definitive.
16. See GSS citation, Chapter 2, note 2.

17. Duane F. Alwin and Jon A. Krosnick, "Aging, Cohorts, and the Stability of Sociopolitical Orientations over the Life Span," *American Journal of Sociology* 97, no. 1 (1991): 169–195.
18. Forty-seven percent of unaffiliated twentysomethings answered "no" to the NSAT question "Do you believe in God or not, or are you unsure?" Twenty-six percent answered "yes," and 27% answered "unsure."
19. Five percent of unaffiliated twentysomethings strongly agreed with this NSAT statement: "I used to believe in a personal God, but now I think of God as a spiritual force." Another 28% agreed.
20. A claim that is spun positively and negatively by various observers. For the former, see Caroline Newman, "Why Millennials Are Leaving Religion but Embracing Spirituality," *UVA Today*, December 14, 2015, https://news.virginia.edu/content/qa-why-millennials-are-leaving-religion-embracing-spirituality; for the latter, see Barna Group, "Meet the 'Spiritual but Not Religious," Research Releases in Faith & Christianity, April 6, 2017, https://www.barna.com/research/meet-spiritual-not-religious/.
21. Classification was tiered. Nones affirming a personal and involved God were Unaffiliated Believers. Nones affirming that spiritual growth was fairly, very, or extremely important, and were not already classified as Unaffiliated Believers, were Spiritual Eclectics. Eclectics believe in a deist God, a cosmic life force, or disbelieve in God. Nones who thought about the meaning of life "fairly" or "very often," and who were not already classified as a Believer or Eclectic, were Philosophical Secularists. All other Nones, not already classified as Believers, Eclectics, or Philosophical Secularists, were Indifferent Secularists.
22. Address at the Freedoms Foundation, Waldorf-Astoria, New York City, New York, December 22, 1952. https://www.dwightdeisenhower.com/193/Religion
23. Alexis de Tocqueville, *Democracy in America*, trans. and ed. Harvey C. Mansfield and Delba Winthrop (Chicago: University of Chicago Press, 2000). See also discussion of Tocqueville in Robert N. Bellah et al., *Habits of the Heart: Individualism and Commitment in American Life*, rev. ed. (Berkeley: University of California Press, 1996).
24. Active participation in "service club or fraternal organization," 3.8% Nones, 3.6% religiously affiliated; "veteran's group," 1.5% Nones, 0.3% religiously affiliated; "senior citizens center or group," 0.4% Nones, 0.2% religiously affiliated; "women's group," 1.7% Nones, 3.3% religiously affiliated. No differences in percentages are statistically significant. Source: NSAT 2013.
25. Involved in "issue-oriented political organization," 1.5% Nones, 1.9% religiously affiliated; "non-partisan civic organization," 0.8% Nones, 1.1% religiously affiliated; "neighborhood association or community group,"

3.2% Nones, 5.1% religiously affiliated; "group representing racial/ethnic interests," 0.9% Nones, 1.1% religiously affiliated. No differences in percentages are statistically significant. Source: NSAT 2013.

26. Active participation in "religious group," 1.5% Nones, 19.5% religiously affiliated. Involved in "hobby, sports team, or youth group," 9.0% Nones, 16.6% religiously affiliated; "school club or association," 7.9% Nones, 13.7% religiously affiliated. Percentages are statistically different ($p < .05$). Source: NSAT 2013.
27. 2016 voter participation figures taken from "Religious Makeup of the Electorate" table in a report by the Pew Research Center (Gregory A. Smith and Jessica Martinez, "How the Faithful Voted: A Preliminary 2016 Analysis," November 16, 2016, http://www.pewresearch.org/fact-tank/2016/11/09/how-the-faithful-voted-a-preliminary-2016-analysis/). Population estimates of Christians and religiously unaffiliated calculated by authors, using the 2016 GSS.

CHAPTER 7

1. See Christian Smith with Patricia Snell, *Souls in Transition: The Religious and Spiritual Lives of Emerging Adults* (New York: Oxford University Press, 2009), Christian Smith and Melinda Denton, *Soul Searching: The Religious and Spiritual Lives of American Teenagers* (New York: Oxford University Press, 2005), Christian Smith et al., *Young Catholic America: Emerging Adults In, Out of, and Gone from the Church* (New York: Oxford University Press, 2014), and http://youthandreligion.nd.edu/research-findings/.
2. "We use eight measures of religiosity from the NSYR survey data: two measures of religious content (belief in God and attitudes toward religious exclusivism), three measures of religious conduct (the frequency of individual prayer, religious service attendance, and helping others outside of organized volunteer work), and three measures of centrality (importance of religion, closeness to God, and frequency of thinking about the meaning of life)," Lisa D. Pearce and Melinda Lundquist Denton, *A Faith of Their Own: Stability and Change in the Religiosity of America's Adolescents* (Oxford: Oxford University Press, 2011), 32.
3. See Jesse M. Smith, "Becoming an Atheist in America: Constructing Identity and Meaning from the Rejection of Theism," *Sociology of Religion* 72, no. 2 (2011): 215–237.
4. Smith with Snell, *Souls in Transition*.
5. The comprehensive scholarly source for sexuality patterns is Edward O. Laumann et al., *The Social Organization of Sexuality: Sexual Practices in the United States* (Chicago: University of Chicago Press, 1994). Between

85% and 90% of Americans, reports Andrew Cherlin, will eventually marry, *The Marriage-Go-Round: The State of Marriage and the Family in America Today* (New York: Vintage, 2010).

6. See Chapter 6, note 8.
7. Martin Seligman, *Flourish: A Visionary New Understanding of Happiness and Well-being* (New York: Free Press, 2013).
8. Kara Zivin et al., "Persistence of Mental Problems and Needs in a College Student Population," *Journal of Affective Disorders* 117, no. 3 (Oct. 2009): 180–185.
9. See Ann Swidler, "Culture in Action: Symbols and Strategies," *American Sociological Review* 51, no. 2 (Apr. 1986): 273–286; Wade Clark Roof, *Spiritual Marketplace: Baby Boomers and the Remaking of American Religion* (Princeton, NJ: Princeton University Press, 2001).
10. Manuel Castells, *The Rise of the Network Society*, vol. 1 of *The Information Age: Economy, Society, and Culture* (Malden, MA; Oxford: Blackwell, 1996); Robert Wuthnow, *Loose Connections: Joining Together in America's Fragmented Communities* (Cambridge, MA: Harvard University Press, 1998).
11. Jae-On Kim and Charles W. Mueller, *Factor Analysis: Statistical Methods and Practical Issues* (Washington, DC: Sage, 1978).
12. Forty-two percent of Active Christian twentysomethings "strongly disagree," and 34% disagree, with the NSAT item "I used to believe in a personal God, but now I think of God as a spiritual force" (authors' analyses of NSAT 2013).
13. We learned this when we did a multivariate statistical analysis called linear regression. Regressing traditional spirituality on demographic and religious predictors, we found age was a significant, negative predictor of traditional spirituality, but that age dropped from significance once we controlled for religious affiliations. We had strongly predictive models for traditional spirituality. Model 1 significant coefficients: household income(-), age(-), employed(-), male(-), cohabit(-), married(+), Black(+), Hispanic(+), community engaged(+), r-sq = .165. Model 2 Significant coefficients: household income (-), employed(-), male(-), black(+), Hispanic(+), community engaged(+), Catholic(-), Evangelical(+), mainline(-), none(-) r-sq = .389. Weaker models for nontraditional spirituality. Model 1, demographic predictors only, significant coefficients: married(+), parent(+), Black(-), Hispanic(-), r-sq = .046. Model 2, and religious categories and Active dummy variable, significant coefficients: household income(+), parent(+), Black(-), Hispanic(-), Catholic(+, borderline), Evangelical(+), none(+), Active (+), r-sq = .109.
14. See p. 206 of Pearce and Denton, *A Faith of Their Own* for adolescent figures. Twentysomething results from author's analyses of NSAT (2013).

15. The operationalization of marriage, cohabitation, parenthood, employment, completion of bachelor's degrees, and voting was straightforward (see Methodological Appendix for NSAT survey items). Social connectedness we defined as disagreeing or strongly disagreeing with the statement, "I often feel lonely"; by this measure, 68% of American twentysomethings feel socially connected. Community engagement was defined expansively—including attending a PTA/school group meeting; attending a community group meeting; donating blood; giving money to a charity, working for a charity or one's church; attending a political protest or rally; contacting a government official; volunteering or working for a presidential campaign; giving money to a political candidate, issue, or cause; working with others in your community to solve a problem; serving on a community board; writing a "letter to the editor"; commenting about politics on a message board or internet site; holding a publicly elected office; participating in any of the following political movements or attending a meeting, protest, rally, or any other event for Tea Party movement, environmental rights, women's rights, racial equality movement, right to life movement, peace/antiwar, LGBT rights, occupy movement. By this expansive definition, 55% of American twentysomethings are civically or politically engaged in their communities.
16. We did not have the data to determine if innovators were friends with other innovators. It is possible, but innovators are relatively rare, so it could go either way.
17. Will Herberg. *Protestant, Catholic, Jew: An Essay in American Religious Sociology* (Chicago: University of Chicago Press, 1955). Phillip E. Hammond, *Religion and Personal Autonomy: The Third Disestablishment in America* (Columbia: University of South Carolina Press, 1992).

METHODOLOGICAL APPENDIX

1. Dean R. Hoge, "Planning New Research on Spiritual Hunger of Young Adult Americans," White Paper no. 2, February 4, 2008.
2. "Dean R. Hoge, "Plan for the Young Adult Project," May 2, 2008.
3. For additional information about panel recruitment and benefits, see the KnowledgePanel website, https://join.knpanel.com/rewards.html.
4. Journal articles include Mick P. Couper "Web Surveys: A Review of Issues and Approaches," *Public Opinion Quarterly* 64 (2000): 464–494; J. M. Dennis, "Are Internet Panels Creating Professional Respondents? A Study of Panel Effects," *Marketing Research* (Summer 2001): 34–38; Timothy Heeren, Erika M. Edwards, J. Michael Dennis, Sergei Rodkin, Ralph W. Hingson, and David L. Rosenbloom, "A Comparison of Results from an Alcohol Survey of a Prerecruited Internet Panel and the National Epidemiologic

Survey on Alcohol and Related Conditions," *Alcoholism: Clinical and Experimental Research* 32, no. 2 (2008): 222–229; Mario Callegaro and Charles DiSogra, "Computing Response Metrics for Online Panels," *Public Opinion Quarterly* 72, no. 5 (2008): 1008–1031; Linchiat Chang and Jon A. Krosnick, "National Surveys Via Rdd Telephone Interviewing Versus the Internet: Comparing Sample Representativeness and Response Quality," *Public Opinion Quarterly* 73, no. 4 (2009): 641–678; Charles A. DiSogra, Curtiss Cobb, Elisa Chan, and J. Michael Dennis, "Calibrating Non-Probability Internet Samples with Probability Samples Using Early Adopter Characteristics," in *JSM Proceedings, Survey Methods Section* (Alexandria, VA: American Statistical Association, 2011), 4501–4515. Copies of dozens of conference papers along with reports by the Knowledge Networks, Inc., staff can be accessed at http://www.knowledgenetworks.com/ganp/reviewer-info.html.

5. Tim Clydesdale, *The Purposeful Graduate: Why Colleges Must Talk to Students about Vocation* (Chicago: University of Chicago Press, 2015).

SELECTED BIBLIOGRAPHY

We list here the scholarly research consulted in the making of this book. For complete citations of all materials used, see Notes.

Alwin, Duane F., and Jon A. Krosnick. "Aging, Cohorts, and the Stability of Sociopolitical Orientations over the Life Span." *American Journal of Sociology* 97, no. 1 (1991): 169–195.

Ammerman, Nancy Tatom. "Golden Rule Christianity: Lived Religion in the American Mainstream." In *Lived Religion in America: Toward a History of Practice*, edited by David D. Hall, 196–216. Princeton, NJ: Princeton University Press, 1997.

Ammerman, Nancy Tatom. *Sacred Stories, Spiritual Tribes: Finding Religion in Everyday Life*. Oxford: Oxford University Press, 2014.

Arnett, Jeffrey Jensen. *Emerging Adulthood: The Winding Road from the Late Teens Through the Twenties*. 2nd ed. New York: Oxford University Press, 2014.

Arnett, Jeffrey Jensen, and Jennifer Lynn Tanner, eds. *Emerging Adults in America: Coming of Age in the 21st Century*. Washington, DC: American Psychological Association, 2006.

Arum, Richard, and Josipa Roksa. *Aspiring Adults Adrift: Tentative Transitions of College Graduates*. Chicago: University of Chicago Press, 2014.

Baggett, Jerome P. *Sense of the Faithful: How American Catholics Live their Faith*. New York: Oxford University Press, 2009.

Baker, Joseph O., and Buster G. Smith. *American Secularism: Cultural Contours of Nonreligious Belief Systems*. New York: New York University Press, 2015.

Bellah, Robert N., Richard Madsen, William M. Sullivan, Ann Swidler, and Steven M. Tipton. *Habits of the Heart: Individualism and Commitment in American Life*. Berkeley: University of California Press, 1985.

Bender, Courtney. *The New Metaphysicals: Spirituality and the American Religious Imagination*. Chicago: University of Chicago Press, 2010.

Bengston, Vern, with Norella M. Putney and Susan Harris. *Families and Faith: How Religion Is Passed Down Across Generations*. Oxford: Oxford University Press, 2013.

Bielo, James. *Emerging Evangelicals: Faith, Modernity, and the Desire for Authenticity*. New York: New York University Press, 2011.

Cadge, Wendy. *Paging God: Religion in the Halls of Medicine*. Chicago: University of Chicago Press, 2012.

Castells, Manuel. *The Rise of the Network Society*. Vol. 1. *The Information Age: Economy, Society, and Culture*. Malden, MA: Blackwell, 1996.

Cherlin, Andrew. *The Marriage-Go-Round: The State of Marriage and the Family in America Today*. New York: Vintage, 2010.

Clark, Lynn Schofield. *From Angels to Aliens: Teenagers, the Media, and the Supernatural*. New York: Oxford University Press, 2003.

Clydesdale, Tim. *The First Year Out: Understanding American Teens After High School*. Chicago: University of Chicago Press, 2007.

Clydesdale, Tim. *The Purposeful Graduate: Why Colleges Must Talk to Students About Vocation*. Chicago: University of Chicago Press, 2015.

Desmond, Matthew. *Evicted: Poverty and Profit in the American City*. New York: Crown, 2016.

Dillon, Michele. *Catholic Identity: Balancing Reason, Faith and Power*. Cambridge: Cambridge University Press, 1999.

Durkheim, Émile. *The Elementary Forms of the Religious Life, a Study in Religious Sociology*. London: G. Allen and Unwin, 1915.

Espinosa, Gaston. "Demographic and Religious Changes Among Hispanics of the United States." *Social Compass* 51, no. 3 (2004): 303–320.

Evans, Rachel Held. *Searching for Sunday: Loving, Leaving, and Finding the Church*. Nashville, TN: Thomas Nelson, 2015.

Freitas, Donna. *Sex and the Soul: Juggling Sexuality, Spirituality, Romance, and Religion on America's College Campuses*. Rev. ed. New York: Oxford University Press 2015.

Furstenberg, Frank F. Jr., Sheela Kennedy, Vonnie C. McLoyd, Ruben G. Rumbaut, and Richard A. Settersen Jr. "Growing Up Is Harder to Do." *Contexts* 3, no. 3 (Summer 2004): 33–41.

Garces-Foley, Kathleen. "Parishes as Homes and Hubs for Young Adult Catholics." In *American Parishes: Remaking Local Catholicism*, edited by Gary Adler, Tricia Bruce, and Brian Stark. New York: Fordham University Press, 2019.

Glanzer, Perry, Jonathan P. Hill, and Todd Ream. "Changing Souls: Higher Education's Influence upon the Religious Lives of Emerging Adults." In *Emerging Adults' Religiousness and Spirituality: Meaning-Making in an Age of Transition*, edited by Carolyn McNamara Barry and Mona M. Abo-Zena, 152–170. New York: Oxford University Press, 2014.

Greeley, Andrew M. *The Catholic Myth: The Behavior and Beliefs of American Catholics*. New York: Touchstone, 1997.

Hacker, Jacob S. *The Great Risk Shift: The Assault on American Jobs, Families, Health Care, and Retirement—And How You Can Fight Back*. New York: Oxford University Press, 2006.

Hadaway, C. Kirk, Penny Long Marler, and Mark Chaves. "Overreporting Church Attendance in America: Evidence That Demands the Same Verdict." *American Sociological Review* 63, no. 1 (Feb. 1998): 122–130.

Hammond, Phillip E. *Religion and Personal Autonomy: The Third Disestablishment in America*. Columbia: University of South Carolina Press, 1992.

Herberg, Will. *Protestant, Catholic, Jew: An Essay in American Religious Sociology*. Chicago: University of Chicago Press, 1955.

Herzog, Patricia, ed. *The Sociology of Emerging Adulthood: Studying Youth in the Context of Public Issues*. San Diego, CA: Cognella Academic, 2017.

Hunter, James Davison. *Evangelicalism: The Coming Generation*. Chicago: University of Chicago Press, 1987.

Johnson, Benton, Dean R. Hoge, and Donald A. Luidens. "Mainline Churches: The Real Reason for Decline." *First Things* 31 (Mar. 1993): 13–18.

Johnson, Marilynn. "'The Quiet Revival': New Immigrants and the Transformation of Christianity in Greater Boston." *Religion and American Culture* 24, no. 2 (Summer 2014): 231–258.

Kinnaman, David, and Gabe Lyons. *Unchristian: What a New Generation Really Thinks About Christianity . . . and Why It Matters*. Grand Rapids, MI: Baker Books, 2012.

Koslow, Sally. *Slouching Toward Adulthood: Observations for the Not-So-Empty Nest*. New York: Viking, 2012.

Laumann, Edward O., John H. Gagnon, Robert T. Michael, and Stuart Michaels. *The Social Organization of Sexuality: Sexual Practices in the United States*. Chicago: University of Chicago Press, 1994.

Loveland, Matthew T. "Religious Switching: Preference Development, Maintenance, and Change." *Journal for the Scientific Study of Religion* 42, no. 1 (Mar. 2003): 147–157.

Kim, Jae-On, and Charles W. Mueller. *Factor Analysis: Statistical Methods and Practical Issues*. Washington, DC: Sage, 1978.

Manning, Christel. *Losing Our Religion: How Unaffiliated Parents Are Raising Their Children*. New York: New York University Press, 2015.

Musick, Marc, and John Wilson. "Religious Switching for Marriage Reasons." *Sociology of Religion* 56, no. 3 (Oct. 1995): 257–270.

Newman, Katherine S. "Ties That Bind: Cultural Interpretations of Delayed Adulthood in Western Europe and Japan." *Sociological Forum* 23, no. 4 (Dec. 2008): 645–669.

Packard, Josh. *The Emerging Church: Religion at the Margins*. Boulder, CO: Lynne Rienner, 2012.

Peacock, James R., and Margaret M. Poloma. "Religiosity and Life Satisfaction Across the Life Course." *Social Indicators Research* 48, no. 3 (Nov. 1999): 321–345.

Pearce, Lisa D., and Melinda Lundquist Denton. *A Faith of Their Own: Stability and Change in the Religiosity of America's Adolescents*. Oxford: Oxford University Press, 2011.

Roof, Wade Clark. *Spiritual Marketplace: Baby Boomers and the Remaking of American Religion*. Princeton, NJ: Princeton University Press, 1999.

Roof, Wade Clark, and William McKinney. *American Mainline Religion: Its Changing Shape and Future*. New Brunswick, NJ: Rutgers University Press, 1987.

Roozen, David A. "Oldline Protestantism: Pockets of Vitality Within a Continuing Stream of Decline." Hartford Institute for Religion Research Working Paper 1104.1. Hartford, CT: Hartford Seminary, 2004. http://hirr.hartsem.edu/bookshelf/roozen_article5.html.

Schwartz, Barry, and Ken Kliban. *The Paradox of Choice: Why More Is Less*. New York: Harper Collins, 2004.

Seidman, Alan, ed. *College Student Retention: Formula for Student* Success. ACE Series on Higher Education. 2nd ed. Lanham, MD: Rowman and Littlefield, 2012.

Seligman, Martin E. P. *Flourish: A Visionary New Understanding of Happiness and Well-Being*. New York: Free Press, 2013.

Settersten, Richard, and Barbara E. Ray. *Not Quite Adults: Why 20-Somethings Are Choosing a Slower Path to Adulthood, and Why It's Good for Everyone*. New York: Bantam Books Trade Paperback, 2010.

Settersten, Richard A. Jr., Frank F. Furstenberg Jr., and Ruben G. Rumbaut, eds. *On the Frontier of Adulthood: Theory, Research, and Public Policy*. Chicago: University of Chicago Press, 2005.

Silverstein, Merril, and Vern L. Bengtson. "Return to Religion? Predictors of Religious Change Among Baby-Boomers in Their Transition to Later Life." *Journal of Population Ageing* 11, no. 1 (Dec. 2018): 7–21.

Smidt, E. Corwin. *American Evangelicals Today*. Lanham, MD: Rowman and Littlefield, 2013.

Smith, Christian. *American Evangelicalism: Embattled and Thriving*. Chicago: University of Chicago Press, 1998.

Smith, Christian, with Kari Christoffersen, Hilary Davidson, and Patricia Snell Herzog. *Lost in Transition: The Dark Side of Emerging Adulthood*. New York: Oxford University Press, 2011.

Smith, Christian, and Melinda Denton. *Soul Searching: The Religious and Spiritual Lives of American Teenagers*. New York: Oxford University Press, 2005.

Smith, Christian, Kyle Longest, Jonathan Hill, and Kari Christoffersen, *Young Catholic America: Emerging Adults In, Out of, and Gone from the Church*. New York: Oxford University Press, 2014.

Smith, Christian, with Patricia Snell. *Souls in Transition: The Religious and Spiritual Lives of Emerging Adults*. New York: Oxford University Press, 2009.

Smith, Jesse M. "Becoming an Atheist in America: Constructing Identity and Meaning from the Rejection of Theism." *Sociology of Religion* 72, no. 2 (2011): 215–237.

Strayhorn, Terrell L. *College Students' Sense of Belonging: A Key to Educational Success for All Students*. New York: Routledge, 2012.

Swidler, Ann. "Culture in Action: Symbols and Strategies." *American Sociological Review* 51, no. 2 (Apr. 1986): 273–286.

Tocqueville, Alexis de. *Democracy in America*. Translated and edited by Harvey C. Mansfield and Delba Winthrop. Chicago: University of Chicago Press, 2000.

Twenge, Jean M. *Generation Me: Why Today's Young Americans Are More Confident, Assertive, Entitled—and More Miserable Than Ever Before.* Rev. ed. New York: Atria, 2014.

Twenge, Jean M. *iGen: Why Today's Super-Connected Kids Are Growing Up Less Rebellious, More Tolerant, Less Happy—and Completely Unprepared for Adulthood.* New York: Atria, 2017.

Uecker, Jeremy, Mark Regnerus, and Margaret Vaaler. "Losing My Religion: The Social Sources of Religious Decline Among Emerging Adults." *Social Forces* 85, no. 4 (2007): 1–26.

Wuthnow, Robert. *After the Baby Boomers: How Twenty- and Thirty-Somethings Are Shaping the Future of American Religion.* Princeton, NJ: Princeton University Press, 2010.

Wuthnow, Robert. *After Heaven: Spirituality in America Since the 1950s.* Berkeley: University of California Press, 1998.

Wuthnow, Robert. *Loose Connections: Joining Together in America's Fragmented Communities.* Cambridge, MA: Harvard University Press, 1998.

Zivin, Kara, Daniel Eisenberg, Sarah E. Gollust, and Ezra Golberstein. "Persistence of Mental Problems and Needs in a College Student Population." *Journal of Affective Disorders* 117, no. 3 (Oct. 2009): 180–185.

INDEX

Tables and figures are indicated by an italic *t* and *f* following the page/paragraph number.